SPEECHES

BY

THE RT. HON. THOMAS BABINGTON MACAULAY, M.P.

AUTHOR OF "THE HISTORY OF ENGLAND FROM THE ACCESSION OF JAMES THE SECOND," "LAYS OF ANCIENT ROME," "ESSAYS FROM THE EDINBURGH REVIEW," ETC., ETC.

IN TWO VOLUMES.

VOL. I.

REDFIELD,
110 & 112 NASSAU STREET, NEW YORK.

1853.

R. CRAIGHEAD, PRINTER AND STEREOTYPER,
53 Vesey street, New York.

PUBLISHER'S PREFACE.

Francis, the author of a collection of portraits of contemporary statesmen, entitled the Orators of the Age, has given in that work a sketch of the Parliamentary manner and successes of Macaulay. He claims for him the first rank of the speakers of the day—no less for the literary and historical illustrations of his speeches, than for their fidelity to the immediate interests of the discussion. In the union of these two qualities may be summed up Macaulay's characteristic merits. "He is a great reconciler of the new with the old. Although he may adorn a subject with the lights afforded by his rare genius, he never trifles with it. His historical research renders him a living link with the old and uncorrupted constitution of the country. * * There is no speaker now before the public who so readily and usefully, and with so little appearance of effort, infuses the results of very extensive reading and very deep research into the common, every-day business of Parliament. But his learning never tyrannizes over his common sense."* The

* Francis's Orators of the Age.

political liberality and principle of free development, the honorable and humanitarian spirit of these speeches are as obvious.

The following speeches, which are now for the first time brought together, are reprinted in a connected and complete series from the standard authority, Hansard's Parliamentary Debates. They embrace the whole of the distinguished orator's course in the House of Commons, from 1830 to the present day. Among them will be found in due chronological order, the several speeches on the Reform Bill, which brought the orator so prominently forward in the arena of the House of Commons and before the world, in his vindication of the extension of the suffrage and the principles of representation, supported by every resource of wit, skilful argument, ingenuity of detail, and historical precedent, including those memorable passages on the lessons of the French and English Revolutions; the discussion of questions growing out of the agitations in Ireland in 1833, and later, the measures of repression, the reform of the Protestant Church Establishment, the Maynooth College Bill; his eloquent review of the East India policy, which recalls the triumphs of Burke; his Copyright speeches, in which he places literary property on the ground of expediency; his views on the Corn Laws, the Ballot, the Charter petition, the Dissenters' Chapel Bill; his remarks on the Treaty of Washington; with many discussions incidental to these and other important topics, springing up during his Parliamentary career.

Thomas Babington Macaulay was born in 1800. In 1818 he entered Trinity College, Cambridge, obtaining a fellowship of that college in 1824. He then became a law student at Lincoln's Inn, and was called to the bar in 1826. At this period he laid the foundation of his literary fame by his celebrated articles in the *Edinburgh Review* (one of the earliest of which, a paper on the Reform Question, is printed in the present volumes), having previously given some brilliant poems and sketches to *Knight's Quarterly Magazine*. We find him in 1830 in Parliament under the nomination system, sitting for the Marquis of Lansdowne's borough of Calne before the Reform Bill. He was elected member for Leeds in 1833, but soon resigned his seat to proceed to India as member of the Supreme Council of Calcutta, where he was at the head of the Commission for the Reform of East India Legislation. In 1838 he returned to England, and shortly afterwards was elected member for Edinburgh. In 1839 he joined the Cabinet as Secretary at War, supporting the Whig cause by some of his most vigorous speeches. His course in the advocacy of the Maynooth Grant probably lost him his election at Edinburgh in 1847. He was installed Rector of the University of Glasgow in 1849, and, as is well known, employed his time out of Parliament up to his re-election in the present year, in the composition of his History of England. His Lays of Ancient Rome, published in 1842, are a noble illustration of the poetic force with which he revivifies the dead facts of history.

As some curiosity may be felt in this connexion to know something of Macaulay's personal manner as a speaker, we may add that, Mr. Francis describes his voice as "monotonous, pitched in alto, shrill, pouring forth words with inconceivable velocity—a voice well adapted to give utterance with precision to the conclusions of the intellect, but in no way naturally formed to express feeling or passion." His face is described as "literally instinct with expression : the eye, above all, full of deep thought and meaning." In stature, he is short and stout.

Macaulay must always be listened to and read with pleasure, for the brilliant light he constantly throws upon his object, whatever its character. Passing over his great efforts in the following collection, we may refer for an example of the force of picturesque treatment, condensing and illuminating the argument, to the very neat little casual speech on the Anatomy Bill, with its prompt disposition of the comparative interests of rich and poor in the question. It shows how a man of genius may give value to every occasion.

New York, January, 1853.

CONTENTS OF VOL. I.

MACAULAY'S SPEECHES.

ENGLISH POLITICS IN 1827.*

The New Antijacobin Review.—Nos. I. and II. 8vo. London. 1827.

We ought to apologize to our readers for prefixing to this article the name of such a publication. The two numbers which lie on our table contain nothing which could be endured, even at a dinner of the Pitt Club, unless, as the newspapers express it, the hilarity had been continued to a very late hour. We have met, we confess, with nobody who has ever seen them; and, should our account excite any curiosity respecting them, we fear that an application to the booksellers will already be too late. Some tidings of them may perhaps be obtained from the trunk-makers. In order to console our readers, however, under this disappointment, we will venture to assure them, that the only subject on which the reasonings of these Antijacobin Reviewers throw any light, is one in which we take very little interest—the state of their own understandings; and that the only feeling which their

* From the Edinburgh Review, Jan. 1827.

Note. This article and the following one, which have not been collected in the edition of Macaulay's Edinburgh Review articles, are here printed as an appropriate introduction of the celebrated Speeches on the Reform Bill, to several of the leading points of which they offer no slight resemblances.

pathetic appeals have excited in us, is that of deep regret for our four shillings, which are gone and will return no more.

It is not a very cleanly, or a very agreeable task, to rake up from the kennels of oblivion the remains of drowned abortions, which have never opened their eyes on the day, or even been heard to whimper, but have been at once transferred from the filth in which they were littered, to the filth with which they are to rot. But unhappily we have no choice. Bad as this work is, it is quite as good as any which has appeared against the present administration. We have looked everywhere, without being able to find any antagonist who can possibly be as much ashamed of defeat as we shall be of victory.

The manner in which the influence of the press has, at this crisis, been exercised, is, indeed, very remarkable. All the talent has been on one side. With an unanimity which, as Lord Londonderry wisely supposes, can be ascribed only to a dexterous use of the secret-service money, the able and respectable journals of the metropolis have all supported the new government. It has been attacked, on the other hand, by writers who make every cause which they espouse despicable or odious,—by one paper which owes all its notoriety to its reports of the slang uttered by drunken lads who are brought to Bow Street for breaking windows —by another, which barely contrives to subsist on intelligence from butlers, and advertisements from perfumers. With these are joined all the scribblers who rest their claim to orthodoxy and loyalty on the perfection to which they have carried the arts of ribaldry and slander. What part these gentlemen would take in the present contest, seemed at first doubtful. We feared, for a moment, that their servility might overpower their malignity, and that they would be even more inclined to flatter the powerful than to calumniate the innocent. It turns out that we were mistaken; and we are most thankful for it. They have been kind enough to spare us the discredit of their alliance. We know not how we should have borne to be of the same party with them. It is bad enough, God knows, to be of the same species.

The writers of the book before us, who are also, we believe, the great majority of its readers, can scarcely be said to belong to this class. They rather resemble those snakes with which Indian jugglers perform so many curious tricks: The bags of venom are left, but the teeth are extracted. That they might omit nothing tending to make them ridiculous, they have adopted a title on which no judicious writer would have ventured; and challenged comparison with one of the most ingenious and amusing volumes in our language. Whether they have assumed this name on the principle which influenced Mr. Shandy in christening his children, or from a whim similar to that which induced the proprietors of the most frightful Hottentot that ever lived, to give her the name of Venus, we shall not pretend to decide; but we would seriously advise them to consider, whether it is for their interest, that people should be reminded of the celebrated imitations of Darwin and Kotzebue, while they are reading such parodies on the Bible as the following:—"In those days, a strange person shall appear in the land, and he shall cry to the people, Behold, I am possessed by the Demon of Ultra-Liberalism; I have received the gift of incoherence; I am a political philosopher, and a professor of paradoxes."

We would also, with great respect, ask the gentleman who has lampooned Mr. Canning in such Drydenian couplets as this—

"When he said if they would but let him in,
He would never try to turn them out again,"

whether his performance gains much by being compared with New Morality? and, indeed, whether such satire as this is likely to make anybody laugh but himself, or to make anybody wince but his publisher?

But we must take leave of the *New Antijacobin Review;* and we do so, hoping that we have secured the gratitude of its conductors. We once heard a schoolboy relate, with evident satisfaction and pride, that he had been horsewhipped by a Duke: we trust that our present condescension will be as highly appreciated.

But it is not for the purpose of making a scarecrow of a ridiculous publication, that we address our readers at the present important crisis. We are convinced, that the cause of the present Ministers is the cause of liberty, the cause of toleration, the cause of political science,—the cause of the people, who are entitled to expect from their wisdom and liberality many judicious reforms,—the cause of the aristocracy, who, unless those reforms be adopted, must inevitably be the victims of a violent and desolating revolution. We are convinced, that the government of the country was never intrusted to men who more thoroughly understood its interest, or were more sincerely disposed to promote it—to men who, in forming their arrangements, thought so much of what they could *do*, and so little of what they could *get*. On the other side, we see a party which, for ignorance, intemperance, and inconsistency, has no parallel in our annals,—which, as an Opposition, we really think, is a scandal to the nation, and, as a Ministry, would speedily be its ruin. Under these circumstances, we think it our duty to give our best support to those with whose power are inseparably bound up all the dearest interests of the community,—the freedom of worship, of discussion, and of trade,—our honour abroad, and our tranquillity at home.

In undertaking the defence of the Ministers, we feel ourselves embarrassed by one difficulty: we are unable to comprehend distinctly of what they are accused. A statement of facts may be contradicted; but the gentlemen of the Opposition do not deal in statements. Reasonings may be refuted; but the gentlemen of the Opposition do not reason. There is something impassive and elastic about their dulness, on which all the weapons of controversy are thrown away. It makes no resistance, and receives no impression. To argue with it, is like stabbing the water, or cudgelling a woolpack. Buonaparte is said to have remarked, that the English soldiers at Waterloo did not know when they were beaten. The Duke of Wellington, equally fortunate in politics and in war, has the rare felicity of being supported a second time by a force of this description,—men whose desperate hardihood in argument sets all assailants at defiance,—who fight on, though borne down on every side by overwhelming proofs, rush enthusiastically into the mouth of an absurdity, or stake themselves with cool intrepidity on the horn of a dilemma. We doubt whether this unconquerable pertinacity be quite as honourable in debate as in battle; but we are sure, that it is a very difficult task for persons trained in the old school of logical tactics to contend with antagonists who possess such a quality.

The species of argument in which the members of the Opposition appear chiefly to excel, is that of which the Marquis, in the *Critique de l'Ecole des Femmes*, showed himself so great a master: —"Tarte à la crême—morbleu, tarte à la crême!" "Hé bien, que veux tu dire, tarte à ta crême?" "Parbleu, tarte à la crême, chevalier!" "Mais encore?" "Tarte à la crême!" Dî-nous un peu tes raisons." "Tarte à la crêmé!" "Mais il faut expliquer ta pensée, ce me semble." "Tarte à la crême, Madam." "Que trouvez-vouz là à redire?" "Moi, rien;—tarte à la crême!" With equal taste and judgment, the writers and speakers of the Opposition repeat their favourite phrases—"deserted principles," "unnatural coalition," "base love of office." They have not, we must allow, been unfortunate in their choice of a topic. The English are but too much accustomed to consider every public virtue as comprised in consistency; and the name of coalition has to many ears a startling and ominous sound. Of all the charges brought against the Ministry, this alone, as far we can discover, has any meaning; and even to this we can allow no force.

To condemn coalitions in the abstract, is manifestly absurd: Since in a popular government, no good can be done without concert, and no concert can be obtained without compromise. Those who will not stoop to compliances which the condition of human nature renders necessary, are fitter to be hermits than to be statesmen. Their virtue, like gold which is too refined to be coined, must be alloyed before it can be of any use in the commerce of society. But most peculiarly inconsistent and unreasonable is the conduct of those who, while they profess strong Party-feelings, yet entertain a superstitious aversion to Coalitions. Every argument which can be urged against coalitions, as such, is also an argument against party connexions. Every argument by which party connexions can be defended, is a defence of coalitions. What coalitions are to parties, parties are to individuals. The members of a party, in order to promote some great common object, consent to waive all subordinate considerations:—That they may co-operate with more effect where they agree, they contrive, by reciprocal concession, to preserve the semblance of unanimity, even where they differ. Men are not thought unprincipled for acting thus; because it is evident that without such mutual sacrifices of individual opinions, no government can be formed, nor any important measures carried, in a world of which the inhabitants resemble each other so little, and depend on each other so much,—in which there are as many varieties of mind as of countenance, yet in which great effects can be produced only by combined exertions. We must extend the same indulgence to a coalition between parties. If they agree on every important practical question, if they differ only about objects which are either insignificant or unattainable, no party man can, on his own principles, blame them for uniting. These doctrines, like all other doctrines, may be pushed to extremes by the injudicious, or employed by the designing as a pretext for profligacy. But that they are not in themselves unreasonable or pernicious, the whole history of our country proves.

The Revolution itself was the fruit of a coalition between parties, which had attacked each other with a fury unknown in later times. In the preceding generation their hostility had covered England with blood and mourning. They had subsequently exchanged the sword for the axe: But their enmity was not the less deadly because it was disguised by the forms of justice. By popular clamour, by infamous testimony, by perverted law, they had shed innocent and noble blood like water. Yet all their animosities were forgotten in the sense of their common danger. Whigs and Tories signed the same associations. Bishops and field-preachers thundered out the same exhortations. The doctors of Oxford and the goldsmiths of London sent in their plate with equal zeal. The administration which, in the reign of Queen Anne, defended Holland, rescued Germany, conquered Flanders, dismembered the monarchy of Spain, shook the throne of France, vindicated the independence of Europe, and established the empire of the sea, was formed by a junction between men who had many political contests and many personal injuries to forget. Somers had been a member of the ministry which had sent Marlborough to the Tower. Marlborough had assisted in harassing Somers by a vexatious impeachment. But would these great men have acted wisely or honourably if, on such grounds, they had refused to serve their country in concert? The Cabinet which conducted the seven years' war with such distinguished ability and success, was composed of members who had a short time before been leaders of opposite parties. The Union between Fox and North is, we own, condemned by that argument which it will never be possible to answer in a manner satisfactory to the great body of mankind,—the argument from the event. But we should feel some surprise at the dislike which some zealous Pittites affect to entertain for coalitions, did we not know that a Pittite means, in the phraseology of the present day, a person who differs from Mr. Pitt on every subject of importance. There are, indeed, two Pitts,—the real and the imaginary,—the Pitt of history, a Parliamentary reformer, (an enemy of the Test and Corporation Acts,) an advocate of Catholic Emancipation and of free trade,—and the canonized Pitt of the legend,—as unlike to his namesake as Virgil the magician to Virgil the Poet, or St. James the slayer of Moors to St. James the fisherman. What may have been the opinions of that unreal being whose birth-day is celebrated by libations to Protestant Ascendency, on the subject of coalitions, we leave it to his veracious hagiographers, Lord Eldon and Lord Westmoreland, to determine. The sentiments of the real Mr. Pitt may be easily ascertained from his conduct. At the time of the revolutionary war he admitted to participation in his power those who had formerly been his most determined enemies. In 1804 he connected himself with Mr. Fox, and, on his return to office, attempted to procure a high situation in the government for his new ally. One more instance we will mention, which has little weight with us, but which ought to have much weight with our opponents. They talk of Mr. Pitt;—but the real object of their adoration is unquestionably the late Mr. Percival, a gentleman whose acknowledged private virtues were but a poor compensation to his country for the narrowness and feebleness of his policy. In 1809 that minister offered to serve not only *with* Lord Grenville and Earl Grey, but even *under* them. No approximation of feeling between the members of the government and their opponents had then taken place: there had not even been the slightest remission of hostilities. On no question of foreign or domestic policy were the two parties agreed. Yet under such circumstances was this proposition made. It was, as might have been anticipated, rejected by the Whigs, and derided by the country. But the recollection of it ought certainly to prevent those who concurred in it, and their devoted followers, from talking of the baseness and selfishness of coalitions.

These general reasonings, it may be said, are superfluous. It is not to coalitions in the abstract, but to the present coalition in particular, that objection is made. We answer, that an attack on the present coalition can only be maintained by succeeding in the most signal way in an attack on coalitions in the abstract. For never has the world seen, and never is it likely to see, a junction between parties agreeing on so many points, and differing on so few. The Whigs and the supporters of Mr. Canning were united in principle. They were separated only by names, by badges, and by recollections. Opposition, on such grounds as these, would have been disgraceful to English statesmen. It would have been as unreasonable and as profligate as the disputes of the blue and green factions in the Hippodrome of Constantinople. One man admires Mr. Pitt, and another Mr. Fox. Are they therefore never to act together? Mr. Pitt and Mr. Fox were themselves willing to coalesce while they were alive; and it would therefore be strange, if, after they have been lying for twenty years in Westminster Abbey, their names should keep parties asunder. One man approves of the revolutionary war. Another thinks it unjust and impolitic. But the war is over. It is now merely a matter of historical controversy. And the statesman who should require his colleagues to adopt his confession of faith respecting it, would act as madly as Don Quixote when he went to blows with Cardenio about the chastity of Queen Madasima. On these points, and on many such points as these, our new ministers, no doubt, hold different opinions. They may also, for aught we know, hold different opinions about the title of Perkin Warbeck, and the genuineness of the Εικων Βασιλικη. But we shall hardly, on such grounds as these, pronounce their union a sacrifice of principle to place.

It is, in short, of very little importance whether the parties which have lately united entertain the same sentiments respecting things which have been done and cannot be undone. It is of as little importance whether they have adopted the same speculative notions on questions which could not at present be brought forward with the slightest chance of success, and which, in all probability, they will never be required to discuss. The real questions are these: Do they differ as to the policy which present circumstances require? Or is any great cause, which they may have heretofore espoused, placed in a more unfavourable situation by their junction?

That this is the case, no person has even attempted to prove. Bold assertions have indeed been made by a class of writers, who seem to think that their readers are as completely destitute of memory as they themselves are of shame. For the last two years they have been abusing Mr. Canning for adopting the principles of the Whigs; and they now exclaim that, in joining Mr. Canning, the Whigs have abandoned all their principles! "The Whigs," said one of their writers, but a few months ago, "are exercising more real power by means of the present Ministers than if they were themselves in office." "The Ministers," said another, "are no longer Tories. What they call conciliation is mere Whiggism." A third observed that the jest of Mr. Canning about Dennis and his thunder had lost all its point, and that it was a lamentable truth, that all the late measures of the government seemed to have been dictated by the Whigs. Yet these very authors have now the effrontery to assert that the Whigs could not possibly support Mr. Canning without renouncing every opinion which they had formerly professed.

We confidently affirm, on the other hand, that no principle whatever has been sacrificed. With respect to our foreign relations and our commercial policy, the two parties have for years been perfectly agreed. On the Catholic question the views of the

Whigs are the same with those of a great majority of their new colleagues. It is true that, in an illustrious assembly, which was formerly suspected of great dulness and great decorum, and which has of late effectually redeemed itself from one half of the reproach, the conduct of the Whigs towards the Catholics has been represented in a very unfavourable light. The arguments employed against them belong, we suppose, to a kind of logic which the privileged orders alone are qualified to use, and which, with their other constitutional distinctions, we earnestly pray that they may long keep to themselves. An ingenious member of this assembly is said to have observed, that the Protestant alarmists were bound to oppose the new Ministers as friends to the Catholic cause, and that the Catholics ought to oppose them as traitors to the same cause. He reminded the former of the infinite danger of trusting power to a Cabinet composed principally of persons favourable to emancipation: and, at the same time, pointed the indignation of the latter against the perfidy of the pretended friends who had not stipulated that emancipation should be made a ministerial measure! We cannot sufficiently admire the exquisite dexterity of an assailant who, in the same breath, blames the same people for doing, and for *not* doing the same thing. To ordinary plebeian understandings we should think it undeniable that the Catholic question must be now—either in the same situation in which it was before the late change; or it must have lost; or it must have gained. If it have gained, the Whigs are justified; if it have lost, the enemies of the claims ought zealously to support the new government; if it be exactly where it was before, no person who acted with Lord Liverpool can, on this ground, consistently oppose Mr. Canning.

In this view, indeed, the cause of the Whigs is the cause of the ministers who have seceded from the Cabinet. Both parties have put in the same plea; and both must be acquitted or condemned together. If it be allowed that the elevation of Mr. Canning was not an event favourable to the Catholic cause, the Whigs will certainly stand convicted of inconsistency. But at the same time, the only argument by which the ex-Ministers have attempted to vindicate their secession, must fall to the ground; and it will be difficult to consider that proceeding in any other light than as a factious expedient to which they have resorted, in order to embarrass a colleague whom they envied. If, on the other hand, the effect of the late change were such, that it became the duty of those who objected to Catholic Emancipation, to decline all connexion with the Ministry, it must surely have become, at the same time, the duty of the friends of Emancipation to support the Ministry. Those who take the one ground, when their object is to vindicate the seceders, and the other, when their object is to blacken the Whigs, who, in the same speech, do not scruple to represent the Catholic cause as triumphant and as hopeless, may, we fear, draw down some ridicule on themselves, but will hardly convince the country. But why did not the Whigs stipulate that some proposition for the relief of the Catholics should be immediately brought forward, and supported by the whole influence of the Administration? We answer, simply because they could not obtain such conditions, and because, by insisting upon them, they would have irreparably injured those whom they meant to serve, and have thrown the government into the hands of men who would have employed all its power and patronage to support a system which, we do not scruple to say, is the shame of England, and the curse of Ireland. By the course which they have taken, they have insured to the sister kingdom every alleviation which its calamities can receive from the lenient administration of an oppressive system. Under their government, it will at least be no man's interest to espouse the side of bigotry. Truth will have a fair chance against prejudice. And whenever the dislike with which the majority of the English people regard the Catholic claims shall have been overcome by discussion, no other obstacle will remain to be surmounted.

The friends of the Catholics have, indeed, too long kept out of sight the real difficulty which impedes the progress of all measures for their relief. There has been a nervous reluctance—perhaps a natural unwillingness, to approach this subject. Yet it is of the utmost importance that it should at last be fully understood. The difficulty, we believe, is neither with the King nor with the Cabinet,—neither with the Commons nor with the Lords. It is with the People of England; and not with the corrupt, not with the servile, not with the rude and uneducated, not with the dissolute and turbulent, but with the great body of the middling orders;—of those who live in comfort, and have received some instruction. Of the higher classes, the decided majority is, beyond all dispute, with the Catholics. The lower classes care nothing at all about the question. It is among those whose influence is generally exerted for the most salutary purposes,—among those from whom liberal statesmen have, in general, received the strongest support,—among those who feel the deepest detestation of oppression and corruption, that erroneous opinions on this subject are most frequent. A faction with which they have no other feeling in common, has, on this question, repeatedly made them its tools, and has diverted their attention more than once from its own folly and profligacy, by raising the cry of No Popery. They have espoused their opinions, not from want of honesty, not from want of sense, but simply from want of information and reflection. They think as the most enlightened men in England thought seventy or eighty years ago. Pulteney and Pelham would no more have given political power to Papists than to ourang-outangs. A proposition for mitigating the severity of the penal laws would, in their time, have been received with suspicion. The full discussion which the subject has since undergone, has produced a great change. Among intelligent men in that rank of life from which our ministers and the members of our legislature are selected, the feeling in favour of concession is strong and general. But, unfortunately, sufficient attention has not been paid to a lower, but most influential and respectable class. The friends of the Catholic claims, content with numbering in their ranks all the most distinguished statesmen of two generations, proud of lists of minorities and majorities adorned by every name which commands the respect of the country, have not sufficiently exerted themselves to combat popular prejudices. Pamphlets against Emancipation are circulated, and no answers appear. Sermons are preached against it, and no pains are taken to obliterate the impression. The rector carries a petition round to every shopkeeper and every farmer in his parish, talks of Smithfield and the inquisition, Bishop Bonner and Judge Jeffries. No person takes the trouble to canvass on the other side. At an election, the candidate who is favonrable to the Catholic claims, is almost always content to stand on the defensive. He shrinks from the odium of a bold avowal. While his antagonist asserts and reviles, he palliates, evades, and distinguishes. He is unwilling to give a pledge: he has not made up his mind: he hopes that adequate securities for the Church may be obtained: he will wait to see how the Catholic States of South America behave themselves! And thus, as fast as he can, he gets away from the obnoxious subject, to retrenchment, reform, or negro slavery. If such a man succeeds, his vote does not benefit the Catholics half so much as his shuffling injures them. How can the people understand the question, when those whose business is to enlighten them, will not state it to them plainly? Is it strange that they should dislike a cause of which almost all its advocates seem to be ashamed? If, at the late election, all our public men who are favourable to Emancipation had dared to speak out, had introduced the subject of their own accord, and discussed it day after day, they might have lost a few votes; they might have been compelled to face a few dead cats; but they would have put down the prejudice effectually. Five or six friends of the claims might have been unseated, but the claims would have been carried.

The popular aversion to them is an honest aversion; according to the measure of knowledge which the people possess, it is a just aversion. It has been reasoned down wherever the experiment has been fearlessly tried. It may be reasoned down everywhere. The war should be carried on in every quarter. No misrepresentation should be suffered to pass unrefuted. When a silly letter from Philo-Melancthon, or Anti-Doyle, about the Coronation Oath, or divided allegiance, makes its appearance in the corner of a provincial newspaper, it will not do merely to say "What stuff!" We must remember that such statements constantly reiterated, and seldom answered, will assuredly be believed. Plain, spirited, moderate treatises on the subject, should find their way into every cottage;—not such rancorous nonsense as that for which the Catholics formerly contracted with the fiercest and basest libeller of the age, the apostate politician, the fraudulent debtor, the ungrateful friend, whom England has twice spewed out to America; whom America, though far from squeamish, has twice vomited back to England. They will not, they may be assured, serve their cause by pouring forth unmeasured abuse on men whose memory is justly dear to the hearts of a great people;—men mighty even in their weaknesses, and wise even in their fanaticism;—the goodly fellowship of our reformers,—the noble army of our martyrs. Their scandal about Queen Elizabeth, and their wood-cuts of the devil whispering in the ear of John Fox, will produce nothing but disgust. They must conduct the controversy with good sense and good temper, and there cannot be the slightest doubt of the issue. But of this they may be fully assured, that, while the general feeling of the Nation remains unchanged, a Ministry which should stake its existence on the success of their claims, would ruin itself, without benefiting them.

The conduct of the Catholics, on the present occasion, deserves the highest praise. They have shown that experience has at last taught them to know their enemies from their friends. Indeed, there are few scenes in this tragicomic world of ours more amusing than that which the leaders of the Opposition are now performing. The very men who have so long obstructed Emancipation—who have stirred up the public feeling in England against Emancipation,—who, in fine, have just resigned their offices, because a supporter of Emancipation was placed at the head of the government,—are now weeping over the disappointed hopes of the poor Papists, and execrating the perfidious Whigs who have taken office without stipulating for their relief! The Catholics are, in the meantime, in the highest spirits, congratulating themselves on the success of their old friends, and laughing at the condoling visages of their new champions.

Something not very dissimilar is taking place with respect to Parliamentary Reform. The reformers are delighted with the new Ministry. Their opponents are trying to convince them that they ought to be dissatisfied with it. The Whigs, we suppose, ought to have insisted that Reform should be made a Ministerial measure. We will not at present inquire whether they have, as a body, ever declared any decided opinion on the subject. A much shorter answer will suffice. Be Reform good or bad, it is at present evidently unattainable. No man can, by coming into office, or by going out of office, either effect it or prevent it. As we are arguing with people who are more influenced by one name than by ten reasons, we will remind them of the conduct pursued by Mr. Pitt with regard to this question. At the very time when he publicly pledged himself to use his whole power, "*as a man and as a minister, honestly and boldly*" to carry a proposition of Parliamentary Reform, he was sitting in the same Cabinet with persons decidedly hostile to every measure of the kind. At the present juncture, we own that we should think it as absurd in any man to decline office for the sake of this object, as it would have been in Sir Thomas More to refuse the Great Seal, because he could not introduce all the institutions of Utopia into England. The world would be in a wretched state indeed, if no person were to accept of power, under a form of government which he thinks susceptible of improvement. The effect of such scrupulosity would be, that the best and wisest men would always be out of place; that all authority would be committed to those who might be too stupid or too selfish to see abuses in any system by which they could profit, and who, by their follies and vices, would aggravate all the evils springing from defective institutions.

But were we to admit the truth of every charge which personal enemies or professional slanderers have brought against the present ministers of the Crown, were we to admit that they had abandoned their principles, that they had betrayed the Catholics and the Reformers, it would still remain to be considered, whether we might not change for the worse. We trust in God that there is no danger. We think that this country never will, never can, be subjected to the rule of a party so weak, so violent, so ostentatiously selfish, as that which is now in Opposition. Has the Cabinet been formed by a coalition? How, let us ask, has the Opposition been formed? Is it not composed of men who have, all their lives, been thwarting and abusing each other, Jacobins, Whigs, Tories, friends of Catholic Emancipation, enemies of Catholic Emancipation,—men united only by their common love of high rents, by their common envy of superior abilities, by their common wish to depress the people and to dictate to the throne? Did Lord Lansdowne at any time differ so widely from Mr. Canning as Lord Redesdale from Lord Lauderdale—sometime needle-maker, and candidate for the shrievalty of London? Are the Ministers charged with deserting their opinions? and can we find no instance of miraculous conversion on the left of the woolsack? What was the influence which transformed the *Friend of the People* into an aristocrat, "resolved to stand or fall with his order?" Whence was the sudden illumination, which at once disclosed to all the discarded Ministers the imperfections of the Corn Bill? Let us suppose that the Whigs had, as a party, brought forward some great measure before the late changes, that they had carried it through the Commons, that they had sent it up, with the fairest prospect of success, to the Lords, and that they had then, in order to gratify Mr. Canning, consented, in the face of all their previous declarations, to defeat it, what a tempest of execration and derision would have burst upon them! Yet the conduct of the Ex-Ministers, according to the best lights we can obtain upon it, was even more culpable than this. Not content with doing a bad thing, they did it in the worst way. The bill which had been prepared by the leader for whom they professed boundless veneration, which had been brought in under their own sanction, which, as they positively declared, had received their fullest consideration, which one of themselves had undertaken to conduct through the House of Lords, that very bill they contrived to defeat:—and, in the act of defeating it, they attempted to lay upon the colleagues whom they had deserted, the burden of public resentment which they alone had incurred. We would speak with indulgence of men who had done their country noble service before—and of many of whom, individually, it must be impossible to think otherwise than with respect. But the scene lately passed in that great assembly has afflicted and disgusted the country at large; and it is not the least of its evil consequences, that it has lessened in the public estimation, not only a body which ought always to be looked up to with respect, but many individuals of whose motives we cannot bring ourselves to judge unfavourably, and from whose high qualities we trust the country may yet receive both benefit and honour. Mr. Peel fortunately did not expose himself quite as effectually as his associates; though we regret that the tone he adopted was so undecided and equivocal. It was not for him to pronounce any judgment on the wisdom of their conduct. He was fully convinced of the purity of their motives. And finally it was the eighteenth of June!—a day on which, it seems, the Duke of Wellington is privileged to commit all sorts of mischief with impunity to the end of his life. The Duke of Wellington, however, though the part which he took was unfortunately prominent, seems to have been comparatively innocent. He might not, while in office, have paid much attention to the measure in its original form. He might not have understood the real nature of his own unlucky amendment. But what were the motives of Earl Bathurst? Or where were they when he undertook the care of the bill in its former shape? Nothing had been changed since, excepting his own situation. And it would be the very madness of charity to believe, that, if he had still been a colleague of Lord Liverpool, or had been able to come to terms with Mr. Canning, he would have pursued such a line of conduct. Culpably as all his coadjutors have acted in this transaction, his share of it is the most indefensible.

And it is for these men,—for men who, before they have been two months out of office, have retracted the declarations which they made on a most important subject just before they quitted office,—that we are to discard the present ministers, as inconsistent and unprincipled! And these men are the idols of those who entertain so virtuous a loathing for unnatural coalitions, and base compromises. These men think themselves entitled to boast of the purity of their public virtues, and to repel, with indignant amazement, any imputation of interested or factious motives.

We dwell long on this event; because it is one which enables the country to estimate correctly the practical principles of those who, if the present ministers should fall, will assuredly take their places. To call their conduct merely factious, is to deal with it far too mildly. It has been factious at the expense of consistency, and of all concern for the wishes and interests of the people. Was there no other mode of embarrassing the government? Could no other opportunity be found or made for a division? Was there no other pledge which could be violated, if not with less awkwardness to themselves, at least with less injury to the state? Was it necessary that they should make a handle of a question on which the passions of the people were roused to the highest point, and on which its daily bread might depend that they should condemn the country to another year of agitation, and expose it to dangers, which, only a few months before, they had themselves thought it necessary to avert, by advising an extraordinary exercise of the prerogative? There is one explanation, and only one. They were out, and they longed to be in. Decency, consistency, the prosperity and peace of the country, were as dust in the balance. They knew this question had divided men who were generally united, and united others who were usually opposed; and though they themselves had already taken their part with their colleagues in office and the more intelligent part of their habitual opponents, they did not scruple, for the sake of embarrassing those they had deserted, to purchase the appearance of a numerous following, by opposing a measure which they had themselves concocted, and pledged themselves to support. From the expedients to which they have resorted in Opposition, we may judge of what we have to expect if they should ever return to office.

They will return too, it must be remembered, not, as before, the colleagues of men by whose superior talents they were overawed, and to whose beneficial measures they were often compelled to yield a reluctant consent. The late change has separated the greater part of them from all such associates for ever: it has divided the light from the darkness: it has set all the wisdom, all the liberality, all the public spirit on one side; the imbecility, the bigotry, and the rashness on the other. If they rule again, they will rule alone.

They will return to situations which they will owe neither to their talents nor to their virtues, neither to the choice of their King nor to the love of their country; but solely to the support of an Oligarchical Faction, richly endowed with every quality which ensures to its possessors the hatred of a nation,—a faction arbitrary, bigoted, and insolent,—a faction which makes parade of its contempt for the dearest interests of mankind, which loves to make the people feel of how little weight, in its deliberations, is the consideration of their happiness.

On this party, and on this alone, must such ministers, returning from such a secession, rely to uphold them against the public opinion, against the wishes of a King who has wisely and nobly performed his duty to the state, against the most beloved and respected portion of the aristocracy, against a formidable union of all the great statesmen and orators of the age. It was believed by those of whose wisdom Lord Eldon and the Duke of Newcastle think with reverence, that, in the bond between a sorcerer and his familiar demon, there was a stipulation that the gifts bestowed by the Powers of Evil should never be employed but for purposes of evil. Omnipotent for mischief, these obligors of the fiend were powerless for good. Such will be the compact between the Ex-Ministers, if ever they should return to power, and the only party which can then support them. That they may be masters, they must be slaves. They will be able to stand only by abject submission and by boundless profusion—by giving up the People to be oppressed, first for the profit of the Great, and then for their amusement,—by corn-laws, and game-laws, and pensions for Lord Robert, and places for Lord John.

They will return pledged to oppose every reform, to maintain a constant struggle against the spirit of the age, to defend abuses to which the nation is every day becoming more quick-sighted. Even Mr. Peel, if, unluckily, he should at last identify himself with their faction, must restrain his propensity to innovation. Mutterings have already been heard in high places against his tendencies to liberality; and all his schemes for the reformation of our code or our courts must be abandoned.

Then will come all those desperate and cruel expedients of which none but bad governments stand in need. The press is troublesome. There must be fresh laws against the press. Secret societies are formed. The Habeas Corpus act must be suspended. The people are distressed and tumultuous. They must be kept down by force. The army must be increased; and the taxes must be increased. Then the distress and tumult are increased: and then the army must be increased again! The country will be governed as a child is governed by an ill-tempered nurse,—first beaten till it cries, and then beaten because it cries!

Our firm conviction is, that if the seceders return to office, they will act thus; and that they will not have the power, even if they should have the inclination, to act otherwise. And what must the end of these things be? We answer, without hesitation, that, if this course be persisted in, if these counsels and these counsellors are maintained, the end must be, a revolution, a bloody and unsparing revolution—a revolution which will make the ears of those who hear of it tingle in the remotest countries, and in the remotest times. The middling orders in England are, we well know, attached to the institutions of their country, but not with a blindly partial attachment. They see the merits of the system; but they also see its faults; and they have a strong and growing desire that these faults should be removed. If, while their wish for improvement is becoming stronger and stronger, the government is to become worse and worse, the consequences are obvious. Even now, it is impossible to disguise, that there is arising in the bosom of that class a Republican sect, as audacious, as paradoxical, as little inclined to respect antiquity, as enthusiastically attached to its ends, as unscrupulous in the choice of its means, as the French Jacobins themselves,—but far superior to the French Jacobins in acuteness and information—in caution, in patience, and in resolution. They are men whose minds have been put into training for violent exertion. All that is merely ornamental—all that gives the roundness, the smoothness, and the bloom, has been exsuded. Nothing is left but nerve, and muscle, and bone. Their love of liberty is no boyish fancy. It is not nourished by rhetoric, and it does not evaporate in rhetoric. They care nothing for Leonidas, and Epaminondas, and Brutus, and Cocles. They profess to derive their opinions from demonstration alone; and are never so little satisfied with them as when they see them exhibited in a romantic form. Metaphysical and political science engage their whole attention. Philosophical pride has done for them what spiritual pride did for the Puritans in a former age; it has generated in them an aversion for the fine arts, for elegant literature, and for the sentiments of chivalry. It has made them arrogant, intolerant, and impatient of all superiority. These qualities will, in spite of their real claims to respect, render them unpopular, as long as the people are satisfied with their rulers. But under an ignorant and tyrannical ministry, obstinately opposed to the most moderate and judicious innovations, their principles would spread as rapidly as those of the Puritans formerly spread, in spite of their offensive peculiarities. The public, disgusted with the blind adherence of its rulers to ancient abuses, would be reconciled to the most startling novelties. A strong democratic party would be formed in the educated class. In the lowest, and most numerous order of the population, those who have any opinions at all are democrats already. In our manufacturing towns, the feeling is even now formidably strong; and it is not strange that it should be so: For it is on persons in this station that the abuses of our system press most heavily; while its advantages, on the other hand, are comparatively little felt by them. An abundant supply of the necessaries of life is, with them, almost the only consideration. The difference between an arbitrary and a limited monarchy vanishes, when compared with the difference between one meal a-day and three meals a-day. It is poor consolation to a man who has had no breakfast, and expects no supper, that the King does not possess a dispensing power, and that troops cannot be raised in time of peace, without the consent of Parliament. With this class, our government, free as it is, is even now as unpopular as if it were despotic,—nay, much more so. In despotic states, the multitude is unaccustomed to general speculations on politics. Even when men suffer most severely, they look no further than the proximate cause. They demand the abolition of a particular duty, or tear an obnoxious individual to pieces. But they never think of attacking the whole system. If Constantinople were in the state in which Manchester and Leeds have lately been, there would be a cry against the Grand Vizier or the bakers. The head of the Vizier would be thrown to the mob, over the wall of the Seraglio—a score of bakers would be smothered in their own ovens; and everything would go on as before. Not a single rioter would think of curtailing the prerogatives of the Sultan, or of demanding a representative divan. But people familiar with political inquiries carry their scrutiny farther; and, justly or unjustly, attribute the grievances under which they labour, to defects in the original constitution of the government. Thus it is with a large proportion of our spinners, our grinders, and our weavers. It is not too much to say, that in a season of distress, they are ripe for any revolution. This, indeed, is acknowledged by all the Tory writers of our time. But all this, they tell us, comes of education—it is all the fault of the Liberals. We will not take up the time of our readers with answering such observations. We will only remind our gentry and clergy, that the question at present is not about the *cause* of the evil, but about its *cure;* and that, unless due precaution be used, let the fault be whose it may, the punishment will inevitably be their own.

The history of our country, since the peace of 1815, is almost entirely made up of the struggles of the lower orders against the government, and of the efforts of the government to keep them down. In 1816, immense assemblies were convened, secret societies were formed, and gross outrages were committed. In 1817, the Habeas Corpus Act was twice suspended. In 1819, the disturbances broke out afresh. Meetings were held, so formidable, from their numbers and their spirit, that the Ministry, and the Parliament, approved of the conduct of magistrates who had dispersed one of them by the sword. Fresh laws were passed against seditious writings and practices. Yet the following year commenced with a desperate and extended conspiracy for the assassination of the cabinet, and the subversion of the government. A few months after this event, the Queen landed. On that occasion, the majority of the middling orders joined with the mob. The effect of the union was irresistible. The Ministers and the Parliament stood aghast; the bill of pains and penalties was dropped; and a convulsion, which seemed inevitable, was averted. But the events of that year ought to impress one lesson on the mind of every public man,—that an alliance between the disaffected multitude and a large portion of the middling orders, is one with which no government can venture to cope, without imminent danger to the constitution.

A government like that with which England would be cursed, if the present Ministry should fall before the present Opposition, would render such an alliance not only inevitable, but permanent. In less than ten years, it would goad every Reformer in the country into a Revolutionist. It would place at the head of the multitude, persons possessing all the education, all the judgment, and all the habits of co-operation, in which the multitude itself is deficient. That great body is physically the most powerful in the state. Like the Hebrew champion, it is yet held in captivity by its blindness. But if once the eyeless Giant shall find a guide to put his hand on the props of the State—if once he shall bow himself upon the pillars, woe to all those who have made him their laughing-stock, or chained him to grind at their mill!

We do, therefore, firmly believe, that, even if no external cause were to precipitate a fatal crisis, this country could not be governed for a single generation by such men as Lord Westmoreland and Lord Eldon, without extreme risk of revolution. But there are other symptoms in the body politic, not less alarming than those which we have described. In Ireland, there are several millions of Catholics, who do not love our government; and who detest, with all their heart, with all their soul, with all their mind, and with all their strength, the party now in Opposition. The accession of that party to power, would be a death-blow to their hopes of obtaining their demands by constitutional means: and we may fairly expect, that all the events which followed the recall of Lord Fitzwilliam, will take place again, on a greater and more formidable scale. One thing, indeed, we have no right to expect, that a second Hoche will be as unfortunate as the former. A civil war in Ireland will lead almost necessarily to a war with France. Maritime hostilities with France, and the clash of neutral and belligerent pretensions, will then produce war with America. Then come expeditions to Canada and expeditions to Java. The Cape of Good Hope must be garrisoned. Lisbon must be defended. Let us suppose the best. That best must be, a long conflict, a dear-bought victory, a great addition to a debt already most burthensome, fresh taxes, and fresh discontents. All these are events which may not improbably happen under any government—events which the next month may bring forth—events, against which no minister, however able and honest, can with perfect certainty provide,—but which Ministers, whose policy should exasperate the people of Ireland, would almost unavoidably bring upon us. A

Cabinet formed by the Ex-ministers could scarcely exist for a year, without incensing the lower classes of the English to frenzy, by giving them up to the selfish tyranny of its aristocratical supporters, without driving Ireland into rebellion, and without tempting France to war.

There is one hope, and one hope only for our country; and that hope is in a liberal Administration,—in an Administration which will follow with cautious, but with constantly advancing steps, the progress of the public mind; which, by promptitude to redress practical grievances, will enable itself to oppose with authority and effect, the propositions of turbulent theorists; which by kindness and fairness in all its dealings with the People, will entitle itself to their confidence and esteem.

The state of England at the present moment bears a close resemblance to that of France at the time when Turgot was called to the head of affairs. Abuses were numerous; public burdens heavy; a spirit of innovation was abroad among the people. The philosophical minister attempted to secure the ancient institutions, by amending them. The mild reforms which he projected, had they been carried into execution, would have conciliated the people, and saved from the most tremendous of all commotions the church, the aristocracy, and the throne. But a crowd of narrow-minded nobles, ignorant of their own interest, though solicitous for nothing else, the Newcastles and the Salisburys of France, began to tremble for their oppressive franchises. Their clamours overpowered the mild good sense of a king who wanted only firmness to be the best of sovereigns. The minister was discarded for councillors more obsequious to the privileged orders; and the aristocracy and clergy exulted in their success.

Then came a new period of profusion and misrule. And then, swiftly, like an armed man, came poverty and dismay. The acclamations of the nobles, and the *Te Deums* of the church, grew fainter and fainter. The very courtiers muttered disapprobation.

The ministers stammered out feeble and inconsistent counsels. But all other voices were soon drowned in one, which every moment waxed louder and more terrible,—in the fierce and tumultuous roar of a great people, conscious of irresistible strength, maddened by intolerable wrongs, and sick of deferred hopes! That cry, so long stifled, now rose from every corner of France, made itself heard in the presence-chamber of her king, in the saloons of her nobles, and in the refectories of her luxurious priesthood. Then, at length, concessions were made which the subjects of Louis the Fourteenth would have thought it impious even to desire,—which the most factious opponent of Louis the Fifteenth had never ventured to ask,—which, but a few years before, would have been received with ecstacies of gratitude. But it was too late!

The imprisoned genie of the Arabian Tales, during the early period of his confinement, promised wealth, empire, and supernatural powers, to the man who should extricate him. But when he had waited long in vain, mad with rage at the continuance of his captivity, he vowed to destroy his deliverer without mercy! Such is the gratitude of nations, exasperated by misgovernment, to rulers who are slow to concede. The first use which they make of freedom is to avenge themselves on those who have been so slow to grant it.

Never was this disposition more remarkably displayed than at the period of which we speak. Abuses were swept away with unsparing severity. The royal prerogatives, the feudal privileges, the provincial distinctions, were sacrificed to the passions of the people. Every thing was given; and every thing was given in vain. Distrust and hatred were not to be thus eradicated from the minds of men who thought that they were not receiving favors but extorting rights; and that, if they deserved blame, it was not for their insensibility to tardy benefits, but for their forgetfulness of past oppression.

What followed was the necessary consequence of such a state of feeling. The recollection of old grievances made the people suspicious and cruel. The fear of popular outrages produced emigrations, intrigues with foreign courts, and, finally, a general war. Then came the barbarity of fear; the triple despotism of the clubs, the committees, and the commune; the organized anarchy, the fanatical atheism, the scheming and far-sighted madness, the butcheries of the Chatelet, and the accursed marriages of the Loire. The whole property of the nation changed hands. Its best and wisest citizens were banished or murdered. Dungeons were emptied by assassins as fast as they were filled by spies. Provinces were made desolate. Towns were unpeopled. Old things passed away. All things became new.

The paroxysm terminated. A singular train of events restored the house of Bourbon to the French throne. The exiles have returned. But they have returned as the few survivors of the deluge returned to a world in which they could recognise nothing; in which the valleys had been raised, and the mountains depressed, and the courses of the rivers changed,—in which sand and seaweed had covered the cultivated fields and the walls of imperial cities. They have returned to seek in vain, amidst the mouldering relics of a former system, and the fermenting elements of a new creation, the traces of any remembered object. The old boundaries are obliterated. The old laws are forgotten. The old titles have become laughing-stocks. The gravity of the parliaments, and the pomp of the hierarchy; the doctors whose disputes agitated the Sorbonne, and the embroidered multitude whose footsteps wore out the marble pavements of Versailles,—all have disappeared. The proud and voluptuous prelates who feasted on silver, and dozed amidst curtains of massy velvet, have been replaced by curates who undergo every drudgery and every humiliation for the wages of lackeys. To those gay and elegant nobles who studied military science as a fashionable accomplishment, and expected military rank as a part of their birthright, have succeeded men born in lofts and cellars; educated in the half-naked ranks of the revolutionary armies, and raised by ferocious valour and self-taught skill, to dignities with which the coarseness of their manners and language forms a grotesque contrast. The government may amuse itself by playing at despotism, by reviving the names and aping the style of the old court—as Helenus in Epirus consoled himself for the lost magnificence of Troy, by calling his brook Xanthus, and the entrance of his little capital the Scæan gate. But the law of entail is gone, and cannot be restored. The liberty of the press is established, and the feeble struggles of the minister cannot permanently put it down. The Bastile is fallen, and can never more rise from its ruins. A few words, a few ceremonies, a few rhetorical topics, make up all that remains of that system which was founded so deeply by the policy of the house of Valois, and adorned so splendidly by the pride of Louis the Great.

Is this a romance? Or is it a faithful picture of what has lately been in a neighboring land—of what may shortly be within the borders of our own? Has the warning been given in vain? Have our Mannerses and Clintons so soon forgotten the fate of houses as wealthy and as noble as their own? Have they forgotten how the tender and delicate woman,—the woman who would not set her foot on the earth for tenderness and delicateness, the idol of gilded drawing-rooms, the pole-star of crowded theatres, the standard of beauty, the arbitress of fashion, the patroness of genius—was compelled to exchange her luxurious and dignified ease for labour and dependence; the sighs of dukes and the flattery of bowing abbés for the insults of rude pupils and exacting mothers;—perhaps, even to draw an infamous and miserable subsistence from those charms which had been the glory of royal circles—to sell for a morsel of bread her reluctant caresses and her haggard smiles—to be turned over from a garret to a hospital, and from a hospital to a parish vault? Have they forgotten how the gallant and luxurious nobleman, sprung from illustrious ancestors, marked out from his cradle for the highest honours of the state and of the army, impatient of control, exquisitely sensible of the slightest affront, with all his high spirit, his polished manners, his voluptuous habits, was reduced to request, with tears in his eyes, credit for half-a-crown,—to pass day after day in hearing the auxiliary verbs misrecited, or the first page of Télémaque misconstrued, by petulant boys, who infested him with nicknames and caricatures, who mimicked his foreign accent, and laughed at his thread-bare coat. Have they forgotten all this? God grant that they may never remember it with unavailing self-accusation, when desolation shall have visited wealthier cities and fairer gardens;—when Manchester shall be as Lyons, and Stowe as Chantilly;—when he who now, in the pride of rank and opulence, sneers at what we have written in the bitter sincerity of our hearts, shall be thankful for a porringer of broth at the door of some Spanish convent, or shall implore some Italian money-lender to advance another pistole on his George!

STATE OF PARTIES.*

[A Sequel to the Preceding Article.]

Spirit of Party. 8vo. London, 1827.

We design to make here a few observations, by way of supplement to the Article in our last Number, which has been in several particulars†, we are sorry to find, exceedingly misunderstood in some respectable quarters, as it has certainly, we are not surprised to remark, been grossly misrepresented in others of a widely different description.

The State of Parties, and the condition of public affairs generally, is, in some respects, materially different from anything ever known in this country. For some years, indeed ever since the termination of the wars arising out of the French Revolution, the opinions favoured by sound reason, and avouched by the practical test of experience, upon all subjects of foreign and domestic policy, had been making a steady and sure, because a quiet and peaceful progress among the more intelligent parts of the community. As intelligence spread wider by the diffusion of knowledge, the dissemination of those opinions became more enlarged, and their operation upon all classes of society more efficacious. They had been making considerable advances both in France and England, during the period between the American and the French Revolutions. But the latter event had cruelly disappointed in its progress

* Edinburgh Review, October, 1827.

† Among other mistakes, we find it ascribed to various persons, eminent statesmen and others, who, if they have ever seen it, which we know not, assuredly never could have seen it before it was published.

the hopes raised by its first fair prospects; and the horrors of the times of Anarchy, followed by the military tyranny of Napoleon, and the dreadful wars in which he involved his country and Europe, otherwise so deeply his debtors, had stampt all change with the most hateful characters, and accustomed men to confound reform with rebellion, reckoning the friend of freedom and improvement, one who would sacrifice order and peace, and all established institutions, to wild extravagant speculation—a victim as it were to the love of change for its own sake. The fall of Napoleon, and the peace that followed the French Restoration, finally put down those groundless prejudices against the safest course of policy, and made an end of the calumnies so long heaped upon the best friends of order and existing establishments—those who, by tranquil amendments, would destroy all the purchase that revolutionists ever can have whereby to work their overthrow. Accordingly, the natural course of education and knowledge has silently been producing its fruits; sound and enlightened views of policy have been gaining ground; truth, no longer counteracted in its progress, has been making way everywhere; and wisdom, no longer overawed by noisy clamour or childish fears, has been teaching her lessons to a willing generation.

For some years of the period on which we are looking back, the Government of this country was intrusted to the management of men, who gave it a direction widely different from the course of public opinion, and conducted it upon all the principles of the most narrow and vicious policy, as if they alone, and the engine in their hands, stood still amidst the general advance of the age. While the Finances, and indeed all the internal affairs of the State, were under the guidance of persons, whose notions were the refuse of the antiquated school; the Foreign Minister, though not by nature deficient in liberal feelings, and certainly gifted with no common talents, and, above all, with great sagacity, had, unhappily for his country and for his reputation, become intimately connected with the Continental Sovereigns and their chief Statesmen, and had imbibed from this intercourse a prejudice against free opinions, and a dislike of Constitutional Government, so strong as almost to renew in our political system, the exploded terrors about Jacobinism and French principles. All improvements in the Constitution of the Continental States were to be discountenanced as revolutionary: everything that could lead to a change, how slowly and peaceably soever, was to be resisted: the strong arm of absolute power was to be deemed the only security for the public peace; and the iron hand of military force, the only means by which that arm could work its destined end. These principles soon embodied themselves in the famous League so universally dreaded at first, then detested, and since despised, under the name of the Holy Alliance. Professing only to have the intention of keeping the peace, those combined Princes, extending their union over almost all Europe, guaranteed to each other, not only the integrity of their dominions, but the unchanged existence of all their internal institutions; and some of them having succeeded in reconquering their dominions from Napoleon, by the aid of their people, to whom they had promised a Representative Government, as the appropriate reward of a constancy worthy of freemen, Europe, with astonishment, saw those very Monarchs become parties to this combination against all improvement, as if for the very purpose of preventing themselves from redeeming pledges so sacred, and which had passed for so mighty a consideration. The wonder, however, stopt not here: The leagued Sovereigns made war at their pleasure to prevent the peace from being disturbed. Wherever a Prince was compelled or induced to adopt free institutions, the Allies marched an army to restore his absolute authority and his people's subjection; and the formal accession of England was alone wanting to make the sway of this grand nuisance universal; nay, to extend its claims, which were once actually preferred, over our own country. In all these unheard of proceedings, infinitely more dangerous to National Independence than the wildest fury of the French Republic, or the mightiest projects of Napoleon himself, it was a miserable sight to behold England, once the patroness of public freedom,—the enemy of aggression,—the refuge of all oppressed nations, stoop to become the willing witness, and even the unresisting tool of the most flagitious conspiracy the world ever saw, excepting, perhaps, the high crime last perpetrated by the same despotic Princes, the partition of Poland. Yet so it was; and such was the price we paid for our Minister having acted as our Ambassador, and kept the high company of absolute Monarchs, and their unconstitutional and irresponsible counsellors. The tone, too, of these foreign Courts was imported into our Parliament and our Cabinet; it became customary to deride everything free and liberal as new-fangled, and low, and dangerous to good government; men extolled all the little drivelling notions of Austrian *Hof-raths* and *Kriegs-raths*, as sound, old, well-wearing maxims, and laughed at the doctrines of the New-School, as wholly unknown to the warriors of Leipsic and Waterloo, or the negotiators of Vienna and of Aix. It is true, that our official statesmen had all this pleasantry to themselves; they made no converts in the country; they found neither sympathy nor support from the people; and as often as they attempted in Parliament to countenance their favourite topic, the sorry reception they met with, seemed adjusted in a nice proportion to its intrinsic merit, and the talents by which it was recommended.

Meanwhile, upon questions of internal policy, the liberal feelings of the country generally prevailed, even in Parliamentary divisions, over the narrow views of the Court. One after another, the Government abandoned many of the most pernicious taxes and lines of mercantile policy, and at length, after long resistance, it adopted sound principles upon the important subject of reform in the system and administration of the laws. While its opponents were preparing new measures, and expecting additional triumphs at home; while its allies abroad were about to carry their aggressions on all national independence farther than ever, by the most iniquitous of all their measures for extirpating liberty; the melancholy event of the minister's decease, who had erred, we believe, much more from want of foresight and deliberate reflection in the early stage of the intercourse, than from any evil designs towards liberty at any period, gave a new and happier aspect to the face of affairs in this country, as far as the Government was concerned, and eventually produced a very sensible change for the better in the policy of other powers, and in the prospects of a large portion of the world. He was succeeded by a statesman of far more enlarged views, and more brilliant talents, his inferior certainly in some of the qualities calculated to gain a following in Parliament, but worthy of all acceptation in comparison of him, because unconnected with the enemies of freedom, and committed to none of the worst principles at least of later times, by which improvement had been stifled abroad and obstructed at home. Catastrophes very different indeed, but almost equally sudden, have now deprived the country of both those statesmen; and we may be enabled calmly to reflect upon their conduct and their merits, without heaping on the one unmerited obloquy, though, unfortunately for his fame, he died when events had brought the policy he was connected with to its lowest pitch in public consideration,—without raising altars to the other's memory, because we lost him when the system he maintained looked the fairest in all men's eyes, and dazzled them into a forgetfulness of all that had happened before.

The progress of liberal opinions was immediately and rapidly accelerated by the conduct, and still more by the language, of the Government in 1823 and the subsequent years. In a few months the disgraceful connexion with the Holy Alliance was at an end, and the further proceedings of that combination were so far checked, that it can hardly now be said to have any real existence.

The recognition of the new commonwealths in South America, and the establishment of political as well as mercantile relations with them, very soon followed; the odious provisions of the Alien Bill were suffered to expire, and a restriction of little or no moment substituted in their place; and the most decisive steps were taken to defend Portugal, harassed by the intrigues, and menaced by the arms of Spain, for the crime of having accepted a Constitutional Government. At home, the policy so long recommended by the *Liberal Party* both in and out of doors, was as steadily and effectually pursued, as that which they had maintained to be the sound, and British, and statesman-like view of Foreign Affairs. Oppressive and impolitic taxes were repealed, among others the duties on law proceedings; the principles of Free Trade were adopted in many important cases, and the way was paved for extending them to all the parts of our mercantile system; some of the reforms in the Criminal Law, which Sir Samuel Romilly had so long in vain laboured to recommend, and which had been resisted with too much success till 1819, when Sir James Mackintosh, his follower in the same honourable career, carried a Committee for examining the state of that Code, were, on the principles of those enlightened individuals, taken up by their former antagonists, and received the sanction of the Legislature; nay, so harmless was the name of judicial reform become, and so popular its pursuit with both court and country, that the same persons stopt not there, but introduced improvements, though more limited in principle, into other branches of jurisprudence.

The effects produced by this fortunate and unexpected change in the conduct of the Ministry, upon the state and distribution of parties, both in Parliament and in the Country, were such as might have been expected, unless men had lost all regard for principle and consistency in their personal animosities, or in the worst abuse of party feelings. The Opposition lent their warm support to Government, as often as they saw a disposition to pursue the sound and enlightened policy always recommended by them. Far from the despicable, unprincipled inclination to discover faults in the manner of executing designs often suggested by themselves, and thus apparently save their consistency as to measures, while they continued their opposition to the men, they were even above the feeling of jealousy which would have kept inferior minds from coming forward to grace the triumphs of a rival; they scarcely ever, certainly never but where the necessity of explaining their conduct to the public required it, reminded either the Government or the country, how long they had supported the policy, now luckily adopted in the quarter most likely to give it effect. All the while, (and we speak of some years, certainly of the Sessions 1824, 1825, and 1826, but in not a few particulars of 1823 too,) there was nothing that indicated the least understanding between the parties who had been so long opposed to each other; no appearance of any intercourse in private among their chiefs; and we believe it is universally understood that no arrangement, nor any treaty for an arrangement, had been so much as talked of in any political circle of the least importance. Indeed one symptom must remove all suspicion on this head; whensoever the measures of the Ministry were objectionable, their adversaries were at their post, as ready as ever for the strife; few more vehement debates, or with more party animation, have ever been carried on, than the discussions on the Catholic Association in 1825; and even trivial matters, from time to time, furnished fuel to maintain the heats which contending parties engender, though oftentimes separated by a narrow space.

Nevertheless, with the symptoms which we have just noted, near observers did not fail to mark others, that seemed to give prognostics of greater change, and more permanent co-operation. The Ministry were known to be much divided among themselves. One class supported the claims of the Catholics, as essentially just in themselves, and maintained the expediency of complying with them, as necessary for the safety of the empire. Another refused upon any account even to consider this great question; they had taken their ground upon it, and from that ground they announced that no lapse of time, no change of circumstances, could move them. There seemed here a sufficient source of disunion to make a disruption of the Ministry not merely a natural, but an unavoidable event. But this was very far from being the only ground. The same parties were divided upon all the great principles of foreign and domestic policy, which having been discountenanced by the late Foreign Minister, both in the Cabinet, in his negotiations, and in Parliament, were now become the favourite maxims of his successor; but on these principles, the individuals who differed with him, were not so inflexible as upon the question, whether Ireland should be saved to the empire; and opposing him on this, on those they only thwarted him, leaving the liberal course, in all or almost all cases but the most important, to be pursued by the State. That their assent was most reluctant; that it often was extorted by the apprehension of breaking up the Ministry; that matters were frequently kept quiet by the common unwillingness of all parties to press them to extremities—not seldom by the controlling influence either of the first person in the Ministry, or the first person in the State—cannot any longer be doubted. But in the course of these altercations two parties had been formed, and differing in all questions, constant dissent had produced frequent dissensions; and, as always happens in such cases, those dissensions were not confined to things, but extended to persons, until as much of animosity, probably, and as little mutual goodwill, prevailed between the two parties that divided the Cabinet, as are found to subsist in ordinary times between the parties that divide the senate or the nation.

Another symptom not unconnected with this, was now more and more perceptible. The Opposition became less vehement, less unremitting, in proportion as the breach was supposed to widen in the Ministry; and their support in great part, their courtesies entirely, were now given with a kind of reserve or discrimination: it was to the 'Liberal part of the Government' that they lent their aid; it was to *them* they looked for the reform of abuses; it was in *their* sound principles that they reposed confidence for the future. To give *them* encouragement in their wise and honourable course, became an object of importance for the good of the country; and aware how their opponents in the Cabinet endeavoured to hinder their progress, the Opposition employed all means for comforting and strengthening *their* hands, and enabling them to overcome the common enemy.

The year 1826 began with the measures rendered necessary by the commercial distress; and the Liberal Parties on both sides of the House agreed fully in the support of them. A Session followed, remarkable for nothing so much as its want of interest; and there had not been within the memory of man, so few points of difference between the contending parties in both Houses of Parliament. The General Election followed, and a marked distinction was everywhere to be traced in the conduct of the Opposition towards the *Liberal*, and towards the *Illiberal* 'portion of his Majesty's Government.' The new Parliament met, and the conduct pursued in Portugal, the grounds upon which it was defended, and the language so worthy of constitutional Ministers, in which that defence was couched, drew forth the most cordial and unqualified approbation from the Opposition Leaders. The period of the Christmas recess arrived, and it is perfectly certain that up to that time no arrangement whatever had been made, or even propounded, or discoursed of between the two great portions of the Liberal Party, those in office, and those in opposition.

Immediately after the recess, the noble Lord at the head of the Government was stricken with a grievous malady, which compelled him in a few weeks to resign his situation. In what way his place should be supplied, was a question calculated to trouble his colleagues at all times; for he had great weight with them; and though, on Irish questions, he adopted the illiberal views of one party to the uttermost extent of impolicy and intolerance, on other matters he leant towards their adversaries, or at any rate, by his personal consideration with all, and his ancient intimacy with the leader of that side, he was enabled to preserve the Government from the violent end it so often seemed near coming to. But if the difficulty would at any time have been great, of finding a successor to that noble person, it was incalculably augmented by the present aspect of affairs abroad, and by the new balance of parties. What had been passing for some time in Parliament, above all, what had passed just before the recess, showed how infallibly the great body of the Opposition, both in and out of Parliament, that is, the only powerful party in both Houses, and an immense majority of all ranks in the country, would give their cordial support to the liberal part of the Cabinet; and it might be safely predicted, that if Mr. Canning were placed at the head of the Government, no remains either of party or of personal animosity would interfere with their desire to give him and his friends, because of the policy they had so wisely adopted and so ably patronised, a cordial, and, if wanted, a systematic support. It was equally clear, that should they be driven out of the Ministry, a cordial and systematic co-operation would be easily established between them and those who had indeed for years been their allies. So that while, on the one hand, the Liberal part of the Cabinet could stand more triumphantly than before, should the Illiberal resign, these had not the most trifling chance of maintaining their ground, should they, by taking the upper hand, drive their adversaries from office.

If it be clear that such was the posture of affairs, the question was manifestly decided; and it only remained for the opponents of Mr. Canning in the Cabinet, either to submit, or to retire, should he be placed by their common Master at the head of the Government. He was plainly in a situation to dictate his own terms, while they had no power over him, either of continuing to govern without his assistance, or of opposing the Ministry he might form. Of the two courses, submission and resignation, they chose the latter, partly upon personal grounds of objection to the individual, partly upon public principles which they held widely differing from his, and which would have been betrayed, by serving under one who openly attached himself to the contrary system. Accordingly, after a short interval spent in fruitless negotiation, and in unavailing attempts to form a purely Tory Ministry—attempts wholly uncountenanced, it is believed, by the Sovereign, and which the most sagacious of themselves knew from the first to be desperate—they resigned in a body, leaving his Majesty without advisers, and the country without a Government.

Far be from us, however, any design of imputing blame to the distinguished persons who suddenly, and, it is said, without any actual concert, took this step. Their feelings of personal honour may have justified it; their differences of opinion upon fundamental points may have required it. We are quite aware of the change in the aspect of the Catholic Question, which the substituting its zealous advocate for its determined opponent, as Prime Minister, was calculated to create. Indeed, we can much more easily comprehend the enemies of that great measure feeling the impossibility of acting under Mr. Canning as their leader, both in the Government and the House of Commons, than we can understand their so long allowing him the preponderance he had in the Cabinet, with the ostensible position he occupied in Parliament, before Lord Liverpool's political demise. But there was one resignation not so easily understood upon any of those grounds, and which remains unexplained, either by personal or political disunion; we mean Lord Melville's—whose conduct in his important office had given satisfaction; whose opinions had uniformly been upon the liberal side in all questions, Irish as well as English; and who was not understood to be separated, by any dislike, from those whose principles were his own. His retirement, therefore, while it was regretted, could only be accounted for upon the supposition of some punctilious notions of duty towards his other colleagues, or towards the Ministry, in the abstract, with which he had so long been connected;—notions certainly in nowise calculated to lessen any one's respect for him, though all might desire to see them give way after a season. Mr. Peel's retirement was also matter of some regret, because he had of late shown a disposition, worthy of all encouragement in official characters, to probe abuses both in the practice and structure of our judicial system,* and had adopted some of

* The Newspapers have been filled with some very singular effusions during the late progress of the Western Circuit, purporting to be charges to various Grand Juries and Petit Juries, and addresses to prisoners, both before and after conviction, and interlocutory observations during the course of trials. To these, the name of the Chief Justice of the Common Pleas is appended; and the reader is frequently tempted to believe that they must be efforts of pleasantry, as where the learned Judge tells a convict, that 'we (of course meaning the prisoner as well as the Judge) are much indebted to the salutary change of the law, whereby the punishment is now raised from seven to fourteen years' transportation.' However, be those productions genuine or not, we (and in *this* plural the learned Judge *is* certainly included) are not indebted to them in any respect whatever. They are distinguished by a great flow of language, eminently spirited, impressive, and often felicitous; by any one judicial quality they assuredly are not marked. A great magistrate, the second in England, travelling the second of its circuits, to read lectures upon what ought to be the law, which he is only sworn to administer as it is; and making every charge the vehicle of unmeasured praises heaped upon one of the leaders of a well-known political party, is not a spectacle which the friends either of the bench or of the law can take great delight in beholding. The

the principles, nay, fostered the very measures of amendment so long recommended, with boundless learning, and unwearied zeal, by the chiefs of the Liberal Party. But though Mr. Peel's conduct in leaving office might be regretted, it could not by any candid man be blamed; neither could the grounds of it be misunderstood; his resignation was widely different from Lord Melville's; he *could* not with any regard to his character, or with any kind of consistency, have remained in office, at least in the Home Department, under one so pledged to the Catholics as Mr. Canning. Until this question should be settled, his retirement from power seemed almost unavoidable, the impossibility of his friends forming a Government being admitted on all hands; and his wish to do so being to our apprehension more than problematical, as we are confident his interest in its being done is anything but doubtful; for upon almost all other questions he has espoused the more liberal policy of those whom he left in office.

We have now given the plain story of the late change, as it appears from facts known to all the world; and we have had no occasion to invoke the aid of secret history for the untying of any knotty passages. Although it has never been pretended among all the silly and the wilful mis-statements which have been put forth, that any private understanding subsisted between the Liberal Ministers and the leaders of the Opposition previous to

absurd exaggeration of all those eulogies, we are convinced, must be far more painful to the distinguished individual who is their subject than to any other person; if he is bepraised in respect of what he has done, he is also lauded for attempts not quite successful; and he is openly extolled for what others did, and not a little for what has never been done by any one. With reference to his own share of the gain derived from this circuit, he may be tempted to say—'*Pessimum inimicorum genus laudatores*'—but of his panegyrist he may truly say—'*Satis eloquentiæ, sapientiæ parum*,' and may thus explain how he has himself contributed to make of a great Advocate, a very moderate Judge.

the Easter recess, the most groundless and even ridiculous charges were advanced of perfidy and intrigue during those holidays, sometimes against the Ministers, sometimes against the Opposition. That not an instant was lost in opening a communication with the chiefs of that party, when the former Administration had been broken up, is very certain; and that such a step was as consistent with the purest honour and fair dealing in the one party, as it was with entire consistency in the other, and perfectly natural in both, no one who has honoured the preceding narrative with his attention can for a moment doubt. Great reluctance was, however, shown in the Opposition to take office. Some of the new Ministry were known to oppose the Catholic claims; some of the leading Whigs felt it impossible to join them officially; and this begot an unwillingness in those who felt no such difficulties, to become members of a Cabinet divided on so great a question, and likely to be opposed by so highly respected friends.

Happily for the country, happily for their own reputation as statesmen of firm, consistent, and manly character, those scruples were overcome. A Cabinet was formed, in which the liberal part of the former Ministry were cordially united with the leading men of the Opposition, and with two or three individuals not attached to the same views of policy, but whose very worst errors, as we must be allowed to call them, afforded, with their high stations, a security to the country against any rash and headlong attempts being made to bring about changes, which, if gradually effected, may yet remedy all the evils of our domestic situation.

The Session opened with much of complaint, and somewhat of menace. We love not to dwell on painful recollections. We are willing to hope that calmer reflection may render the retrospect for ever as unnecessary as it is unpleasing. In a very short time, the attacks upon the new Ministry were left in the hands of those, of whom, wishing to speak with all *possible* respect, we may be permitted to say, that their weight in the country, and the place they occupy in the annals of its Council, are proportioned to their intrinsic merits; and that their adversaries must always feel contentment, if they should feel little pride, in being opposed to their hostility.

The close of the Session was speedily followed by the death of the Prime Minister,—too early for his country, though not for his own fame; and the Sovereign, in strict accordance with the universal desire of the people, directed the Government to be reconstructed upon the same principle as before. One change, though not in the Cabinet, attended this event; the command of the army was again given to its most distinguished ornament, who never, in our opinion, should have for a day stooped from the loftier height he had scaled by his wisdom, his valour, and his brilliant fortune, to join in the little details and low intrigues of vulgar politics. We have said nothing of some of the Ministers who resigned; but we suspect that no very deep affliction was suffered by the country from their loss. After the very long period during which they had lived in office, their departure could hardly be deemed untimely; and though one of those veterans retired with a great name, and all of them in the full possession of their faculties, there seemed a prevailing disposition, in the public mind, to express no sorrow for the loss, until they saw whether they could* be worse governed by their successors. They sunk gradually into a kind of watching Opposition—a corps of observation; and one thing must be admitted on all hands, whatever opinion may be entertained of the new Opposition from the recollection of their past services, that no man looked forward to much occasion for them in their new capacity, since the new Ministry stands unrivalled by any former Government in popularity with the country, and surpassed by none in favour with the Crown.

* In this country, we are often puzzled with *will*, and *shall*, *would*, *should*, and *could*, so we don't venture to suggest any alteration.

It must be evident to every person of ordinary understanding, and be admitted by any one of moderate candour, that, in the effectual assistance which some of the Opposition render to the new Government, by taking part in it officially, and the disinterested, though necessarily less efficient, support which others give it out of place, nothing is done by either class inconsistent with the strictest notions of party principle, or which, tried by the most rigorous standard of party duty, could be found wanting. Suppose the whole principles and distribution of political parties to have remained unaltered of late years, we affirm, nor indeed has it ever been in terms denied, that the late Coalition was framed on the most approved models known in the best times of our history.

The only justification of party unions has always been found in their necessity, sometimes for curbing the influence of the executive power, sometimes for promoting certain other principles held by the members of such associations in common, and deemed by them essential to the good of the country. Men have, through ambition, or avarice, or the other forms of selfishness, abused this privilege, or rather duty of public men; they have leagued themselves together to extort better terms from their Sovereign, their opponents, or the public; they have in reality been holding out and keeping together for some personal reasons, and not because they differed from their adversaries, and agreed among themselves in holding certain opinions—but they were never yet shameless enough to avow such motives: their profligacy has always paid the homage to political virtue, of pretending to act together because they concurred in maintaining principles different from those of other parties. Even where the ground of contention seemed the most narrow, and reduced as it were to a mere personal point, they sedulously magnified this by all the powers of refining and sophistry, if they could put forward a larger justification, and conceal the reason. Thus, when the great body of the Whigs, in an evil hour for their public reputation and their influence in the country, joined Lord North against Lord Shelburne, and opposed the peace which they had so long been urging, they were far from admitting that the mere assumption of the Treasury by one of their number instigated them to this ill-omened step, much less that they had sacrificed their principles on the American Question to gratify their spleen against a former colleague, and obtain the highest station of power. They alleged that the new Minister had changed his principles upon the recognition of American independence; that he was resolved to screen Indian delinquency; that he owed his elevation to unconstitutional designs entertained by the Court against all the great parties of the country, for the purpose of governing more absolutely through creatures of its own. It was their adversaries who charged them with personal motives, and urged as an accusation against them, that the appointment of the Prime Minister was the real cause of their secession. Does it not follow from such principles, rather is it not a proposition of the very same purport, that when a body of men originally collected and banded against others by a political faith, in holding which it differed from them, finds all differences at an end, and former adversaries acting upon its own much cherished principles, a new line of conduct ought straightway to be pursued? Common honesty to the country, as well as a regard for consistency, requires that there should be an end of the Opposition, when there is an end of the only diversity that called for it, or indeed could justify it. Whoever would still keep aloof in such circumstances, and continue in Opposition when there is no longer any public ground of difference, plainly admits his real motives all along to have been personal and selfish, however cunningly he may have varnished them over with the pretence of principle. To this charge it is manifest the Whigs would have exposed themselves, had they held back from Mr. Canning's party, whom they had no tangible ground of differing with.

But we may put the case still more strongly upon mere party grounds. Coalitions have ever been held allowable, and sometimes admitted to be the duty of statesmen, when necessary to further some great object of public good. To frame a strong Government in 1757, Lord Chatham's Ministry was formed out of every conflicting party; and it carried the country to the highest pitch of glory. This precedent was cited by Mr. Fox and Mr. Burke in defence of the coalition with Lord North; and though the diversity of facts did not well justify the application, there can be no doubt of the principle in proof of which it was referred to. The coalition sought by many, to be effected between Mr. Fox and Mr. Pitt in 1784 and 1804, could only be grounded upon the necessity of giving the country a good and vigorous Government; and the junction of Lord Grenville and the Whigs in 1804, and afterwards in office, was dictated, as it was triumphantly defended, by their agreement on some great questions, and their disposition to sacrifice lesser points of opinion, and all personal considerations, to the important object of promoting those grand principles in which they coincided. But in all these cases, and in none more than the last, there were various differences of principle; not only were Whig and Tory, Alarmist and Reformer, to coalesce; but during the war, and for the sake of carrying it on to a better issue, they who were the authors of it, were united with its constant and sturdy opponents. Yet all men approved of the union, because lesser things should yield to greater, and upon one or two great questions there was a fortunate concurrence of opinion. It would be very difficult, however, in the present case, to find the subject upon which the new allies did not agree —Catholic Question—Currency—Free Trade—Judicial Reform—Foreign Policy—South American Independence—on all these they had for years fought side by side; on all these they had been combating together against the Ministers who lately resigned; while, with the exception of Parliamentary Reform, upon which the members of the same party differed among themselves, there was not a single practical point of dissension to be descried. Any two, almost any one of those great subjects was important enough to justify a union, even had the parties differed upon most of the others; but when the agreement extended over the whole, can any man seriously maintain that it was not their duty to coalesce, if their cordial co-operation could alone secure the success of their common principles, and the exclusion from power of their common adversaries?

It has been said, that there is in the Cabinet, as now composed, an admixture of members unfavourable to the Catholic Claims, and reports have reached us of very strong, but not perhaps very well considered objections being taken on this head. Beside our former general argument, we shall content ourselves with two observations in reply. The first is, that three members in the whole Cabinet, and these in no way connected, either with the head of the Administration, or with the management of Irish affairs, do not alter the features of tolerance and liberality impressed upon it by the union which has created the rest of the body. The other is, that such a criticism proceeds with a strange air from the ancient friends and associates of Mr. Fox, who, in 1783, took office with Lord Shelburne, differing from him, as he afterwards avowed, on many points, and extremely reluctant ever to join him, and with Lord Thurlow, whom he had all his life been opposing upon all points, and who had held the Great Seal during the American war. But still more marvellous is such a remark from any who held office in Mr. Fox's last Administration! Is it really forgotten already how the Cabinet of 1806 was composed? There was at its head Lord Grenville—the colleague and kinsman of Mr. Pitt—the main promoter of the first war, and instigator to the second—the author of the letter to Bonaparte, which prolonged it from 1800—the staunch enemy of reform—the avowed friend and protector of the Wellesleys in India. Against him were to be set Mr. Fox and Mr. Grey, peacemakers, reformers, managers of Indian Impeachments. Then came Mr. Windham and Lord Fitzwilliam, the administrators of Mr. Burke's fury, as their new colleagues had often termed them, and going as much beyond the Grenvilles in hatred of peace, as they exceeded the Foxites in fondness of war. It is true, that all these great men strenuously supported the Catholic Claims; but those claims were as vehemently opposed by other members of the Cabinet, by Lord Ellenborough, and by Lord Sidmouth, whose former accession to office had been expressly grounded upon his hostility to the question. Yet the exigencies of the State induced Mr. Fox and Mr. Grey to form parts of this Cabinet, where the interest of Ireland was so little consulted, that by common consent the subject was not to be mentioned, unless in order to bring forward a small measure, no sooner attempted than abandoned. It is true, that one great and righteous deed was done, in spite of all the divisions which variegated the aspect of this motley piece of Cabinet-making; they abolished the Slave Trade; but not because they agreed upon this any more than upon those penal laws which they left unrepealed; for Lord Sidmouth, Lord Moira, and Lord Fitzwilliam, were determined enemies of the measure, and Mr. Windham was perhaps the most zealous of all its antagonists, not to be a planter.*

We have been meeting the two opposite objections made to the late coalition, by two very different classes of adversaries, the High Tories, who exclaimed against it as an unnatural and unprincipled league for power, at the expense of constancy; and a few much respected members of the old Whig party, whose accusations were less precise, but who seemed to dislike it only because persons once their antagonists formed a branch of it; an objection to which

* It will not be supposed that we are painting the Administration of 1806 as we ourselves view it: we are showing in what light the facts would justify its enemies in now representing it, upon the grounds on which some of its members are opposing the present Government.

every coalition must be equally liable. The answer to all these attacks is plain and simple. The inconsistency would have been in men continuing the conflict when they were no longer divided in their sentiments; the unnatural conduct would have been for men to attack their natural allies and join their natural enemies; the disregard of principle would have been shown by those who sacrificed their public duty to personal views, and regardless of their pledged opinions, sought the gratification of personal feelings, not the less personal, nor the more amiable, because they were those of hatred, jealousy, or vexation.

But suppose we come down to a more humble level in the argument, and listen to the suggestion, why did the Whigs join Mr. Canning, when, by holding out, they must have occasioned a total change? We are far from being satisfied that such a change was preferable to the united Ministry; we are sure the union was more acceptable to the country as well as to the court; but we answer the question as it is put, and after the manner of our nation, we answer it by propounding another—What was to hinder Mr. Canning from joining his former colleagues, and submitting to fill a second place, a submission which the Whigs would then have forced him to? If he found himself disappointed in the estimate he had formed of his new allies; if he found that all their regard for their common principles could not overcome their selfish lust of power, or mitigate their equally selfish hatred of him, had he not a right to distrust them, and to prefer any government which perpetuated their exclusion? Then, suppose he had been driven out of office, was there no chance of his rejoining his former colleagues, and no possibility of this union effecting at court the downfall of a party, which had showed so little moderation as to gain no credit with the Sovereign, and so little regard for its long professed principles, as to lose all respect in the country? As for the only other event that can be stated, it may be spoken of, but it surely cannot be conceived possible; we allude to the Whigs joining those ministers who had resigned, and uniting with them in opposing their liberal colleagues. We at once pronounce so prodigious an inconsistency impossible. It would have been abandoning all their principles either to storm the government, or spite a former opponent, whose recent conduct upon all great questions of policy they had loudly applauded. It was as impossible for them to think of such a course, as it now would be for those most eminent and respected individuals, whose alienation from the government we join the whole country in deploring, to unite themselves with men, whom they differ from upon every question of public policy, and to seek with them the overthrow of a Ministry, all whose principles they profess.

In the remarks which we have made, nothing, we trust, has escaped us, tending to evince the least disrespect for the principles of party, so essential to the existence of a free government. Those attachments arising from similarity of principle, are in truth the very ground-work of our argument. They have in all good times, and among the best men, been held pure and patriotic bonds of union; honourable to the individuals, profitable to the commonwealth. Nevertheless, it is impossible to deny, that in proportion as the body of the people become more enlightened, and take a more constant interest in the management of their own affairs, such combinations becoming less necessary, lose somewhat of the public favour; and we believe that at no period of our history, did, what is called 'Party,' enjoy less popularity and exert less influence with the bulk of the community. It may indeed be affirmed with safety, that the efforts and the personal weight of individuals, have, of late years, done far more to keep alive the power and authority of Parties, than the influence of party has done for the protection of their particular members. A new casting also of political sects has taken place; the distinctions, and almost the names, of Loyalist and Jacobin, Whig and Tory, Court and Country Faction, are fast wearing away. Two great divisions of the community will, in all likelihood, soon be far more generally known; the *Liberal* and the *Illiberal*, who will divide, but we may be sure most unequally, the suffrages of the Nation.

Nor is it in name only that this arrangement will be new; the people will be differently distributed; the coalition, which has been gradually forming among the public men whose personal respect and mutual confidence has brought about so fortunate a union, extends to the community at large. Some of the older questions, by which Whig and Tory were wont to be divided, retain all their importance; but, upon these, the Liberal party, of whatever denomination, are well agreed. Indeed, it used to be a saying of Mr. Wilberforce, when he regarded the importance of those questions, compared with the ones they still differed about, that he would not answer to the name of Tory; conveying thereby, as that great man is wont, a lesson of his mild wisdom with the relish of attractive and harmless wit. The only consequence with respect to doctrines which such a junction can produce, is likely to be beneficial both to the State and to the progress of sound opinion. Extremes will be avoided; alterations in our system will be gradual; and the only risk which the existence, or the measures of a Liberal Government could run, will be avoided—that of a reaction against them,—when it is distinctly perceived by all men, that we are governed by individuals, whose great parts are under the control of sound discretion, and whose conduct is, in all things, tempered with the moderation of practical wisdom.

SPEECH IN THE HOUSE OF COMMONS,

APRIL 5, 1830,

On the "Bill to Repeal the Civil Disabilities affecting British-born Subjects professing the Jewish Religion."

In spite of the parallel which my hon. friend (the member for Oxford) has attempted—I think in vain—to draw between this case and the Roman Catholic measure before the House during the last Session of Parliament, I trust that we shall not have to forego the votes of many of those hon. Gentlemen who in the last Session were opposed to the concession of the Catholic claims. Indeed, many of those Gentlemen will be precluded, by the course they then took, from offering any opposition to the present measure. The general principle of religious toleration was involved in the question of last year, as it is now: but most of those Gentlemen who voted against the Roman Catholics declared in favour of this general principle, only they found that there were special circumstances which took the case of the Roman Catholics out of the pale of that principle. But, Sir, there are no such circumstances here. In this instance, there is no foreign power to be feared. There is no divided allegiance threatening the State—there are no bulls—there are no indulgencies—there are no dispensations—there is no priesthood exercising an absolute authority over the consciences of those who are under their spiritual control—there are no agitators rousing and exciting the people to a course contrary to all good government—there are no associations assembling, or

Hansard's Parliamentary Debates, 2d series, vol. xxiii. 1830, p. 1308–1314.

charged with assembling, for the purpose of assuming a power which ought only to belong to legally recognized functionaries—there are no mobs, disciplined to their task, and almost in the regular training of arms—there is no rent levied with the regularity of a tax. It was the fashion last year to declaim about a government that yielded to clamor, opposition, or threats, having betrayed the sacredness of its office, but there can be none such here; for even those most opposed to the present measure cannot deny that the Jews have borne their deprivations long in silence, and are now complaining with mildness and decency. As a contrast to this, the Roman Catholics were always described as an insinuating, restless, cunning, watchful sect, ever on the search how they might increase their power and the number of their sect, pressing for converts in every possible way, and only withheld by the want of power from following up their ancient persecutions. But the sect with which we now have to deal are even more prone to monopolize their religion than the others are to propagating the Catholic faith. Never has such a thing been heard of as an attempt on the part of the Jews to gain proselytes; and we may conclude, that with such rites and forms as belong to their faith, it could scarcely be expected by any one that a scheme of proselytism could succeed with them. Be that, however, as it may, it is a thing at which they never appear to have aimed. On the contrary, they have always discouraged such an idea. Let the history of England be examined, and it will furnish topics enough against the Catholics. Those who have looked for such things have always found enough to talk about as to the crimes they have committed: the fires in Smithfield—the Gunpowder Plot—the Seven Bishops—have always afforded copious matter upon which to launch out in invective against the Catholics. But with respect to the Jews, the history of England affords events exactly opposite: its pages, as to these people, are made up of wrongs suffered and injuries endured by them, without a trace of any wrong or injury committed in return; they are made up, from the beginning to the end, of atrocious cruelties inflicted on the one hand, and grievous privations endured for conscience-sake on the other. With respect to all Christian sects, their changes of situation have always afforded scope for charges of mutual recrimination against one another; but every one allows the side on which the balance between the Jew and the Christian is weighed down. As to the opposition offered to this Bill by my hon. friend, I am at a loss to see on what he has grounded it, unless he takes the broad principle, that no one who is not a Christian is to be entrusted with power, as his rule of action; I am at a loss to see how he can refuse his assent to or oppose this measure without throwing himself open to the charge of inconsistency. If this Bill, like the Roman Catholic one of last Session, is to be opposed, it is condemning the strong and the weak, the violent and the patient, the proselyting and the exclusive, the political and the religious. If this is the course that is to be taken for our guide, persecution will never want an excuse, and the wolf will ever be able to invent a pretence to bear down and destroy the lamb. If this is to be the maxim set up for our land-mark, it will soon appear that every thing may be a reason with the aggressor, as every thing is shown to be a crime in the aggressed. In all the opposition that was lately evinced against the Catholics, it was never once assumed or pretended that the opposition was religious; it was political, and nothing else. When the object was to excite ill blood and rancour in the country—when red-hot speeches and tub-sermons went forth on the subject, the people were told that the question was, whether they should be compelled to worship stocks and stones, instead of the true God? But this was a point of view never alluded to by the more distinguished and candid opponents of the Catholic claims. I myself remember having heard the Earl of Eldon declare that it was not on religious but on political grounds, that he was opposed to the measure. The question just at that time under consideration was that of Transubstantiation; and the noble and learned Lord observed that it was not because the Catholics believed in the real presence that they were objected to, but that being the test by which they were kept out, they were through that kept out, because they were not good subjects. But now the whole case is changed. Political objection is fairly given up; and in its place religious persecution is avowed. In all that my hon. friend, the member for Oxford, has offered to the House, I have traced but two political objections; and neither of them appears to me to be entitled to the weight which my hon. friend would give to them. The first political argument that my hon. friend has adduced against this measure is, that the Jews of this country are more attached to their nation—wandering and scattered as they are over the face of the earth—than they are to the people of England. The only answer that I shall offer to this, is, that at all events it is exceedingly unfair to lay down this as an objection till we have tried the experiment whether, by making Englishmen of them, they will not become members of the community. Till that has been done, all we can say is, that as long as they are not Englishmen they are nothing but Jews. The other objection of my hon. friend appears to me to be more extraordinary still. He says that if this measure be granted, the power of the Jews will be such that they will come into Parliament in a much greater number than is proportioned to their relative number in the country, and the consequence of this will be to destroy the present system of representation, which will be rendered odious to the people, and a reform in Parliament must ensue. All that I can see in this argument is, that the Jews will not get into Parliament, because we are labouring under a bad system of representation. At all events, the system that we have at present must be either good or bad. If the system is bad, it is evident that the sooner we get rid of it the better. If the system is good, why should we complain of that to which it naturally tends? These objections seem to be the only political objections that my hon. friend has urged against the measure now before the House, and all the rest may be characterised as purely religious persecution. But even when my hon. friend has brought himself to that, he does not pretend to say that he opposes the Bill because the religion of the Jews is dangerous. No such pretence is put forth at all. No such outcry as that raised last session is heard now. The opposition which has made its appearance now is, if I may use the phrase without giving offence to my hon. friend, nothing but the offal—nothing but the leavings of the intolerance which was so abundant last year. All that tho House has been told is, that the Jews are not Christians, and that therefore they must not have power. But this has not been declared openly and ingenuously, as it once was. Formerly the persecution of the Jews was at least consistent. The thing was made complete once by taking away their property, their liberty, and their lives. My hon. friend is now equally vehement as to taking away their political power; and yet, no doubt, he would shudder at what such a measure would really take away. The only power that my hon. friend seems to wish to deprive the Jews of is to consist in maces, gold chains, and skins of parchment, with pieces of wax dangling at the ends of them. But he is leaving them all the things that bestow real power. He allows them to have property, and in these times property is power, mighty and overwhelming power—he allows them to have knowledge, and knowledge is no less power. Then why is all this power poisoned by intolerance? Why is the Jew to have the power of a principal over his clerk—of a master over his servant—of a landlord over his tenant? Why is he to have all this, which is power, and yet to be deprived of the fair and natural consequences of this power? Why, having conceded all this, is my hon. friend afterwards to turn round and say, "You shall have all these real effects and advantages of your situation, but in the fair sequence of their possession, you shall be crippled and borne down." As things now stand, a Jew may be the richest man in England—he may possess the whole of London—his interest may be the means of raising this party or depressing that—of making East-India directors, or sending members into Parliament—the influence of the Jew may be of the first consequence in a war which shall be the means of shaking all Europe to its centre. His power may come into play in assisting or retarding the greatest plans of the greatest Princes; and yet, with all this confessed, acknowledged, undenied, my hon. friend would have them deprived of power! If, indeed, my hon. friend would have things thus arranged, I would put a question to him thus:—Does he not think that wealth confers power? If it do, can he be prepared to say that the Jews shall not have power? If it do not, where are we to draw the line? How are we to permit all the consequences of their wealth but one? I cannot conceive the nature of an argument that is to bear out such a position. If it was to be full and entire persecution, after the consistent example of our ancestors, I could understand it. If we were called on to revert to the days, when, as a people, they were pillaged—when their warehouses were torn down—when their every right was sacrificed, the thing would be comprehensible. But this is a delicate persecution, with no abstract rule for its guidance. As to the matter of right, if the word "legal" is to be attached to it, I am bound to acknowledge that the Jews have no legal right to power; but in the same way, 300 years ago, they had no legal right to be in England; and 600 years ago they had no right to the teeth in their heads: but if it is the moral right we are to look at, I say, that on every principle of moral obligation, I hold that the Jew has a right to political power. Every man has a right to all that may conduce to his pleasure, if it does not inflict pain on any one else. This is one of the broadest maxims of human nature, and I cannot therefore see how its supporters can be fairly called upon to defend it—the *onus probandi* lies, not on the advocates of freedom, but on the advocates of restraint. Let my hon. friend first show that there is some danger—some injury to the State, likely to arise from the admission of the Jews, and then will be the time to call upon us to answer the case that he has made out. Till such an argument, however, is fully made out, I shall contend for the moral right of the Jews. That they wish to have access to the privilege of sitting in Parliament has already been shown; it now remains to show that some harm is calculated to result from that admission. Unless this is shown, the refusal is neither more nor less than persecution. My hon. friend put a different interpretation upon the particular word I have used; but the meaning will still remain the same; and when we come to define the sense, it must be found, that we are only quibbling about a word. Any person may build a theory upon phrases: with some, perhaps, burning would be persecution, while the screwing of thumbs would not be persecution; others may call the screwing of thumbs persecution, and deny the justice of that expression when used to whipping. But according to my impression, the infliction of any penalties on account of religious opinions, and on account of religious opinions alone, is generally understood as coming within the meaning of the term, for all the purposes of political argument. It is as much persecution in principle as an *auto da fé*, the only difference is in degree. Defining persecution, then, as I do, I cannot conceive any argument to be adduced in favour of the mildest degree of this injustice, which, logically speaking, though not morally, indeed, might not be used with equal force in favour of the most cruel inflictions from similar motives. I have to make my apology for having occupied so much of the time of the hon. gentlemen present; but I could not refrain from making known my sentiments to this House of Commons, which has done more for the rights of conscience than any Parliament that ever sat. Its sessions of 1828 and 1829 have been marked by a glorious course in favour of religious liberty; and I hope that, before our separation, this Session of 1830 will put the finishing hand to that work which so many great and good men wish to see accomplished, but which cannot be, till this most desirable measure shall be carried into effect.

NOTE. In his speech on this subject, which followed, Sir James Macintosh said, "The speech which they had heard from his Honourable and Learned Friend was one which, he had no doubt, would make its full impression on the House, it being every way worthy of the name he bore."

SLAVERY IN THE WEST INDIES.*

DEC. 13, 1830.

On the Presentation of a Petition from West India Planters, and others interested in Property in the West Indies.

If the petitioners who ask for compensation, and if the noble Marquis who presented the petition, and the hon. Member who spoke last but one, had confined themselves to the subject of compensation, he should not have thought it necessary to say one word on the subject. He thought—he believed the public also thought —that compensation ought to be given. He agreed with the noble Lord and the hon. Gentleman, and he agreed, too, with the petitioners, that whenever slavery was extinguished, all the loss of property which might arise should be made good by the Government. He agreed in this opinion, not because he agreed with what fell from the hon. Member for Dumfries, which, by the by, he did not understand, about the compact of society. He did not see from that species of metaphysical argument how protection for property was necessary; but it was found by experience that it was bad for men that property should not be secured, and that great inconvenience resulted from violating property, and on that ground, it was said, that men ought to have their property protected. After the public had declared, by Acts of Parliament, that men should be property, after they had been bought and sold, deposited as pledges, and made to answer for dowers, great inconvenience would result from taking away that species of property, and the masters and

* Hansard, 3d Series, vol. i. p. 1054–6.

owners ought to be compensated. He declared, that he thought, in common with most of those who petitioned the House, that slavery ought to be extinguished; but he and the petitioners all contemplated, on its extinction, giving a reasonable compensation to the masters of slaves. If, therefore, the noble Lord and the hon. Gentleman had confined themselves to compensation, which he admitted was just, he should not have said one word on the subject; but they had mingled other matters with that which he always wished to see separated from it. He agreed that exaggeration could not do any good, and he regretted, as much as the noble Lord and the hon. Member for Dumfries, that either anger or exaggeration should have been displayed on either side. It was a charge against the petitions for the abolition, that they were all got up under the influence of the Anti-Slavery Society. The petitions were got up under that influence—was that extraordinary? Who should inform the people of England, busily employed in their own domestic occupations, of what occurred in the West Indies, if some such Society did not undertake the task? But the influence the Society possessed was over the public mind. It had no other. It appealed to the public reason. It had no monopoly of the public Press. Its reports and proceedings were open to cavil and objection. The periodical literature was as much in the hands of the West Indians as their opponents. Magazines and Reviews were on their side; of celebrated works, he believed that The Quarterly Review had always been in their favour. He did not believe that there was one of those periodical publications which were most read—he meant the newspapers—he did not believe that there was one of the London newspapers that was fully and completely on the side of the abolitionists. The organs of the West-India body were as numerous as those of the other side, and their funds were at least equal to those of the Anti-Slavery Society. It was not long ago that the West-India body gave as much to one writer as the Anti-Slavery Society received and employed in a year. The fact was, that the West-India body was in the wrong. All men were active to embrace the opposite opinions. They had been progressively gaining ground, and all the efforts of the West-Indians had failed to stem the tide of public opinion. They had been trying since 1802, and were carried further and further away every year from their object. The public feeling since that time had ebbed and flowed somewhat, but, on the whole, it had been much strengthened. After every ebb it had only run upwards with double vigour. It required that slavery should be abolished; it required, in the interest of the West-Indians themselves, as well as in the interest of the slaves, and in the interest of the country generally, that the question should be brought to a speedy conclusion, and that the slaves should be emancipated. The petitions, it was said, were violent; but, though nobody supposed violence was good, what good cause had escaped being disfigured by violence? The Christian religion itself at its origin was disfigured by many pious frauds, and fanatics then abounded. Such was the case, too, at the Reformation, and much violence was instrumental in bringing it to a conclusion. For his part, he did not charge the West-India body with the calumny that was uttered against the abolitionists. The body, he knew, contained many honourable men, who were free from all suspicion of such a charge, and who scouted as much as any honourable men could, those people who lived by slander and traded in violent abuse, and in whom the ideas of calumny and their dinner were inseparably associated. He would do justice to the West-Indians, and let them do justice to their opponents. Let neither party recriminate any longer. Let them all consider the matter like statesmen and legislators. Let them ask themselves, was there any evil, and was there a remedy for it? Were they the people who ought to apply the remedy, and was this the time? If this were the time, and they were the people, he would implore them to apply the remedy. He saw that there were many difficulties in the way of it; but he thought those difficulties would readily vanish if the subject were taken up by statesmen of a capacious intellect and resolute heart. The statesmen who had lately taken office were of that character: in them he had great confidence, and he had no doubt that they would bring forward the question in a proper manner. When it was brought forward, he, for one, wished that it should be with a view to extinguish the system of slavery; but he wished it brought forward carefully, with temperance, avoiding all causes of irritation, and all violence of language; he wished the question looked at as a whole, and that it should be discussed with a sincere desire to come to a calm and deliberate decision, and to do every interest justice.

ON PARLIAMENTARY REFORM.*

MARCH 2, 1831.

In the adjourned Debate on the motion, "that leave be given to bring in a Bill to amend the Representation of the people of England and Wales."

It is a circumstance, Sir, of happy augury for the measure before the House, that almost all those who have opposed it have declared themselves altogether hostile to the principle of Reform. Two Members, I think, have professed, that though they disapprove of the plan now submitted to us, they yet conceive some alteration of the Representative system to be advisable. Yet even those Gentlemen have used, as far as I have observed, no arguments which would not apply as strongly to the most moderate change, as to that which has been proposed by his Majesty's Government. I say, Sir, that I consider this as a circumstance of happy augury. For what I feared was, not the opposition of those who shrink from all Reform,—but the disunion of reformers. I knew, that during three months every reformer had been employed in conjecturing what the plan of the Government would be. I knew, that every reformer had imagined in his own mind a scheme differing doubtless in some points from that which my noble friend, the Paymaster of the Forces, has developed. I felt therefore great apprehension that one person would be dissatisfied with one part of the Bill, that another person would be dissatisfied with another part, and that thus our whole strength would be wasted

* Hansard, 3d Series, Vol. ii. 1830–31, p. 1190–1205.

in internal dissensions. That apprehension is now at an end. I have seen with delight the perfect concord which prevails among all who deserve the name of reformers in this House, and I trust that I may consider it as an omen of the concord which will prevail among reformers throughout the country. I will not, Sir, at present express any opinion as to the details of the Bill; but having during the last twenty-four hours, given the most diligent consideration to its general principles, I have no hesitation in pronouncing it a wise, noble, and comprehensive measure, skilfully framed for the healing of great distempers, for the securing at once of the public liberties and of the public repose, and for the reconciling and knitting together of all the orders of the State. The hon. Baronet (Sir John Walsh) who has just sat down has told us, that the Ministers have attempted to unite two inconsistent principles in one abortive measure. He thinks, if I understand him rightly, that they ought either to leave the representative system such as it is, or to make it symmetrical. I think, Sir, that they would have acted unwisely if they had taken either of these courses. Their principle is plain, rational, and consistent. It is this,—to admit the middle class to a large and direct share in the Representation, without any violent shock to the institutions of our country [*hear!*] I understand those cheers—but surely the Gentlemen who utter them will allow, that the change made in our institutions by this measure is far less violent than that which, according to the hon. Baronet, ought to be made if we make any Reform at all. I praise the Ministers for not attempting, under existing circumstances, to make the Representation uniform—I praise them for not effacing the old distinction between the towns and the counties,—for not assigning Members to districts, according to the American practice, by the Rule of Three. They have done all that was necessary for the removing of a great practical evil, and no more than was necessary. I consider this, Sir, as a practical question. I rest my opinion on no general theory of government—I distrust all general theories of government. I will not positively say, that there is any form of polity which may not, under some conceivable circumstances, be the best possible. I believe that there are societies in which every man may safely be admitted to vote [*hear!*] Gentlemen may cheer, but such is my opinion. I say, Sir, that there are countries in which the condition of the labouring classes is such that they may safely be intrusted with the right of electing Members of the Legislature. If the laborers of England were in that state in which I, from my soul, wish to see them,—if employment were always plentiful, wages always high, food always cheap,—if a large family were considered not as an encumbrance, but as a blessing—the principal objections to Universal Suffrage would, I think, be removed. Universal Suffrage exists in the United States without producing any very frightful consequences; and I do not believe, that the people of those States, or of any part of the world, are in any good quality naturally superior to our own countrymen. But, unhappily, the lower orders in England, and in all old countries, are occasionally in a state of great distress. Some of the causes of this distress are, I fear, beyond the control of the Government. We know what effect distress produces, even on people more intelligent than the great body of the laboring classes can possibly be. We know that it makes even wise men irritable, unreasonable, and credulous—eager for immediate relief—heedless of remote consequences. There is no quackery in medicine, religion, or politics, which may not impose even on a powerful mind, when that mind has been disordered by pain or fear. It is therefore no reflection on the lower orders of Englishmen, who are not, and who cannot in the nature of things be highly educated, to say that distress produces on them its natural effects, those effects which it would produce on the Americans, or on any other people,—that it blunts their judgment, that it inflames their passions, that it makes them prone to believe those who flatter them, and to distrust those who would serve them. For the sake, therefore, of the whole society, for the sake of the labouring classes themselves, I hold it to be clearly expedient, that in a country like this, the right of suffrage should depend on a pecuniary qualification. Every argument, Sir, which would induce me to oppose Universal Suffrage, induces me to support the measure which is now before us. I oppose Universal Suffrage, because I think that it would produce a destructive revolution. I support this measure, because I am sure that it is our best security against a revolution. The noble Paymaster of the Forces hinted, delicately indeed and remotely, at this subject. He spoke of the danger of disappointing the expectations of the nation; and for this he was charged with threatening the House. Sir, in the year 1817, the late Lord Londonderry proposed a suspension of the Habeas Corpus Act. On that occasion he told the House, that, unless the measures which he recommended were adopted, the public peace could not be preserved. Was he accused of threatening the House? Again, in the year 1819, he brought in the bills known by the name of the Six Acts. He then told the House, that, unless the executive power were reinforced, all the institutions of the country would be overturned by popular violence. Was he then accused of threatening the House? Will any Gentleman say, that it is parliamentary and decorous to urge the danger arising from popular discontent as an argument for severity; but that it is unparliamentary and indecorous to urge that same danger as an argument for conciliatory measures? I, Sir, do entertain great apprehension for the fate of my country. I do in my conscience believe, that unless this measure, or some similar measure, be speedily adopted, great and terrible calamities will befal us. Entertaining this opinion, I think myself bound to state it, not as a threat, but as a reason. I support this measure as a measure of Reform: but I support it still more as a measure of conservation. That we may exclude those whom it is necessary to exclude, we must admit those whom it may be safe to admit. At present we oppose the schemes of revolutionists with only one half, with only one quarter of our proper force. We say, and we say justly, that it is not by mere numbers, but by property and intelligence, that the nation ought to be governed. Yet, saying this, we exclude from all share in the government vast masses of property and intelligence,—vast numbers of those who are most interested in preserving tranquillity, and who know best how to preserve it. We do more. We drive over to the side of revolution those whom we shut out from power. Is this a time when the cause of law and order can spare one of its natural allies? My noble friend, the Paymaster of the Forces, happily described the effect which some parts of our representative system would produce on the mind of a foreigner, who had heard much of our freedom and greatness. If, Sir, I wished to make such a foreigner clearly understand what I consider as the great defects of our system, I would conduct him through that great city which lies to the north of Great Russell-street and Oxford-street,—a city superior in size and in population to the capitals of many mighty kingdoms; and probably superior in opulence, intelligence, and general respectability, to any city in the world. I would conduct him through that interminable succession of streets and squares, all consisting of well-built and well-furnished houses. I would make him observe the brilliancy of the shops, and the crowd of well-appointed equipages. I would lead him round that magnificent circle of palaces which surrounds the Regent's-park. I would tell him, that the rental of this district was far greater than that of the whole kingdom of Scotland, at the time of the Union. And then I would tell him, that this was an unrepresented district! It is needless to give any more instances. It is needless to speak of Manchester, Birmingham, Leeds, Sheffield, with no representation; or of Edinburgh and Glasgow with a mock representation. If a property-tax were now imposed on the old principle, that no person who had less than 150*l.* a year should contribute, I should not be surprised to find, that one-half in number and value of the contributors had no votes at all; and it would, beyond all doubt, be found, that one-fiftieth part in number and value of the contributors had a larger share of the representation than the other forty-nine fiftieths. This is not government by property. It is government by certain detached portions and fragments of property, selected from the rest, and preferred to the rest, on no rational principle whatever. To say that such a system is ancient is no defence. My hon. friend, the member for the University of Oxford (Sir R. Inglis), challenges us to show, that the Constitution was ever better than it is. Sir, we are legislators, not antiquaries. The question for us is, not whether the Constitution was better formerly, but whether we can make it better now. In fact, however, the system was not in ancient times by any means so absurd as it is in our age. One noble Lord (Lord Stormont) has to-night told us, that the town of Aldborough, which he represents, was not larger in the time of Edward I. than it is at present. The line of its walls, he assures us, may still be traced. It is now built up to that line. He argues, therefore, that, as the founders of our representative institutions gave Members to Aldborough when it was as small as it now is, those who would disfranchise it on account of its smallness have no right to say, that they are recurring to the original principle of our representative institutions. But does the noble Lord remember the change which has taken place in the country during the last five centuries? Does he remember how much England has grown in population, while Aldborough has been standing still? Does he consider, that in the time of Edward I. this part of the island did not contain two millions of inhabitants? It now contains nearly fourteen millions. A hamlet of the present day would have been a place of some importance in the time of our early Parliaments. Aldborough may be absolutely as considerable a place as ever.

But compared with the kingdom, it is much less considerable, by the noble Lord's own showing, than when it first elected burgesses. My hon. friend, the member for the University of Oxford, has collected numerous instances of the tyranny which the kings and nobles anciently exercised, both over this House, and over the electors. It is not strange, that, in times when nothing was held sacred, the rights of the people, and of the Representatives of the people, should not have been held sacred. The proceedings which my hon. friend has mentioned, no more prove, that, by the ancient constitution of the realm, this House ought to be a tool of the king and of the aristocracy, than the Benevolences and the Ship-money prove their own legality; or than those unjustifiable arrests, which took place long after the ratification of the great Charter, and even after the Petition of Right, prove that the subject was not anciently entitled to his personal liberty. We talk of the wisdom of our ancestors—and in one respect at least they were wiser than we. They legislated for their own times. They looked at the England which was before them. They did not think it necessary to give twice as many Members to York as they gave to London, because York had been the capital of Britain in the time of Constantius Chlorus; and they would have been amazed indeed if they had foreseen, that a city of more than a hundred thousand inhabitants would be left without Representatives in the nineteenth century, merely because it stood on ground which, in the thirteenth century, had been occupied by a few huts. They framed a representative system, which was not indeed without defects and irregularities, but which was well adapted to the state of England in their time. But a great revolution took place. The character of the old corporations changed. New forms of property came into existence. New portions of society rose into importance. There were in our rural districts rich cultivators, who were not freeholders. There were in our capital rich traders, who were not liverymen. Towns shrank into villages.

Villages swelled into cities larger than the London of the Plantagenets. Unhappily, while the natural growth of society went on, the artificial polity continued unchanged. The ancient form of the representation remained; and precisely because the form remained, the spirit departed. Then came that pressure almost to bursting—the new wine in the old bottles—the new people under the old institutions. It is now time for us to pay a decent, a rational, a manly reverence to our ancestors—not by superstitiously adhering to what they, under other circumstances, did, but by doing what they, in our circumstances, would have done. All history is full of revolutions, produced by causes similar to those which are now operating in England. A portion of the community which had been of no account, expands and becomes strong. It demands a place in the system, suited, not to its former weakness, but to its present power. If this is granted, all is well. If this is refused, then comes the struggle between the young energy of one class, and the ancient privileges of another. Such was the struggle between the Plebeians and the Patricians of Rome. Such was the struggle of the Italian allies for admission to the full rights of Roman citizens. Such was the struggle of our North American colonies against the mother country. Such was the struggle which the *Tiers Etat* of France maintained against the aristocracy of birth. Such was the struggle which the Catholics of Ireland maintained against the aristocracy of creed. Such is the struggle which the free people of colour in Jamaica are now maintaining against the aristocracy of skin. Such, finally, is the struggle which the middle classes in England are maintaining against an aristocracy of mere locality—against an aristocracy, the principle of which is to invest 100 drunken pot-wallopers in one place, or the owner of a ruined hovel in another, with powers which are withheld from cities renowned to the furthest ends of the earth, for the marvels of their wealth and of their industry. But these great cities, says my hon. friend, the member for

Oxford, are virtually, though not directly represented. Are not the wishes of Manchester, he asks, as much consulted as those of any town which sends Members to Parliament? Now, Sir, I do not understand how a power which is salutary when exercised virtually, can be noxious when exercised directly. If the wishes of Manchester have as much weight with us, as they would have under a system which should give Representatives to Manchester, how can there be any danger in giving Representatives to Manchester? A virtual Representative is, I presume, a man who acts as a direct Representative would act: for surely it would be absurd to say, that a man virtually represents the people of property in Manchester, who is in the habit of saying No, when a man directly representing the people of property in Manchester would say Aye. The utmost that can be expected from virtual Representation is, that it may be as good as direct Representation. If so, why not grant direct Representation to places which, as every body allows, ought, by some process or other, to be represented? If it be said, that there is an evil in change as change, I answer, that there is also an evil in discontent as discontent. This, indeed, is the strongest part of our case. It is said that the system works well. I deny it. I deny that a system works well, which the people regard with aversion. We may say here, that it is a good system and a perfect system. But if any man were to say so to any 658 respectable farmers or shop-keepers, chosen by lot in any part of England, he would be hooted down, and laughed to scorn. Are these the feelings with which any part of the Government ought to be regarded? Above all, are these the feelings with which the popular branch of the Legislature ought to be regarded? It is almost as essential to the utility of a House of Commons, that it should possess the confidence of the people, as that it should deserve that confidence. Unfortunately, that which is in theory the popular part of our Government, is in practice the unpopular part. Who wishes to dethrone the King? Who wishes to turn the Lords out of their House? Here and there a crazy radical, whom the boys in the street point at as he walks along. Who wishes to alter the constitution of this House? The whole people. It is natural that it should be so. The House of Commons is, in the language of Mr. Burke, a check for the people—not on the people, but for the people. While that check is efficient, there is no reason to fear that the King or the nobles will oppress the people. But if that check requires checking, how is it to be checked? If the salt shall lose its savour, wherewith shall we season it? The distrust with which the nation regards this House may be unjust. But what then? Can you remove that distrust? That it exists cannot be denied. That it is an evil cannot be denied. That it is an increasing evil cannot be denied. One Gentleman tells us that it has been produced by the late events in France and Belgium; another, that it is the effect of seditious works which have lately been published. If this feeling be of origin so recent, I have read history to little purpose. Sir, this alarming discontent is not the growth of a day or of a year. If there be any symptoms by which it is possible to distinguish the chronic diseases of the body politic from its passing inflammations, all these symptoms exist in the present case. The taint has been gradually becoming more extensive and more malignant, through the whole life-time of two generations. We have tried anodynes. We have tried cruel operations. What are we to try now? Who flatters himself that he can turn this feeling back? Does there remain any argument which escaped the comprehensive intellect of Mr. Burke, or the subtlety of Mr. Wyndham? Does there remain any species of coercion which was not tried by Mr. Pitt and by Lord Londonderry? We have had laws. We have had blood. New treasons have been created. The Press has been shackled. The Habeas Corpus Act has been suspended. Public meetings have been prohibited. The event has proved that these expedients were mere palliatives. You are at the end of your palliatives. The evil remains. It is more formidable than ever. What is to be done? Under such circumstances, a great measure of reconciliation, prepared by the Ministers of the Crown, has been brought before us in a manner which gives additional lustre to a noble name, inseparably associated during two centuries with the dearest liberties of the English people. I will not say, that the measure is in all its details precisely such as I might wish it to be; but it is founded on a great and a sound principle. It takes away a vast power from a few. It distributes that power through the great mass of the middle order. Every man, therefore, who thinks as I think, is bound to stand firmly by Ministers, who are resolved to stand or fall with this measure. Were I one of them, I would sooner—infinitely sooner—fall with such a measure than stand by any other means that ever supported a Cabinet. My hon. friend, the member for the University of Oxford, tells us, that if we pass this law, England will soon be a republic. The reformed House of Commons will, according to him, before it has sat ten years, depose the King, and expel the Lords from their House. Sir, if my hon. friend could prove this, he would have succeeded in bringing an argument for democracy, infinitely stronger than any that is to be found in the works of Paine. His proposition is in fact this—that our monarchical and aristocratical institutions have no hold on the public mind of England; that these institutions are regarded with aversion by a decided majority of the middle class. This, Sir, I say, is plainly deducible from his proposition; for he tells us, that the Representatives of the middle class will inevitably abolish royalty and nobility within ten years: and there is surely no reason to think that the Representatives of the middle class will be more inclined to a democratic revolution than their constituents. Now, Sir, if I were convinced that the great body of the middle class in England look with aversion on monarchy and aristocracy, I should be forced, much against my will, to come to this conclusion, that monarchical and aristocratical institutions are unsuited to this country. Monarchy and aristocracy, valuable and useful as I think them, are still valuable and useful as means, and not as ends. The end of government is the happiness of the people: and I do not conceive that, in a country like this, the happiness of the people can be promoted by a form of government, in which the middle classes place no confidence, and which exists only because the middle classes have no organ by which to make their sentiments known. But, Sir, I am fully convinced that the middle classes sincerely wish to uphold the Royal prerogatives, and the constitutional rights of the Peers. What facts does my hon. friend produce in support of his opinion? One fact only—and that a fact which has absolutely nothing to do with the question. The effect of this Reform, he tells us, would be, to make the House of Commons all-powerful. It was all-powerful once before, in the beginning of 1649. Then it cut off the head of the King, and abolished the House of Peers. Therefore, if this Reform should take place, it will act in the same manner. Now, Sir, it was not the House of Commons that cut off the head of Charles I.; nor was the House of Commons then all-powerful. It had been greatly reduced in numbers by successive expulsions. It was under the absolute dominion of the army. A majority of the House was willing to take the terms offered by the King. The soldiers turned out the majority; and the minority—not a sixth part of the whole House—passed those votes of which my hon. friend speaks—votes of which the middle classes disapproved then, and of which they disapprove still. My hon. friend, and almost all the Gentlemen who have taken the same side with him in this Debate, have dwelt much on the utility of close and rotten boroughs. It is by means of such boroughs, they tell us, that the ablest men have been introduced into Parliament. It is true that many distinguished persons have represented places of this description. But, Sir, we must judge of a form of government by its general tendency, not by happy accidents. Every form of government has its happy accidents. Despotism has its happy accidents. Yet we are not disposed to abolish all constitutional checks, to place an absolute master over us, and to take our chance whether he may be a Caligula or a Marcus Aurelius. In whatever way the House of Commons may be chosen, some able men will be chosen in that way who would not be chosen in any other way. If there were a law that the hundred tallest men in England should be Members of Parliament, there would probably be some able men among those who would come into the House by virtue of this law. If the hundred persons whose names stand first in the alphabetical list of the Court Guide were made Members of Parliament, there would probably be able men among them. We read in ancient history, that a very able king was elected by the neighing of his horse. But we shall scarcely, I think, adopt this mode of election. In one of the most celebrated republics of antiquity—Athens—the Senators and Magistrates were chosen by lot; and sometimes the lot fell fortunately. Once, for example, Socrates was in office. A cruel and unjust measure was brought forward. Socrates resisted it at the hazard of his own life. There is no event in Grecian history more interesting than that memorable resistance. Yet who would have officers assigned by lot, because the accident of the lot may have given to a great and good man a power which he would probably never have attained in any other way? We must judge, as I said, by the general tendency of a system. No person can doubt that a House of Commons chosen freely by the middle classes will contain many very able men. I do not say, that precisely the same able men who would find their way into the present House of Commons, will find their way into the reformed House—but that is not the question. No particular man is necessary to the State. We may depend on it, that if we provide the country with free institutions, those institutions will provide it with great men. There is another objection, which, I think, was first raised by the hon. and learned member for Newport (Mr. H. Twiss). He tells us that the elective franchise is property—that to take it away from a man who has not been judicially convicted of any malpractices is robbery—that no crime is proved against the voters in the close boroughs—that no crime is even imputed to them in the preamble of the Bill—and that to disfranchise them without compensation, would therefore be an act of revolutionary tyranny. The hon. and learned Gentleman has compared the conduct of the present Ministers to that of those odious tools of power, who, towards the close of the reign of Charles II. seized the charters of the Whig Corporations. Now there was another precedent, which I wonder that he did not recollect, both because it was much more nearly in point than that to which he referred, and because my noble friend, the Paymaster of the Forces, had previously alluded to it. If the elective franchise is property—if to disfranchise voters without a crime proved, or a compensation given, be robbery—was there ever such an act of robbery as the disfranchising of the Irish forty-shilling freeholders? Was any pecuniary compensation given to them? Is it declared in the preamble of the bill which took away their votes, that they had been convicted of any offence? Was any judicial inquiry instituted into their conduct? Were they even accused of any crime? Or say, that it was a crime in the electors of Clare to vote for the hon. and learned Gentleman who now represents the county of Waterford—was a Protestant forty-shilling freeholder in Louth, to be punished for the crime of a Catholic forty-shilling freeholder in Clare? If the principle of the hon. and learned member for Newport be sound, the franchise of the Irish peasant was property. That franchise, the Ministry under which the hon. and learned Member held office, did not scruple to take away. Will he accuse the late Ministers of robbery? If not, how can he bring such an accusation against their successors? Every Gentleman, I think, who has spoken from the other side of the House, has alluded to the opinions which some of his Majesty's Ministers formerly entertained on the subject of Reform. It would be officious in me, Sir, to undertake the defence of Gentlemen who are so well able to defend themselves. I will only say, that, in my opinion, the country will not think worse either of their talents or of their patriotism, because they have shown that they can profit by experience, because they have learned to see the folly of delaying inevitable changes. There are others who ought to have learned the same lesson. I say, Sir, that there are those who, I should have thought, must have had enough to last them all their lives of that humiliation which follows obstinate and boastful resistance to measures rendered necessary by the progress of society, and by the development of the human mind. Is it possible that those persons can wish again to occupy a position, which can neither be defended, nor surrendered with honour? I well remember, Sir, a certain evening in the month of May, 1827. I had not then the honour of a seat in this House; but I was an attentive observer of its proceedings. The right hon. Baronet opposite, (Sir R. Peel) of whom personally I desire to speak with that high respect which I feel for his talents and his character, but of whose public conduct I must speak with the sincerity required by my public duty, was then, as he is now, out of office. He had just resigned the Seals of the Home Department, because he conceived that the Administration of Mr. Canning was favourable to the Catholic claims. He rose to ask whether it was the intention of the new Cabinet to repeal the Test and Corporation Acts, and to Reform the Parliament. He bound up, I well remember, those two questions together; and he declared, that if the Ministers should either attempt to repeal the Test and Corporation Acts, or bring forward a measure of Parliamentary Reform, he should think it his duty to oppose them to the utmost. Since that declaration was made nearly four years have elapsed; and what is now the state of the three questions which then chiefly agitated the minds of men? What is become of the Test and Corporation Acts? They are repealed. By whom? By the late Administration. What has become of the Catholic disabilities? They are removed. By whom? By the late Administration. The question of Parliamentary Reform is still behind. But signs, of which it is impossible to misconceive the import, do most clearly indicate, that, unless that question also be speedily settled, property and order, and all the institutions of this great monarchy, will be exposed to fearful peril. Is it possible, that Gentlemen long versed in high political affairs cannot read these signs? Is it possible that they can really believe that the Representative system of England, such as it now is, will last till the year 1860? If not, for what would they have us wait? Would they have us wait merely that we may show to all the world how little we have profited by our own recent experience? Would they have us wait, that we may once again hit the exact point where we can neither refuse with authority, nor concede with grace? Would they have us wait, that the numbers of the discontented party may become larger, its demands higher, its feelings more acrimonious, its organization more complete? Would they have us wait till the whole tragi-comedy of 1827 has been acted over again; till they have been brought into office by a cry of "No Reform!" to be reformers, as they were once before brought into office by a cry of "No Popery!" to be emancipators? Have they obliterated from their minds—gladly perhaps would some among them obliterate from their minds—the transactions of that year? And have they forgotten all the transactions of the succeeding year? Have they forgotten how the spirit of liberty in Ireland, debarred from its natural outlet, found a vent by forbidden passages? Have they forgotten how we were forced to indulge the Catholics in all the license of rebels, merely because we chose to withhold from them the liberties of subjects? Do they wait for associations more formidable than that of the Corn Exchange,—for contributions larger than the Rent,—for agitators more violent than those who, three years ago, divided with the King and the Parliament, the sovereignty of Ireland? Do they wait for that last and most dreadful paroxysm of popular rage,—for that last and most cruel test of military fidelity? Let them wait, if their past experience shall induce them to think that any high honour or any exquisite pleasure is to be obtained by a policy like this. Let them wait, if this strange and fearful infatuation be indeed upon them,—that they should not see with their eyes, or hear with their ears, or understand with their heart. But let us know our interest and our duty better. Turn where we may,—within,—around,—the voice of great events is proclaiming to us, Reform, that you may preserve. Now, therefore, while every thing at home and abroad forebodes ruin to those who persist in a hopeless struggle against the spirit of the age,—now, while the crash of the proudest throne of the continent is still resounding in our ears,—now, while the roof of a British palace affords an ignominious shelter to the exiled heir of forty kings,—now, while we see on every side ancient institutions subverted, and great societies dissolved,—now, while the heart of England is still sound,—now, while the old feelings and the old associations retain a power and a charm which may too soon pass away,—now, in this your accepted time,—now, in this your day of salvation,—take counsel, not of prejudice,—not of party spirit,—not of the ignominious pride of a fatal consistency,—but of history,—of reason,—of the ages which are past,—of the signs of this most portentous time. Pronounce in a manner worthy of the expectation with which this great Debate has been anticipated, and of the long remembrance which it will leave behind. Renew the youth of the State. Save property divided against itself. Save the multitude, endangered by their own ungovernable passions. Save the aristocracy, endangered by its own unpopular power. Save the greatest, and fairest, and most highly civilized community that ever existed, from calamities which may in a few days sweep away all the rich heritage of so many ages of wisdom and glory. The danger is terrible. The time is short. If this Bill should be rejected, I pray to God that none of those who concur in rejecting it may ever remember their votes with unavailing regret, amidst the wreck of laws, the confusion of ranks, the spoliation of property, and the dissolution of social order.

ON PARLIAMENTARY REFORM.*

July 5, 1831.

On the Adjourned Debate on the Second Reading of Lord John Russell's Parliamentary Reform Bill for Ireland.

Before I proceed to examine what may be termed the political arguments applicable to the question, I wish to notice one position, which, if it were a sound one, I admit would be decisive against Reform. That position is—that the elective franchise is property—as much property as the dividends of the fundholder, or the rents of the landowner. It must either be property or not property; and if it be property, to seize what belongs to the rich man, in order to give it to the poor man, would be to break up the very foundation of social order. I support this measure because I am convinced that the elective franchise is not property, and that the Bill ought not, therefore, to give compensation. Looking back to the earliest times, we shall find, that if the elective franchise be property, the present system is founded upon the most monstrous system of injustice and robbery. The great disfranchisement of the reign of Henry VI., was an act of unheard-of plunder, and the same remark will apply to the Reform introduced by Oliver Cromwell. I will not argue on the merit or demerit of his system, but this I will say, that the best and wisest men of that, and subsequent times, never treated the elective franchise as property. I speak of all the debates in which Maynard and Hale partook under the vigorous Oliver, and his feeble successor. Sir Henry Vane said,

* Hansard, 3d Series, vol. iv. 1831, p. 773–783.

that it was a Reform which the Long Parliament would have made had it lasted; and Lord Clarendon declared, that it was a Reform which the King ought to have made had he then come to the Crown. Lord Clarendon, the most distinguished of royalists, who leaned too much to legal refinements on political questions, describes it as a Reform which was fit to be made by a more warrantable method, and in better times. This, then, I say, is that more warrantable method; this that better time. What Cromwell attempted in a country lately convulsed by civil war, and still agitated by religious factions, we are now called upon to accomplish in a state of perfect peace, and under a Prince whose title is as undisputed, as his person is beloved. The only circumstances which, in the opinion of Lord Clarendon, were wanting in the Reform of Cromwell, we find in the Reform of William the Fourth. If the elective franchise were property, these, I contend, were most extensive and sweeping confiscations; but, for the sake of the great institution of property, for which all other institutions exist, which is the source of all knowledge and of all industry, I do most deeply lament to hear the sanctity that belongs to property claimed by that which is not property. If you mix political abuses with the institution of property, you must expect, that property will contract the odium of political abuses; and people will imagine that there is no more immorality in taking away a man's estate, than in disfranchising Old Sarum. If you bind them up that they may stand together, take care that they do not fall together. Many have before used the argument which we heard repeated last night, and which, if I mistake not, was originally employed by the right hon. Baronet (Sir R. Peel). It is true, say they, that the Act of 1829 was a confiscation of the property of the 40*s.* freeholders of Ireland, and show us a case of necessity equally urgent, and we will vote for Reform. Let them, however, beware how they set a precedent for the invasion of property on the ground of political convenience. Considering the elective franchise as not property, we have only to discuss and decide this question—whether it is expedient at the present moment to touch it. The only argument I have heard on this subject was that used by a noble Lord (Porchester) who spoke for the first time last night, and whom it gave me great pleasure to hear. The noble Lord referred to the history of France, and particularly to recent events in that country; but I must question the noble Lord's arguments, as well as his facts. I must deny, that there was a fluctuation from a desire for a violent change from monarchical to a republican form of government, or that it was the fluctuation of the same party. Different opinions did, no doubt, prevail under different administrations—under de Cazes, Villèle, and other administrations; but then these different opinions were expressed by Chambers differently constituted. The Chamber of Deputies of 1815 was differently constituted from that of 1819, and that of 1824 differed from both. The Chamber of 1827, indeed, though chosen in the same manner as the Chamber of 1824, took a very different course. But this difference of political feeling in the Representative body, chosen under different circumstances, was an every-day case. When Queen Anne discharged her Whig Ministry, she succeeded also in getting a House of Commons, the majority of which were Tories. On the accession of George 1st, another change took place, and a House of Commons, chiefly Whigs, were returned. In the same way a total change took place in the political character of the Commons in the election of 1784. I protest against the analogy drawn by the noble Lord, and I deny that the cases of England and France are alike. I deny, that we have had any parties here even remotely resembling the revolutionary and counter-revolutionary parties of France. I deny that there is any analogy between the two Houses of Peers. I regard the Chamber of Peers of France as an unfortunate experiment—as a kind of forced production—an exotic: there was nothing in the property or in the state of society in France, which required such an institution; it had no root in the soil, and its decline and fall need not give the aristocracy of England the slightest alarm. The principal, and most plausible argument against the Reform Bill is this—mark how rich, how great, how happy, this country is, and has been; the admired of all men, and the envied of foreign nations; will you, then, change a system which has produced so many, and such lasting benefits? I am far from denying that England is a great and prosperous country. I am as far from denying, that she owes much of her greatness and prosperity to the form of her government; but government and society are cause and effect—they re-act on each other. No doubt the government of the Czar Peter did much for Russia; but would it be an argument against giving her free institutions, that despotism had procured her civilization? The whole of history shews, that all great revolutions have been produced by a disproportion between society and its institutions; for while society has grown, its institutions have not kept pace and accommodated themselves to its improvements. When we are told of the admiration of distinguished foreigners of all ages for the Constitution of England, it seems to be thought, that their applause has been bestowed upon the same institutions which, in the lapse of centuries, have undergone no change. Philip de Comines said, that the English were the best-governed people in the world, and when Montesquieu gave them the same praise, were both writers speaking of the same institutions? Certainly not. The history of England is the history of a succession of Reforms; and the very reason that the people of England are great and happy is, that their history is the history of Reform. The great Charter, the first assembling of Parliament, the Petition of Right, the Revolution, and lastly, this great measure—are all proofs of my position—are all progressive stages in the progress of society—and I am fully convinced that every argument urged against the step we are now called upon to take might have been advanced with equal justice against any of the other changes I have enumerated. It is the principle of "Hume's History," as every body knows, that the Stuarts governed better than the Tudors; but, suppose any man had risen in the Convention Parliament, and said, "how great and happy we are—we have ten times as many inhabitants, and merchants ten times as wealthy as under the Tudors; we have been most admirably governed—we are not slaves under the Dey of Tripoli, but free subjects of a generous Monarch, and why should we change?" The answer is plain. If we had been the slaves of the Dey of Tripoli, we should not have known better, but the change in our situations has educated us for improvements in our institutions. At the present moment we everywhere see society outgrowing our institutions. Wherever we turn our eyes, we behold a nation great and civilized—with a soil cultivated to a degree of fertility unknown to other countries—with the perfection of all discoveries in physical science, to promote the conveniences of life—standing pre-eminent among the civilized world in everything that depends upon the skill and intelligence of individuals, or combinations of individuals—and yet, with laws and institutions that little command the respect and admiration of mankind. Our roads, our bridges, our steam-engines, our manufactures, our modes of conveyance, our demand for labor, and our rewards of ingenuity, surpass those of any nation in the ancient or modern world, and extort the admiration of rival States; but, let me ask, are foreigners equally struck with the excellence of our legislative enactments—with the modes of conveying land, or of conducting actions—and with a Penal Code that seems purposely contrived to puzzle and ensnare? These are matters in which the Legislature has shown its skill, as our manufacturers have shown theirs, but with a far different result. Let us contrast our commerce, wealth, and perfect civilization, with our Penal Laws—at once barbarous and inefficient—the preposterous fictions of pleading—the mummery of fines and recoveries—the chaos of precedents, and the bottomless pit of Chancery. Here we see the barbarism of the thirteenth century coupled with the civilization of the nineteenth, and we see too, that the barbarism belongs to the Government, and the civilization to the people. Then I say, that this incongruous state of things cannot continue; and if we do not terminate it with wisdom, ere long we shall find it ended by violence. Because I think we have arrived at the point, when a change is both wise and necessary, I support this Bill with heart and soul; and I shall be proud to the last hour of my life, of the part I have been able to take in this great act of reconciliation between the state of society and the condition of its institutions. We were told in the last Parliament, that this is not the Reform for which the people petitioned; and if it be not, looking at the manner in which it has been received, nothing can prove more decisively the blessed effect of seasonable concession. Never was there so signal an example of that wise policy which conducts the great revolutions of public opinion to a happy and peaceful conclusion, and renders the very act of extending liberty the security for social order. It is not strange, that the people, denied their reasonable claims, should become unreasonable; and, when repulsed by those who ought to hear them, should fly to demagogues. We have seen how excitement was created, and we have seen, too, how it may be allayed. The true secret of the power of agitators is, the obstinacy of rulers; and liberal governments make a moderate people. Did w. not hear in the beginning of the last Session the Prime Minister declare, that there should be no Reform, and what was the consequence? The people were excited to such a state, that it seemed as if a dissolution of social order was at hand. So near at hand was it thought, that the Minister of the Crown did not dare to show his Sovereign in his capital. I will venture to say, that now there is not a nation in the world more sincerely or more justly attached to the person and government of their King than the English, or more disposed to strengthen the hands of the public authorities in the enforcement of the law. I do not, however, wonder that a measure which removes discontent should excite the hatred of two classes—the friends of corruption, and the agents of sedition. All who love abuses because they profit by them, and all who take advantage of disaffection which abuses occasion, are naturally leagued against a Bill, which, by making the Government pure, renders the people attached. Those who stand at the two extremities of political opinions play into each other's hands on an occasion like the present; the friends of despotism, on the one hand, are furnished by Jacobin agitators with pretexts for oppression; and Jacobin agitators, on the other hand, are provided by the friends of despotism with arguments against Government. I am rejoiced to see, that the people of England know how to appreciate the monstrous coalition between the enemies of all order and the opponents of all liberty. England has spoken, and spoken out, from every part of the kingdom where the voice of the people was allowed to be heard; it has been heard from our mightiest sea-ports—from our manufacturing towns—from the capital—from our populous counties. As far as my calculations have gone on the late returns, from almost all those situations a suitable answer has been returned to that truly royal voice which demands the opinion of the nation. Here we are now, nearly all Reformers—all Reformers in some sense or other—in some degree or other—for not one Member has declared himself opposed to the principle of Reform; at least some hint has been thrown out that he is not adverse to all change—and I most thoroughly and cordially agree with the noble Paymaster of the Forces, that, like the Scotch army at Dunbar, the enemies of Reform have placed themselves at the mercy of their adversaries. Their arguments and their abuse might be equally directed against all Reforms, for all might be asserted to be revolutionary, anarchical, and demoralizing. It has been said, that the Reform Bill introduced for England is not the Reform for which the people petitioned. Will that Reform Bill which is to be proposed by hon. Gentlemen opposite, be that Reform for which the people have petitioned? If this Bill, now brought forward by the ancient friends and advocates of the people, be not the Reform which is consonant with popular feeling, what will it be if brought forward by those who have been always opposed to popular feeling, and who can adduce no reason for presenting it except intimidation? The hon. member for Aldborough, and other hon. Members, have complained of certain anomalies in the Bill. They object to the measure, that it gives one county twelve Members, while a larger has got only ten—that such a town as Brighton is to have only one Member, while another less considerable is to have two. This may be an excellent argument against the details of the measure; but it cannot in the slightest degree affect the principle. Will they bring forward an Amendment to remove these anomalies? Or do they mean to assert that a new Rule of Three sum must be worked upon the occasion of every census? If not, why do they censure the Bill because it contains anomalies? But, after all, it contains fewer anomalies than exist in the present system [*cries of* "*No, no*"]. I speak with arithmetical precision. In the proposed system there is no disproportion so great—none which can make up the difference between Old Sarum and Manchester. Hon. Gentlemen opposite would, in my mind, do better to answer arguments than to interrupt speeches. If there be anomalies, it is you, and not we, who are bound to propose the remedy —so that—

> "Each fair burgh, numerically free,
> Shall choose its Members by the Rule of Three."

It is asked by the hon. Gentlemen on the other side, will this Reform be final? In return, I ask you, will your Reform be final? The same, and stronger reasons against a Reform being final, apply themselves to any you would make. Last year, when there was a question of giving Representatives to the greatest manufacturing towns in the world, the same argument was brought forward. It was said, it would only be the prelude to greater changes. Such a Reform could not be final; how, then, could you pretend to say, that any Reform you propose would be final? Now, Sir, if I am asked my opinion, I do declare that this Reform of ours is final; but that any which fell short of it would not be. When I say final, I mean that it will be final for that space of time to which we can look forward, and for which alone we can attempt to legislate. In the course of one hundred years, we may chance to have docks as extensive as those of Liverpool in the Hebrides; and a manufacturing town as large as Manchester, in the county of Galway. The same causes are still in action, which, in many places, have converted hamlets into great towns, and barren heaths into cornfields and meadows. For a country so altered and improved in its condition, we cannot pretend to legislate; all that we can do is to set those who shall then exist the signal example of the mode and spirit in which such a reform as their circumstances require should take place. In the only way, therefore, in which a public man ought to use the word final, I use it; and thus I declare this Reform Bill will be final. But as to the other Bill, if the hon. Gentlemen opposite should succeed in any branch of the Legislature in throwing out this measure of ours—if they should succeed in displacing the present Administration—and if they should succeed in obtaining a House of Commons which would support a new ministry—I ask them what they would do? Sir, there can be no difficulty in foreseeing and describing the progress downwards. First, there would be a mock Reform—a Bassetlaw Reform, worthy of those who, when a delinquent borough was to be punished, refused to transfer the franchise to a populous manufacturing town, but threw it into neighboring hundreds—worthy of those who refused to give Representatives to the three greatest manufacturing towns in the world—a Reform fraught with all the evils of change, and not a single benefit—a Reform depriving the Government of the foundation of prescription, without substituting the foundation of reason and the public good—a Reform which would unsettle establishments, without appeasing discontent—a Reform by which the people would be at once encouraged and exasperated—encouraged by the sense of their own importance, and the evident effect of their power, and exasperated because what they obtained was not what they had demanded. Then would come agitation—libels would abound—the Press would be excited —and demagogues would harangue in every street. Coercion would only aggravate the evil. This is no age, this is no country for the war of power against the war of opinions. Those enemies to the public quiet—agitators and demagogues, who would be driven back by this Reform Bill to their proper insignificance—would become truly powerful, till, at the last, the law would be evaded and opposed till it became a mockery, and England would be reduced to the same condition in which Ireland was placed at the end of the year 1828. Then amidst the cheers of the Whigs, who would be occupying their old places on that side of the House, and the grief and dismay of the Tories, who are now again trusting, to be again betrayed, some right hon. Gentleman would rise from these benches—as did, on the 1st of March, the Paymaster of the Forces, to propose that Bill on which the hearts of the people are fixed. Then should we flatter ourselves that all had been done; but not so. The gratitude and delight with which the measure would be now received, could no longer exist when the materials of agitation were ready. They would find themselves in the condition of those in the old stories, who evoked the fiends. When once the evil spirit is called up, you must find him work, or he will tear you in pieces. The noble Lord opposite spoke of the Day of Sacrifices. Let him remember it was afterwards named the Day of Dupes, not because it was a Day of Sacrifices, but of sacrifices delayed too long. It was because the French aristocracy refused Reform in 1783, that there was Revolution in 1789. But we need not go far to see the danger of delaying inevitable concessions. Let us look to Ireland. Is not one such instance, when made practically, enough to convince one generation? I feel, that some apology is due for the tone I have assumed; I fear, that it may be deemed unbecoming in me to make any application to the fears of Members of this House. But surely I may, without reproach, address myself to their honest fears. It is well to talk of opposing a firm front to sedition, and of using vigorous means to put down agitation. Those phrases are used very properly, when they refer to some temporary excitement—to some partial disturbances, as in 1780—to stifle which, the show of force and determination on the part of a Government is alone needed—then it is well to show a bold front; but woe to the Government that cannot distinguish between a nation and a mob—woe to the Government that thinks a great and steady movement of mind is to be put down like a riot. This error has been twice fatal to the Bourbons—it may be fatal to the Legislature of this country if they should venture to foster it. I do believe, that the irrevocable moment has arrived. Nothing can prevent the passing of this noble law—this second Bill of Rights. I do call it the second Bill of Rights; and so will the country call it; and so will our children. I call it a greater Charter of the liberties of England. Eighteen hundred and thirty-one is destined to exhibit the first example of an established, of a deep-rooted system removed without bloodshed, or violence, or rapine—all points being debated—every punctilio observed—the peaceful industry of the country never for a moment checked or compromised—and the authority of the law not for one instant suspended. These are things of which we may well be proud. These are things which make us look with confidence and good hope to the future destinies of the human race. These are things that enable us to look forward to a long series of tranquil and happy years, in which we shall have a popular Government and a loyal people; and in which war, if war be inevitable, shall find us a united nation—of years pre-eminently distinguished by the progress of art and science, and of knowledge generally ; by the diminution of the public burthens, and by all those victories of peace in which, more than in the most splendid military successes, consist the true prosperity of States and the glory of Statesmen. Sir, it is with these feelings, and with these hopes, that I give my most cordial assent to the measure, considering it desirable in itself, and at the present moment, and in the present temper of the people, indispensably necessary to the repose of the empire and the stability of the Throne.

ON PARLIAMENTARY REFORM.*

SEPTEMBER 20, 1831.

On the third reading of the Reform Bill for England.

It is not without great diffidence, Sir, that I rise to address you on a subject which has been nearly exhausted. Indeed, I should not have risen had I not thought that though the arguments on this question are for the most part old, our situation at present is in a great measure new. At length the Reform Bill, having passed without vital injury through all the dangers which threatened it during a long and minute discussion, from the attacks of its enemies and from the dissensions of its friends, comes before us for our final ratification, altered, indeed, in some of its details for the better, and in some for the worse, but in its great principles still the same Bill which, on the 1st of March, was proposed to the late Parliament—the same Bill which was received with joy and gratitude by the whole nation—the same Bill which, in an instant, took away the power of interested agitators, and united in one firm body sects of sincere Reformers—the same Bill which, at the late election, received the approbation of almost every great constituent body in the empire. With a confidence which discussion has only strengthened—with an assured hope of great public blessings if the wish of the nation shall be gratified—with a deep and solemn apprehension of great public calamities if that wish shall be disappointed—I for the last time give my most hearty assent to this noble law, destined, I trust, to be the parent of many good laws,

* Hansard, 3d Series, vol. vii. 1831, p. 297–311.

and, through a long series of years, to secure the repose and promote the prosperity of my country. When I say that I expect this Bill to promote the prosperity of the country, I by no means intend to encourage those chimerical hopes which the hon. and learned member for Rye, who has so much distinguished himself in this debate, has imputed to the Reformers. The people, he says, are for the Bill, because they expect that it will immediately relieve all their distresses. Sir, I believe that very few of that large and respectable class which we are now about to admit to a share of political power, entertain any such absurd expectation. They expect relief, I doubt not, and I doubt not also that they will find it. But sudden relief they are far too wise to expect. The Bill, says the hon. and learned Gentleman, is good for nothing—it is merely theoretical—it removes no real and sensible evil—it will not give the people more work, or higher wages, or cheaper bread. Undoubtedly, Sir, the Bill will not immediately give all those things to the people. But will any institutions give them all those things? Do the present institutions of the country secure to them these advantages? If we are to pronounce the Reform Bill good for nothing, because it will not at once raise the nation from distress to prosperity, what are we to say of that system under which the nation has been of late sinking from prosperity into distress? The defect is not in the Reform Bill, but in the very nature of government. On the physical condition of the great body of the people, government acts not as a specific, but as an alterative. Its operation is powerful, indeed, and certain, but gradual and indirect. The end of government is not directly to make the people rich, but to protect them in making themselves rich—and a Government which attempts more than this is precisely the Government which is likely to perform less. Governments do not and cannot support the people. We have no miraculous powers—we have not the rod of the Hebrew lawgiver—we cannot rain down bread on the multitude from Heaven—we cannot smite the rock and give them to drink. We can give them only freedom to employ their industry to the best advantage, and security in the enjoyment of what their industry has acquired. These advantages it is our duty to give at the smallest possible cost. The diligence and forethought of individuals will thus have fair play; and it is only by the diligence and forethought of individuals that the community can become prosperous. I am not aware that his Majesty's Ministers, or any of the supporters of the Bill, have encouraged the people to hope, that Reform will remove their distresses, in any other way than by this indirect process. By this indirect process the Bill will, I feel assured, conduce to the national prosperity. If it had been passed fifteen years ago, it would have saved us from our present embarrassments. If we pass it now, it will gradually extricate us from them. It will secure to us a House of Commons, which, by preserving peace, by destroying monopolies, by taking away unnecessary public burthens, by judiciously distributing necessary public burthens, will, in the progress of time, greatly improve our condition. This it will do; and those who blame it for not doing more, blame it for not doing what no Constitution, no code of laws, ever did or ever will do; what no legislator, who was not an ignorant and unprincipled quack, ever ventured to promise. But chimerical as are the hopes which the hon. and learned member for Rye imputes to the people, they are not, I think, more chimerical than the fears which he has himself avowed. Indeed, those very Gentlemen who are constantly telling us that we are taking a leap in the dark—that we pay no attention to the lessons of experience—that we are mere theorists—are themselves the despisers of experience—are themselves the mere theorists. They are terrified at the thought of admitting into Parliament Members elected by £10 householders. They have formed in their own imaginations a most frightful idea of these Members. My hon. and learned friend, the member for Cockermouth, is certain that these Members will take every opportunity of promoting the interests of the journeyman in opposition to those of the capitalist. The hon. and learned member for Rye is convinced that none but persons who have strong local connexions, will ever be returned for such constituent bodies. My hon. friend, the member for Thetford, tells us, that none but mob-orators, men who are willing to pay the basest court to the multitude, will have any chance. Other speakers have gone still further, and have described to us the future borough Members as so many Marats and Santerres—low, fierce, desperate men—who will turn the House into a bear-garden, and who will try to turn the monarchy into a republic—mere agitators, without honour, without sense, without education, without the feelings or the manners of gentlemen. Whenever, during the course of the fatiguing discussions by which we have been so long occupied, there has been a cry of "question," or a noise at the bar, the orator who has been interrupted has remarked, that such proceedings will be quite in place in the Reformed Parliament, but that we ought to remember that the House of Commons is still an assembly of Gentlemen. This, I say, is to set up mere theory, or rather mere prejudice, in opposition to long and ample experience. Are the Gentlemen who talk thus, ignorant that we have already the means of judging what kind of men the £10 householders will send up to Parliament? Are they ignorant that there are even now large towns with very popular rights of election—with rights of election even more democratic than those which will be bestowed by the present Bill? Ought they not, on their own principles, to look at the results of the experiments which have already been made, instead of predicting frightful calamities at random? How do the facts which are before us agree with their theories? Nottingham is a city with a franchise even more democratic than that which this Bill establishes. Does Nottingham send hither men of local connexions? It returns two distinguished men—the one an advocate, the other a soldier—both unconnected with the town. Every man paying scot-and-lot has a vote at Leicester. This is a lower franchise than the £10 franchise. Do we find that the members for Leicester are the mere tools of the journeymen? I was at Leicester during the contest in 1826, and I recollect that the suffrages of the scot-and-lot voters were pretty equally divided between two candidates—neither of them connected with the place—neither of them a slave of the mob—the one a Tory Baronet from Derbyshire—the other a most respectable and excellent friend of mine, connected with the manufacturing interest, and also an inhabitant of Derbyshire. Look at Norwich—Look at Northampton, with a franchise more democratic than even the scot-and-lot franchise. Northampton formerly returned Mr. Perceval, and now returns Gentlemen of high respectability—Gentlemen who have a great stake in the prosperity and tranquillity of the country. Look at the metropolitan districts. This is an *à fortiori* case. Nay it is—the expression, I fear, is awkward—an *à fortiori* case at two removes. The £10 householders of the metropolis are persons in a lower station of life than the £10 householders of other towns. The scot-and-lot franchise in the metropolis is again lower than the £10 franchise—yet have Westminster and Southwark been in the habit of sending us Members of whom we have had reason to be ashamed—of whom we have not had reason to be proud? I do not say that the inhabitants of Westminster and Southwark have always expressed their political sentiments with proper moderation. That is not the question—the question is this—what kind of men have they elected? The very principle of all Representative government is, that men who do not judge rightly of public affairs may be quite competent to choose others who will judge better. Whom, then, have Westminster and Southwark sent us during the last fifty years—years full of great events—years of intense popular excitement? Take any one of those nomination-boroughs, the patrons of which have conscientiously endeavoured to send fit men into this House.

Compare the Members for that borough with the members for Westminster and Southwark, and you will have no doubt to which the preference is due. It is needless to mention Mr. Fox, Mr. Sheridan, Mr. Tierney, Sir Samuel Romilly. Yet I must pause at the name of Sir Samuel Romilly. Was he a mob-orator? Was he a servile flatterer of the multitude? Sir, if he had any fault—if there was any blemish on that most serene and spotless character—that character which every public man, and especially every professional man engaged in politics, ought to propose to himself as a model—it was this, that he despised popularity too much and too visibly. The hon. Member for Thetford told us that the hon. and learned member for Rye, with all his talents, would have no chance of a seat in the Reformed Parliament, for want of the qualifications which succeed on the hustings. Did Sir Samuel Romilly ever appear on the hustings? He never solicited one vote—he never shewed himself to the electors till he had been returned at the head of the poll. Even then—as I have heard from one of his nearest relatives—it was with reluctance that he submitted to be chaired. He shrank from being made a shew. He loved the people, and he served them; but Coriolanus himself was not less fit to canvass them. I will mention one other name—that of a man of whom I have only a childish recollection, but who must have been intimately known to many of those who hear me—Mr. Henry Thornton. He was a man eminently upright, honourable, and religious—a man of strong understanding—a man of great political science—but, in all respects, the very reverse of a mob-orator. He was a man who would not have yielded to what he considered as unreasonable clamour—I will not say to save his seat—but to save his life. Yet he continued to represent Southwark, Parliament after Parliament, for many years. Such has been the conduct of the scot-and-lot voters of the metropolis, and there is clearly less reason to expect democratic violence from £10 householders than from scot-and-lot householders; and from £10 householders in the country-towns than from £10 householders in London. The experience, I say, therefore, is on our side; and on the side of our opponents nothing but mere conjecture, and mere assertion. Sir, when this Bill was first brought forward, I supported it not only on the ground of its intrinsic merits, but, also, because I was convinced that to reject it would be a course full of danger. I believe that the danger of that course is in no respect diminished. I believe, on the contrary, that it is increased. We are told that there is a reaction. The warmth of the public feeling, it seems, has abated. In this story both the sections of the party opposed to Reform are agreed—those who hate Reform, because it will remove abuses, and those who hate it, because it will avert anarchy—those who wish to see the electing body controlled by ejectments, and those who wish to see it controlled by constitutional squeezes. They must now, I think, be undeceived. They must have already discovered that the surest way to prevent a reaction is, to talk about it, and that the enthusiasm of the people is at once rekindled by any indiscreet mention of their seeming coolness. This, Sir, is not the first reaction which the sagacity of the Opposition has discovered since the Reform Bill was brought in. Every Gentleman who sat in the late Parliament—every Gentleman who, during the sitting of the late Parliament, paid attention to political speeches and publications, must remember how, for some time before the debate on General Gascoyne's motion, and during the debate on that motion, and down to the very day of the dissolution, we were told that public feeling had cooled. The right hon. Baronet, the member for Tamworth, told us so. All the literary organs of the Opposition, from the *Quarterly Review* down to the *Morning Post*, told us so. All the members of the Opposition with whom we conversed in private told us so. I have in my eye a noble friend of mine, who assured me, on the very night which preceded the dissolution, that the people had ceased to be zealous for the Ministerial plan, and that we were more likely to lose than to gain by the elections. The appeal was made to the people; and what was the result? What sign of a reaction appeared among the Livery of London? What sign of a reaction did the hon. Baronet who now represents Okehampton find among the free-holders of Cornwall? How was it with the large represented towns? Had Liverpool cooled?—or Bristol? or Leicester? or Coventry? or Nottingham? or Norwich? How was it with the great seats of manufacturing industry—Yorkshire, and Lancashire, and Staffordshire, and Warwickshire, and Cheshire? How was it with the agricultural districts—Northumberland and Cumberland, Leicestershire and Lincolnshire, Kent and Essex, Oxfordshire, Hampshire, Somersetshire, Dorsetshire, Devonshire? How was it with the strong-holds of aristocratical influence, Newark, and Stamford, and Hertford, and St. Alban's? Never did any people display, within the limits prescribed by law, so generous a fervour, or so steadfast a determination, as that very people whose apparent languor had just before inspired the enemies of Reform with a delusive hope. Such was the end of the reaction of April; and, if that lesson shall not profit those to whom it was given, such and yet more signal will be the end of the reaction of September. The two cases are strictly analogous. In both cases the people were eager when they believed the Bill to be in danger, and quiet when they believed it to be in security. During the three or four weeks which followed the promulgation of the Ministerial plan, all was joy, and gratitude, and vigorous exertion. Everywhere meetings were held—everywhere resolutions were passed—from every quarter were sent up petitions to this House, and addresses to the Throne—and then the nation, having given vent to its first feelings of delight—having clearly and strongly expressed its opinions—having seen the principle of the Bill adopted by the House of Commons on the second reading—became composed, and awaited the result with a tranquillity which the Opposition mistook for indifference. All at once the aspect of affairs changed. General Gascoyne's amendment was carried—the Bill was again in danger—exertions were again necessary. Then was it well seen whether the calmness of the public mind was any indication of slackness! The depth and sincerity of the prevailing sentiments were proved, not by mere talking, but by actions, by votes, by sacrifices. Intimidation was defied—expenses were rejected—old ties were broken—the people struggled manfully—they triumphed gloriously—they placed the Bill in perfect security, as far as this House was concerned, and they returned to their repose. They are now, as they were on the eve of General Gascoyne's motion, awaiting the issue of the deliberations of Parliament, without any indecent shew of violence, but with anxious interest and immovable resolution. And because they are not exhibiting that noisy and rapturous enthusiasm, which is in its own nature transient—because they are not as much excited as on the day when the plan of the Government was first made known to them, or on the day when the late Parliament was dissolved—because they do not go on week after week, hallooing, and holding meetings, and marching about with flags, and making bonfires, and illuminating their houses—we are again told that there is a reaction. To such a degree can men be deceived by their wishes, in spite of their own recent experience! Sir, there is no reaction; and there will be no reaction. All that has been said on this subject convinces me only that those who are now, for the second time, raising this cry, know nothing of the crisis in which they are called on to act, or of the nation which they aspire to govern—all their opinions respecting this Bill are founded on one great error. They imagine that the public feeling concerning Reform is a mere whim which sprang up suddenly out of nothing, and which will as suddenly vanish into nothing. They, therefore, confidently expect a reaction. They are always looking out for a reaction. Everything that they see, or that they hear, they construe into a sign of the approach of this reaction. They resemble the man in Horace, who lies on the bank of the river, expecting that it will every moment pass by and leave him a clear passage—not knowing the depth and abundance of the fountain which feeds it—not knowing that it flows, and will flow on for ever. They have found out a hundred ingenious devices by which they deceive themselves. Sometimes they tell us that the public feeling about Reform was caused by the events which took place at Paris about fourteen months ago; though every observant and impartial man knows, that the excitement which the late French revolution produced in England, was not the cause but the effect of that progress which liberal opinions had made amongst us. Sometimes they tell us, that we should not have been troubled with any complaints on the subject of the Representation, if the House of Commons had agreed to a certain motion, made in the Session of 1830, for inquiry into the causes of the public distress. I remember nothing about that motion, except that it gave rise to the dullest debate ever known; and the country, I am firmly convinced, cared not one straw about it. But is it not strange that men of real talents can deceive themselves so grossly, as to think that any change in the Government of a foreign nation, or the rejection of any single motion, however popular, could all at once raise up a great, rich, enlightened nation, against its representative institutions? Could such small drops have produced an overflowing, if the vessel had not already been filled to the very brim? These explanations are incredible, and if they were credible, would be anything but consolatory. If it were really true that the English people had taken a sudden aversion to a representative system which they had always loved and admired, because a single division in Parliament had gone against their wishes, or because, in a foreign country, under circumstances bearing not the faintest analogy to those in which we are placed, a change of dynasty had happened, what hope could we have for such a nation of madmen? How could we expect that the present form of government, or any form of government, would be durable amongst them?—Sir, the public feeling concerning Reform is of no such recent origin, and springs from no such frivolous causes. Its first faint commencement may be traced far—very far—back in our history. During seventy years it has had a great influence on the public mind. Through the first thirty years of the reign of George III., it was gradually increasing. The great leaders of the two parties in the State were favourable to Reform. It was supported by large and most respectable minorities in the House of Commons. The French Revolution, filling the higher and middle classes with an extreme dread of change, and the war calling away the public attention from internal to external politics, threw the question back; but the people never lost sight of it. Peace came, and they were at leisure to think of domestic improvements. Distress came, and they suspected, as was natural, that their distress was the effect of unfaithful stewardship and unskilful legislation. An opinion favourable to Parliamentary Reform grew up rapidly, and became strong among the middle classes. But one tie—one strong tie—still bound those classes to the Tory party, I mean the Catholic Question. It is impossible to deny, that on that subject a large proportion—a majority, I fear—of the middle class of Englishmen, conscientiously held opinions opposed to those which I have always entertained, and were disposed to sacrifice every other consideration to what they considered as a religious duty. Thus the Catholic Question hid, so to speak, the question of Parliamentary Reform: the feeling in favour of Parliamentary Reform grew, but it grew in the shade. Every man, I think, must have observed the progress of that feeling in his own social circle. But few Reform meetings were held, and few petitions in favour of Reform presented. At length the Catholics were emancipated; the solitary link of sympathy which attached the people to the Tories was broken; the cry of "No Popery" could no longer be opposed to the cry of "Reform."

That which, in the opinion of the two great parties in Parliament, and of a vast portion of the community, had been the first question, suddenly disappeared; and the question of Parliamentary Reform took the first place; then was put forth all the strength which that question had gathered in secret; then it appeared that Reform had on its side a coalition of interests and opinions unprecedented in our history—all the liberality and intelligence which had supported the Catholic claims, and all the clamour which had opposed them. This, I believe, is the true history of that public feeling on the subject of Reform, which has been ascribed to causes quite inadequate to the production of such an effect. If ever there was in the history of mankind a national sentiment which was the very opposite of a caprice—with which accident had nothing to do—which was produced by the slow, steady, certain progress of the human mind, it is the feeling of the English people on the subject of Reform. Accidental circumstances may have brought that feeling to maturity in a particular year, or a particular month. That point I will not dispute, for it is not worth disputing; but those accidental circumstances have brought on Reform, only as the circumstance that, at a particular time, indulgences were offered to sale in a particular town in Saxony, brought on the great separation from the Church of Rome. In both cases the public mind was prepared to move on the slightest impulse. Thinking thus of the public opinion concerning Reform—being convinced that this opinion is the mature product of time and of discussion—I expect no reaction. I no more expect to see my countrymen again content with the mere semblance of a Representation, than to see them again drowning witches or burning heretics—trying causes by red-hot plough-shares, or offering up human sacrifices to wicker idols. I no more expect a reaction in favour of Gatton and Old Sarum, than a reaction in favour of Thor and Odin. I should think such a reaction almost as much a miracle, as that the shadow should go back upon the dial. Revolutions produced by violence are often followed by reactions; the victories of reason once gained, are gained for eternity. In fact, if there be in the present aspect of public affairs, any sign peculiarly full of evil omen to the opponents of Reform, it is that very calmness of the public mind on which they found their expectations of success. They think that it is the calmness of indifference. It is the calmness of confident hope; and in proportion to the confidence of hope will be the bitterness of disappointment. Disappointment, indeed, I do not anticipate. That we are certain of success in this House is now acknowledged; and our opponents have, in consequence, during the whole of our Session, and particularly during the present debate, addressed their arguments and exhortations rather to the Lords than to the assembly of which they are themselves Members. Their principal argument has always been, that the Bill will destroy the peerage. The hon. and learned member for Rye has, in plain terms, called on the Barons of England to save their order from democratic encroachments, by rejecting this measure. All these arguments—all these appeals being interpreted, mean this: "Proclaim to your countrymen that you have no common interests with them, no common sympathies with them; that you can be powerful only by their weakness, and exalted only by their degradation; that the corruptions which disgust them, and the oppression against which their spirit rises up, are indispensable to your authority; that the freedom and purity of election are incompatible with the very existence of your House. Give them clearly to understand that your power rests, not as they have hitherto imagined, on their rational conviction, or their habitual veneration, or your own great property, but on a system fertile of political evils, fertile also of low iniquities of which ordinary justice takes cognizance. Bind up, in inseparable union, the privileges of your estate with the grievances of ours; resolve to stand or fall with abuses visibly marked out for destruction; tell the people that they are attacking you in attacking the three holes in the wall, and that they shall never get rid of the three holes in the wall till they have got rid of you—that a hereditary peerage, and a representative assembly, can co-exist only in name—that, if they will have a House of Peers, they must be content with a mock House of Commons." This, I say, is the advice, bestowed on the Lords, by those who call themselves the friends of aristocracy. That advice so pernicious will not be followed, I am well assured; yet I cannot but listen to it with uneasiness. I cannot but wonder that it should proceed from the lips of men who are constantly lecturing us on the duty of consulting history and experience. Have they ever heard what effects counsels like their own, when too faithfully followed, have produced? Have they ever visited that neighbouring country, which still presents to the eye, even of a passing stranger, the signs of a great dissolution and renovation of society? Have they ever walked by those stately mansions, now sinking into decay, and portioned out into lodging-rooms, which line the silent streets of the Fauxbourg St. Germain? Have they ever seen the ruins of those castles whose terraces and gardens overhang the Loire? Have they ever heard that from those magnificent hotels, from those ancient castles, an aristocracy as splendid, as brave, as proud, as accomplished as ever Europe saw, was driven forth to exile and beggary—to implore the charity of hostile Governments and hostile creeds—to cut wood in the back settlements of America—or to teach French in the school-rooms of London? And why were those haughty nobles destroyed with that utter destruction? Why were they scattered over the face of the earth, their titles abolished, their escutcheons defaced, their parks wasted, their palaces dismantled, their heritage given to strangers? Because they had no sympathy with the people—no discernment of the signs of their time—because, in the pride and narrowness of their hearts, they called those whose warnings might have saved them, theorists and speculators, because they refused all concession till the time had arrived when no concession would avail. I have no apprehension that such a fate awaits the nobles of England. I draw no parallel between our aristocracy and that of France. Those who represent the Lords as a class whose power is incompatible with the just influence of the middle orders in the State, draw the parallel, and not I. They do all in their power to place the Lords and Commons of England in that position with respect to each other in which the French gentry stood with respect to the Tiers Etat. But I am convinced that these advisers will not succeed. We see, with pride and delight, among the friends of the people, the Talbots, the Cavendishes, the princely house of Howard. Foremost among those who have entitled themselves, by their exertions in this House, to the lasting gratitude of their countrymen, we see the descendants of Marlborough, of Russell, and of Derby. I hope, and firmly believe, that the Lords will see what their interest and their honour require. I hope, and firmly believe, that they will act in such a manner as to entitle themselves to the esteem and affection of the people. But if not, let not the enemies of Reform imagine that their reign is straightway to recommence, or that they have obtained anything more than a short and weary respite. We are bound to respect the constitutional rights of the Peers; but we are bound also not to forget our own. We, too, have our privileges—we, too, are an estate of the realm. A House of Commons, strong in the love and confidence of the people—a House of Commons which has nothing to fear from a dissolution, is something in the Government. Some persons, I well know, indulge a hope that the rejection of the Bill will at once restore the domination of that party which fled from power last November, leaving everything abroad and everything at home in confusion—leaving the European system, which it had built up at a vast cost of blood and treasure, falling to pieces in every direction—leaving the dynasties which it had restored, hastening into exile—leaving the nations which it had joined together, breaking away from each other—leaving the fund-holders in dismay—leaving the peasantry in insurrection—leaving the most fertile counties lighted up with the fires of incendiaries—leaving the capital in such a state, that a royal procession could not safely pass through it. Dark and terrible, beyond any season within my remembrance of political affairs, was the day of their flight. Far darker and far more terrible will be the day of their return; they will return in opposition to the whole British nation, united as it was never before united on any internal question—united as firmly as when the Armada was sailing up the channel—united as when Bonaparte pitched his camp on the cliffs of Boulogne. They will return pledged to defend evils which the people are resolved to destroy; they will return to a situation in which they can stand only by crushing and trampling down public opinion, and from which, if they fall, they may, in their fall, drag down with them the whole frame of society. Against such evils, should such evils appear to threaten the country, it will be our privilege and our duty to warn our gracious and beloved Sovereign. It will be our privilege and our duty to convey the wishes of a loyal people to the throne of a patriot king. At such a crisis the proper place for the House of Commons is in the front of the nation; and in that place this House will assuredly be found. Whatever prejudice or weakness may do elsewhere to ruin the empire, here, I trust, will not be wanting the wisdom, the virtue, and the energy that may save it.

ON THE STATE OF THE NATION.*

OCTOBER 10, 1831.

I DOUBT, Sir, whether any person who had merely heard the speech of the right hon. member for the University of Cambridge, would have been able to conjecture what the question is which we are discussing, and what the occasion on which we are assembled. For myself I can with perfect sincerity declare, that never in the whole course of my life did I feel my mind oppressed by so deep and solemn a sense of responsibility as at the present moment. I firmly believe that the country is now in danger of calamities greater than ever threatened it, from domestic misgovernment or from foreign hostility. The danger is no less than this—that there may be a complete alienation of the people from their rulers. To soothe the public mind, to reconcile the people to the delay—the short delay—which must intervene before their wishes can be legitimately gratified; and in the mean time, to avert civil discord, and to uphold the authority of law—these are, I conceive, the objects of my noble friend, the member for Devonshire—these ought, at the present crisis, to be the objects of every honest Englishman. They are objects which will assuredly be attained, if we rise to this great occasion—if we take our stand in the place which the Constitution has assigned to us—if we employ, with becoming firmness and dignity, the powers which belong to us as trustees of the nation, and as advisers of the Throne. Sir, the Resolution of my noble friend consists of two parts. He calls upon us to declare our undiminished attachment to the principles of the Reform Bill, and also our undiminished confidence in his Majesty's Ministers. I con-

* Hansard, 3d Series, vol. viii. p. 390–399.

sider these two declarations as identical. The Question of Reform is, in my opinion, of such paramount importance, that, approving the principles of the Ministerial Bill, I must think the Ministers who have brought that Bill forward, although I may differ from them on some minor points, entitled to the strongest support of Parliament. The right hon. Gentleman, the member for the University of Cambridge, has attempted to divert the course of the Debate to questions comparatively unimportant. He has said much about the coal-duty, about the candle-duty, about the budget of the present Chancellor of the Exchequer. On most of the points to which he has referred, it would be easy for me, were I so inclined, to defend the Ministers; and where I could not defend them, I should find it easy to recriminate on those who preceded them. The right hon. member for the University of Cambridge has taunted the Ministers with the defeat which their measure respecting the timber trade sustained in the last Parliament. I might, perhaps, at a more convenient season, be tempted to inquire whether that defeat was more disgraceful to them or to their predecessors. I might, perhaps, be tempted to ask the right hon. Gentleman, whether, if he had not been treated, while in office, with more fairness than he has shown while in opposition, it would have been in his power to carry his best measure—the Beer Bill? He has accused the Ministers of bringing forward financial measures, and then withdrawing those measures. Did not he bring forward, during the Session of 1830, a plan respecting the sugar duties? and was not that plan withdrawn? But, Sir, this is mere trifling. I will not be seduced from the matter in hand by the right hon. Gentleman's example. At the present moment I can see only one question in the State—the Question of Reform; only two parties—the friends of the Bill and its enemies. It is not my intention, Sir, again to discuss the merits of the Reform Bill. The principle of that Bill received the approbation of the late House of Commons after ten nights' discussion; and the Bill, as it now stands, after a long and most laborious investigation, passed the present House of Commons by a majority which was nearly half as large again as the minority. This was a little more than a fortnight ago. Nothing has since occurred to change our opinion. The justice of the case is unaltered. The public enthusiasm is undiminished. Old Sarum has grown no larger, Manchester has grown no smaller. In addressing this House, therefore, I am entitled to assume that the Bill is in itself a good Bill. If so, ought we to abandon it merely because the Lords have rejected it? We ought to respect the lawful privileges of their House; but we ought also to assert our own. We are constitutionally as independent of their Lordships, as their Lordships are of us; we have precisely as good a right to adhere to our opinion as they have to dissent from it. In speaking of their decision, I will attempt to follow that example of moderation which was so judiciously set by my noble friend, the member for Devonshire; I will only say that I do not think them more competent to form a correct judgment on a political question than we are. It is certain that on all the most important points on which the two Houses have for a long time past differed, the Lords have at length come over to the opinion of the Commons. I am therefore entitled to say, that with respect to all those points, the Peers themselves being judges, the House of Commons was in the right and the House of Lords in the wrong. It was thus with respect to the Slave-trade—it was thus with respect to Catholic Emancipation—it was thus with several other important Questions. I, therefore, cannot think that we ought, on the present occasion, to surrender our judgment to those who have acknowledged that, on former occasions of the same kind, we have judged more correctly than they have. Then again, Sir, I cannot forget how the majority and the minority in this House were composed; I cannot forget that the majority contained almost all those Gentlemen who are returned bv large bodies of electors. It is, I believe, no exaggeration to say, that there were single Members of the majority who had more constituents than the whole minority put together. I speak advisedly and seriously; I believe that the number of freeholders of Yorkshire exceeds that of all the electors who return the Opposition. I cannot with propriety comment here on any reports which may have been circulated concerning the majority and minority in the House of Lords. I may, however, mention these notoriously historical facts—that during the last forty years the powers of the executive Government have been, almost without intermission, exercised by a party opposed to Reform; and that a very great number of Peers have been created, and all the present Bishops raised to the bench during those years. On this Question, therefore, while I feel more than usual respect for the judgment of the House of Commons, I feel less than usual respect for the judgment of the House of Lords. Our decision is the decision of the nation; the decision of their Lordships can scarcely be considered as the decision even of that class from which the Peers are generally selected, and of which they may be considered as virtual Representatives—the great landed gentlemen of England. I think, therefore, that we ought to adhere to our opinion concerning the Reform Bill. The next question is this—ought we to make a formal declaration that we adhere to our opinion? I think that we ought to make such a declaration; and I am sure that we cannot make it in more temperate or more constitutional terms than those which my noble friend asks us to adopt. I support the Resolution which he has proposed with all my heart and soul; I support it as a friend to Reform; but I support it still more as a friend to law, to property, to social order. No observant and unprejudiced man can look forward without great alarm to the effects which the recent decision of the Lords may possibly produce. I do not predict—I do not expect—open, armed insurrection. What I apprehend is this—that the people may engage in a silent, but extensive and persevering war against the law. What I apprehend is, that England may exhibit the same spectacle which Ireland exhibited three years ago—agitators stronger than the Magistrate, associations stronger than the law, a Government powerful enough to be hated, and not powerful enough to be feared, a people bent on indemnifying themselves by illegal excesses for the want of legal privileges. I fear, that we may before long see the tribunals defied, the tax-gatherer resisted, public credit shaken, property insecure, the whole frame of society hastening to dissolution. It is easy to say—"Be bold—be firm—defy intimidation—let the law have its course—the law is strong enough to put down the seditious." Sir, we have heard this blustering before; and we know in what it ended. It is the blustering of little men whose lot has fallen on a great crisis. Xerxes scourging the winds, Canute commanding the waves to recede from his footstool, were but types of the folly of those who apply the maxims of the Quarter Sessions to the great convulsions of society. The law has no eyes; the law has no hands; the law is nothing—nothing but a piece of paper printed by the King's printer, with the King's arms at the top—till public opinion breathes the breath of life into the dead letter. We found this in Ireland. The Catholic Association bearded the Government. The Government resolved to put down the Association. An indictment was brought against my hon. and learned friend, the member for Kerry. The Grand Jury threw it out. Parliament met. The Lords Commissioners came down with a speech recommending the suppression of the self-constituted legislature of Dublin. A bill was brought in; it passed both Houses by large majorities; it received the Royal assent. And what effect did it produce? Exactly as much as that old Act of Queen Elizabeth, still unrepealed, by which it is provided that every man who, without a special exemption, shall eat meat on Fridays and Saturdays, shall pay a fine of 20*s.* or go to prison for a month. Not only was the Association not destroyed; its power was not for one day suspended; it flourished and waxed strong under the law which had been made for the purpose of annihilating it. The elections of 1826—the Clare election two years later—proved the folly of those who think that nations are governed by wax and parchment—and, at length, in the close of 1828, the Government had only one plain alternative before it—concession or civil war. Sir, I firmly believe, that if the people of England shall lose all hope of carrying the Reform Bill by constitutional means, they will forthwith begin to offer to the Government the same kind of resistance which was offered to the late Government, three years ago, by the people of Ireland—a resistance by no means amounting to rebellion—a resistance rarely amounting to any crime defined by the law—but a resistance nevertheless which is quite sufficient to obstruct the course of justice, to disturb the pursuits of industry, and to prevent the accumulation of wealth. And is not this a danger which we ought to fear? And is not this a danger which we are bound, by all means in our power, to avert? And who are those who taunt us for yielding to intimidation? Who are those who affect to speak with contempt of associations, and agitators, and public meetings? Even the very persons who, scarce two years ago, gave up to associations, and agitators, and public meetings, their boasted Protestant Constitution, proclaiming all the time that they saw the evils of Catholic Emancipation as strongly as ever. Surely—surely—the note of defiance which is now so loudly sounded in our ears, proceeds with a peculiarly bad grace from men whose highest glory it is that they abased themselves to the dust before a people whom their policy had driven to madness—from men the proudest moment of whose lives was that in which they appeared in the character of persecutors scared into toleration. Do they mean to indemnify themselves for the humiliation of quailing before the people of Ireland by trampling on the people of England? If so, they deceive themselves. The case of Ireland, though a strong one, was by no means so strong a case as that with which we have now to deal. The Government, in its struggle with the Catholics of Ireland, had Great Britain at its back.

Whom will it have at its back in the struggle with the Reformers of Great Britain? I know only two ways in which societies can permanently be governed—by public opinion, and by the sword. A Government having at its command the armies, the fleets, and the revenues of Great Britain, might possibly hold Ireland by the sword. So Oliver Cromwell held Ireland; so William III. held it; so Mr. Pitt held it; so the Duke of Wellington might perhaps have held it. But to govern Great Britain by the sword—so wild a thought has never, I will venture to say, occurred to any public man of any party; and, if any man were frantic enough to make the attempt, he would find, before three days had expired, that there is no better sword than that which is fashioned out of a ploughshare. But, if not by the sword, how is the country to be governed? I understand how the peace is kept at New York. It is by the assent and support of the people. I understand also how the peace is kept at Milan. It is by the bayonets of the Austrian soldiers. But how the peace is to be kept when you have neither the popular assent nor the military force—how the peace is to be kept in England by a Government acting on the principles of the present Opposition, I do not understand. There is in truth a great anomaly in the relation between the English people and their Government. Our institutions are either too popular or not popular enough. The people have not sufficient power in making the laws; but they have quite sufficient power to impede the execution of the laws once made. The Legislature is almost entirely aristocratical; the machinery by which the decrees of the Legislature are carried into effect is almost entirely popular; and, therefore, we constantly see all the power which ought to execute the law, employed to counteract the law. Thus, for example, with a criminal code which carries its rigour to the length of atrocity, we have a criminal judicature which often carries its lenity to the length of perjury. Our law of libel is the most absurdly severe that ever existed—so absurdly severe that, if it were carried into full effect, it would be much more oppressive than a censorship. And yet, with this severe law of libel, we have a Press which practically is as free as the air. In 1819 the Ministers complained of the alarming increase of seditious and blasphemous publications. They proposed a law of great rigour to stop the growth of the evil; and they obtained their law. It was enacted, that the publisher of a seditious libel might, on a second conviction, be banished, and that if he should return from banishment, he might be transported. How often was this law put in force? Not once. Last year we repealed it; but it was already dead, or rather it was dead born. It was obsolete before *le Roi le veut* had been pronounced over it. For any effect which it produced it might as well have been in the Code Napoleon as in the English Statute-book. And why did the Government, having solicited and produced so sharp and weighty a weapon, straightway hang it up to rust? Was there less sedition, were there fewer libels, after the passing of the Act than before it? Sir, the very next year was the year 1820—the year of the Bill of Pains and Penalties—the very year when the public mind was most excited—the very year when the public Press was most scurrilous. Why then did not the Ministers use their new law? Because they durst not; because they could not. They had obtained it with ease; for in obtaining it they had to deal with a subservient Parliament. They could not execute it; for in executing it they would have to deal with a refractory people. These are instances of the difficulty of carrying the law into effect when the people are inclined to thwart their rulers. The great anomaly, or, to speak more properly, the great evil which I have described, would, I believe, be removed by the Reform Bill. That Bill would establish perfect harmony between the people and the Legislature. It would give a fair share in the making of laws to those without whose co-operation laws are mere waste paper. Under a reformed system we should not see, as we now often see, the nation repealing Acts of Parliament as fast as we and the Lords can pass them.

As I believe that the Reform Bill would produce this blessed and salutary concord, so I fear that the rejection of the Reform Bill, if that rejection should be considered as final, will aggravate the evil which I have been describing to an unprècedented, to a terrible extent. To all the laws which might be passed for the collection of the revenue, or for the prevention of sedition, the people would oppose the same kind of resistance by means of which they have succeeded in mitigating—I might say in abrogating—the law of libel. There would be so many offenders, that the Government would scarcely know at whom to aim its blow. Every offender would have so many accomplices and protectors, that the blow would almost always miss the aim. The veto of the people—a veto not pronounced in set form, like that of the Roman Tribunes, but quite as effectual as that of the Roman Tribunes—for the purpose of impeding public measures, would meet the Government at every turn. The Administration would be unable to preserve order at home, or to uphold the national honour abroad: and at length men who are now moderate, who now think of revolution with horror, would begin to wish that the lingering agony of the State might be terminated by one fierce, sharp, decisive crisis? Is there a way of escape from these calamities? I believe that there is. I believe that if we do our duty—if we give the people reason to believe that the accomplishment of their wishes is only deferred—if we declare our undiminished attachment to the Reform Bill, and our resolution to support no Minister who will not support that Bill, we shall avert the fearful disasters which impend over the country. There is danger that, at this conjuncture, men of more zeal than wisdom may obtain a fatal influence over the public mind. With these men will be joined others, who have neither zeal nor wisdom—common barrators in politics—dregs of society which, in times of violent agitation, are tossed up from the bottom to the top, and which, in quiet times, sink again from the top to their natural place at the bottom. To these men nothing is so hateful as the prospect of a reconciliation between the orders of the State. A crisis like that, which now makes every honest citizen sad and anxious, fills these men with joy, and with a detestable hope. And how is it that such men, formed by nature and education to be objects of mere contempt, can ever inspire terror? How is it that such men, without talents or acquirements sufficient for the management of a vestry, sometimes become dangerous to great empires? The secret of their power lies in the indolence or faithlessness of those who ought to take the lead in the redress of public grievances. The whole history of low traders in sedition is contained in that fine old Hebrew fable which we have all read in the Book of Judges. The trees meet to choose a king. The vine, and the fig-tree, and the olive tree, decline the office. Then it is that the sovereignty of the forest devolves upon the bramble: then it is that from a base and noxious shrub goes forth the fire which devours the cedars of Lebanon. Let us be instructed. If we are afraid of Political Unions, and Reform Associations, let the House of Commons become the chief point of political union; let the House of Commons be the great Reform association. If we are afraid that the people may attempt to accomplish their wishes by unlawful means, let us give them a solemn pledge that we will use in their cause all our high and ancient privileges—so often victorious in old conflicts with tyranny—those privileges which our ancestors invoked, not in vain, on the day when a faithless King filled our house with his guards, took his seat, Sir, on your chair, and saw your predecessor kneeling on the floor before him. The Constitution of England, thank God, is not one of those Constitutions which are past all repair, and which must, for the public welfare, be utterly destroyed. It has a decayed part; but it has also a sound and precious part. It requires purification; but it contains within itself the means by which that purification may be effected. We read that in old times, when the villeins were driven to revolt by oppression, when the castles of the nobility were burned to the ground—when the warehouses of London were pillaged—when a hundred thousand insurgents appeared in arms on Blackheath—when a foul murder perpetrated in their presence had raised their passions to madness—when they were looking round for some captain to succeed and avenge him whom they had lost—just then, before Hob Miller, or Tom Carter, or Jack Straw, could place himself at their head, the King rode up to them and exclaimed, "I will be your leader"—and at once the infuriated multitude laid down their arms, submitted to his guidance—dispersed at his command. Herein let us imitate him. Our countrymen are, I fear, at this moment, but too much disposed to lend a credulous ear to selfish impostors. Let us say to them, "We are your leaders—we, your own House of Commons—we, the constitutional interpreters of your wishes—the knights of forty English shires, the citizens and burgesses of all your largest towns. Our lawful power shall be firmly exerted to the utmost in your cause; and our lawful power is such, that when firmly exerted in your cause it must finally prevail." This tone it is our interest and our duty to take. The circumstances admit of no delay. Is there one among us who is not looking with breathless anxiety for the next tidings which may arrive from the remote parts of the kingdom? Even while I speak the moments are passing away—the irrevocable moments pregnant with the destiny of a great people. The country is in danger; it may be saved; we can save it. This is the way—this is the time. In our hands are the issues of great good and great evil—the issues of the life and death of the State. May the result of our deliberations be the repose and prosperity of that noble country which is entitled to all our love; and for the safety of which we are answerable to our consciences, to the memory of future ages, to the Judge of all hearts!

ON PARLIAMENTARY REFORM.*

DECEMBER 16, 1831.

I CAN assure my noble friend, for whom I entertain sentiments of respect and kindness, which no political difference will, I trust, ever disturb, that his remarks have given me no pain, except, indeed, the pain which I feel at being compelled to say a few words about myself. Those words shall be very few. I know how unpopular egotism is in this House. My noble friend says, that, in the debates of last March, I declared myself opposed to the ballot, and that I have since recanted, for the purpose of making myself popular with the inhabitants of Leeds. My noble friend is altogether mistaken. I never said in any debate, that I was opposed to the ballot. The word ballot never passed my lips within this House. I observed strict silence respecting it on two accounts: in the first place, because my own opinions were, till very lately, undecided; in the second place, because I knew that the agitation of that question, a question of which the importance appears to me to be greatly overrated, would divide those on whose firm and cordial union the safety of the empire depends. My noble friend has taken this opportunity of replying to a speech which I made last October. The doctrines which I then laid down were, according to him, most intemperate and dangerous. Now, Sir, it happens curiously enough, that my noble friend has himself asserted, in his speech of this night, those very doctrines, in language so nearly resembling mine, that I might fairly accuse him of plagiarism. I said, that laws have no force in themselves, and that unless supported by

* Hansard, 3d Series, vol. ix. p. 378–392.

public opinion, they are a mere dead letter. The noble Lord has said exactly the same thing to-night. "Keep your old Constitution," is his argument; "for whatever may be its defects in theory, it has more of the public veneration than your new constitution will have; and no laws can be efficient, unless they have the public veneration." I said, that statutes are in themselves only wax and parchment, and I was called an incendiary by the Opposition. The noble Lord has said to-night, that statutes in themselves are only ink and parchment; and those very persons who reviled me, have enthusiastically cheered him. It is, evidently, not from the principle which I laid down, but from the application of the principle that they dissent. But, Sir, it is time that I should address myself to the momentous question before us. I shall certainly give my best support to this Bill through all its stages; and in so doing, I conceive that I shall act in strict conformity with the resolution by which this House, towards the close of the late Session, declared its unabated attachment to the principles and to the leading provisions of the first Reform Bill. All those principles, all those leading provisions, I find in the present measure. In the details there are, undoubtedly, considerable alterations. Most of the alterations appear to me to be improvements; and even those alterations which I cannot consider as being in themselves improvements, will yet be most useful, if their effect shall be to conciliate opponents, and to facilitate the adjustment of a question which, for the sake of order, for the sake of peace, for the sake of trade, ought to be not only satisfactorily, but speedily settled. We have been told, Sir, that, if we pronounce this Bill to be a better Bill than the last, we recant all the doctrines which we maintained during the last Session; we sing our palinode; we allow that we have had a great escape; we allow that our own conduct was deserving of censure; we allow that the party which was the minority in this House, and, most unhappily for the country, the majority in the other House, has saved the country from a great calamity. Sir, even if this charge were well-founded, there are those who should have been prevented by prudence, if not by magnanimity, from bringing it forward. I remember an Opposition which took a very different course. I remember an Opposition which, while excluded from power, taught all its doctrines to the Government; which, after labouring long, and sacrificing much, in order to effect improvements in various parts of our system, saw the honuor of those improvements appropriated by others. But the members of that Opposition had, I believe, a sincere desire to promote the public good. They, therefore, raised no shout of triumph over the recantations of their neophytes. They rejoiced, but with no ungenerous joy, when their principles of trade, of jurisprudence, of foreign policy, of religious liberty, became the principles of the Administration. They were content that he who came into fellowship with them at the eleventh hour should have a far larger share of the reward than those who had borne the burthen and heat of the day. In the year 1828, a single division in this House changed the whole policy of the Government with respect to the Test and Corporation Acts. My noble friend, the Paymaster of the Forces, then sat where the right Hon. Baronet, the member for Tamworth, now sits. I do not remember that when the right hon. Baronet announced his change of purpose, my noble friend sprang up to talk about palinodes, to magnify the wisdom and virtue of the Whigs, and to sneer at his new coadjutors. Indeed, I am not sure that the members of the late Opposition did not carry their indulgence too far—that they did not too easily suffer the fame of Grattan and Romilly to be transferred to less deserving claimants—that they were not too ready, in the joy with which they welcomed the tardy and convenient repentance of their converts, to grant a general amnesty for the errors or the insincerity of years. If it were true that we had recanted, this ought not to be made matter of charge against us by men whom posterity will remember by nothing but recantations. But, in truth, we recant nothing—we have nothing to recant.—We support this Bill—we may possibly think it a better Bill than that which preceded it. But are we therefore bound to admit that we were in the wrong—that the Opposition was in the right—that the House of Lords has conferred a great benefit on the nation? We saw—who did not see—great defects in the first Bill? —But did we see nothing else? Is delay no evil? Is prolonged excitement no evil? Is it no evil that the heart of a great people should be made sick by deferred hope? We allow that many of the changes which have been made are improvements. But we think that it would have been far better for the country to have had the last Bill, with all its defects, than the present Bill, with all its improvements. Second thoughts are proverbially the best, but there are emergencies which do not admit of second thoughts. There probably never was a law which might not have been amended by delay. But there have been many cases in which there would have been more mischief in the delay, than benefit in the amendments. The first Bill, however inferior it may have been in its details to the present Bill, was yet herein far superior to the present Bill—that it was the first. If the first Bill had passed, it would, I firmly believe, have produced a complete reconciliation between the aristocracy and the people. It is my earnest wish and prayer that the present Bill may produce this blessed effect; but I cannot say that my hopes are so sanguine as they were at the beginning of the last Session. The decision of the House of Lords has, I fear, excited in the public mind feelings of resentment which will not soon be allayed. What then, it is said, would you legislate in haste? Would you legislate in times of great excitement concerning matters of such deep concern? Yes, Sir, I would: and if any bad consequences should follow from the haste and the excitement, let those be held answerable who, when there was no need of haste, when there existed no excitement, refused to listen to any project of Reform—nay, who made it an argument against Reform, that the public mind was not excited. When few meetings were held, when few petitions were sent up to us, these politicians said, "Would you alter a Constitution with which the people are perfectly satisfied?" And now, when the kingdom from one end to the other is convulsed by the question of Reform, we hear it said by the very same persons, "Would you alter the Representative system in such agitated times as these?" Half the logic of misgovernment lies in this one sophistical dilemma:—If the people are turbulent, they are unfit for liberty: if they are quiet, they do not want liberty. I allow, that hasty legislation is an evil. I allow that there are great objections to legislating in troubled times. But Reformers are compelled to legislate fast, because bigots will not legislate early. Reformers are compelled to legislate in times of excitement, because bigots will not legislate in times of tranquillity. If, ten years ago—nay, if only two years ago, there had been at the head of affairs, men who understood the signs of the times and the temper of the nation, we should not have been forced to hurry now. If we cannot take our time, it is because we have to make up their lost time. If they had reformed gradually, we might have reformed gradually; but we are compelled to move fast, because they would not move at all. Though I admit, Sir, that this Bill is in its details superior to the former Bill, I must say, that the best parts of this Bill—those parts for the sake of which principally I support it—those parts for the sake of which I would support it, however imperfect its details might be, are parts which it has in common with the former Bill. It destroys nomination; it admits the great body of the middle orders to a share in the government; and it contains provisions which will, as I conceive, greatly diminish the expense of elections. Touching the expense of elections, I will say a few words, because that part of the subject has not, I think, received so much attention as it deserves. Whenever the nomination boroughs are attacked, the opponents of Reform produce a long list of eminent men who have sat for those boroughs, and who, they tell us, would never have taken any part in public affairs but for those boroughs.

Now, Sir, I suppose no person will maintain that a large constituent body is likely to prefer ignorant and incapable men, to men of information and ability? Whatever objections there may be to democratic institutions, it was never, I believe, doubted that those institutions are favourable to the development of talents. We may prefer the constitution of Sparta to that of Athens, or the constitution of Venice to that of Florence, but no person will deny that Athens produced more great men than Sparta, or that Florence produced more great men than Venice. But to come nearer home: the five largest English towns which now have the right of returning two Members each by popular election, are Westminster, Southwark, Liverpool, Bristol, and Norwich. Now let us see what Members those places have sent to Parliament. I will not speak of the living, though among the living are some of the most distinguished ornaments of the House. I will confine myself to the dead. Among many respectable and useful members of Parliament, whom these towns have returned, during the last half century, I find Mr. Burke, Mr. Fox, Mr. Sheridan, Mr. Windham, Mr. Tierney, Sir Samuel Romilly, Mr. Canning, Mr. Huskisson. These were eight of the most illustrious parliamentary leaders of the generation which is passing away from the world. Mr. Pitt was, perhaps, the only person worthy to make a ninth with them. It is, surely, a remarkable circumstance that, of the nine most distinguished Members of the House of Commons who have died within the last forty years, eight should have been returned to Parliament by the five largest represented towns. I am, therefore, warranted in saying, that great constituent bodies are quite as competent to discern merit, and quite as much disposed to reward merit, as the proprietors of boroughs. It is true that some of the distinguished statesmen whom I have mentioned would never have been known to large constituent bodies if they had not first sate for nomination boroughs. But, why is this? Simply, because the expense of contesting popular places, under the present system, is ruinously great. A poor man cannot defray it; an untried man cannot expect his constituents to defray it for him. And this is the way in which our Representative system is defended. Corruption vouches corruption. Every abuse is made the plea for another abuse. We must have nomination at Gatton, because we have profusion at Liverpool. Sir, these arguments convince me, not that no Reform is required, but that a very deep and searching Reform is required. If two evils serve in some respects to counterbalance each other, this is a reason, not for keeping both, but for getting rid of both together. At present you close against men of talents that broad, that noble entrance which belongs to them, and which ought to stand wide open to them; and in exchange you open to them a bye-entrance—low and narrow—always obscure—often filthy—through which, too often, they can pass only by crawling on their hands and knees, and from which they too often emerge sullied with stains never to be washed away. But take the most favourable case. Suppose that the Member who sits for a nomination borough, owes his seat to a man of virtue and honour, to a man whose service is perfect freedom, to a man who would think himself degraded by any proof of gratitude which might degrade his nominee. Yet, is it nothing that he comes into this House wearing the badge, though not feeling the chain of servitude? Is it nothing that he cannot speak of his independence without exciting a smile? Is it nothing that he is considered, not as a Representative, but as an adventurer? This is what your system does for men of genius. It admits them to political power, not as, under better institutions, they would be admitted to power, erect—independent—unsullied—but by means which corrupt the virtue of many, and in some degree diminish the authority of all. Could any system be devised, better fitted to pervert the principles and break the spirit of men formed to be the glory of their country? And, can we mention no instance in which this system has made such men useless, or worse than useless, to the country of which their talents were the ornament, and might, under happier circumstances, have been the salvation? Ariel—the beautiful and kindly Ariel, doing the bidding of the loathsome and malignant Sycorax, is but a faint type of genius enslaved by the spells, and employed in the drudgery, of corruption—

> "A spirit too delicate
> "To act those earthy and abhorred commands."

We cannot do a greater service to men of real merit, than by destroying that system which has been called their refuge—which is their house of bondage; by taking from them the patronage of the great, and giving to them in its stead the respect and confidence of the people. The Bill now before us will, I believe, produce that happy effect. It facilitates the canvass; it reduces the expense of legal agency; it shortens the poll; above all, it disfranchises the out-voters. It is not easy to calculate the precise extent to which these changes will diminish the cost of elections. I have attempted, however, to obtain some information on this subject. I have applied to a gentleman of great experience in affairs of this kind—a gentleman who, at the three last general elections, managed the finances of the popular party in one of the largest boroughs in the kingdom. He tells me, that at the general election of 1826, when the borough was contested, the expenses of the popular candidate amounted to 18,000*l.*; and that by the best estimate which can now be made, the borough may, under the reformed system, be as effectually contested for one-tenth part of that sum. In the new constituent bodies there are no ancient rights reserved. In those bodies, therefore, the expense of an election will be still smaller. I firmly believe, that it will be possible to poll out Manchester for less than the market price of Old Sarum. Sir, I have, from the beginning of these discussions, supported reform on two grounds, first, because I believe it to be in itself a good thing—and secondly, because I think the dangers of withholding it to be so great, that even if it were an evil, it would be the less of two evils. The dangers of the country have in no wise diminished. I believe that they have greatly increased. It is, I fear, impossible to deny, that what has happened with respect to almost every great question that ever divided mankind has happened also with respect to the Reform Bill. Wherever great interests are at stake there will be much excitement, and wherever there is much excitement there will be some extravagance. The same great stirring of the human mind which produced the Reformation produced also the follies and crimes of the Anabaptists. The same spirit which resisted the Ship-money, and abolished the Star-chamber, produced the Levellers and the Fifth-monarchy men. And so, it cannot be denied that bad men, availing themselves of the agitation produced by the question of Reform, have promulgated, and promulgated with some success, doctrines incompatible with the existence—I do not say of monarchy, or of aristocracy—but of all law, of all order, of all property, of all civilization, of all that makes us to differ from Mohawks or Hottentots. I bring no accusation against that portion of the working classes which has been imposed upon by these doctrines. Those persons are what their situation has made them—ignorant from want of leisure—irritable from the sense of distress. That they should be deluded by impudent assertions, and gross sophisms—that, suffering cruel privations, they should give ready credence to promises of relief—that, never having investigated the nature and operation of government, they should expect impossibilities from it, and should reproach it for not performing impossibilities—all this is perfectly natural. No errors which they may commit, ought ever to make us forget that it is in all probability owing solely to the accident of our situation that we have not fallen into errors precisely similar. There are few of us who do not know from experience, that, even with all our advantages of education, pain and sorrow can make us very querulous and very unreasonable. We ought not, therefore, to be surprised that, as the Scotch proverb says, "it should be ill talking between a full man and a fasting;" that the logic of the rich man who vindicates the rights of property, should seem very inconclusive to the poor man who hears his children cry for bread. I bring, I say, no accusation against the working classes. I would withhold from them nothing which it might be for their good to possess. I see with pleasure that, by the provisions of the Reform Bill, the most industrious and respectable of our labourers will be admitted to a share in the government of the State. If I would refuse to the working people that larger share of power which some of them have demanded, I would refuse it, because I am convinced that, by giving it, I should only increase their distress. I admit that the end of government is their happiness. But, that they may be governed for their happiness, they must not be governed according to the doctrines which they have learned from their illiterate, incapable, low-minded flatterers. But, Sir, the fact that such doctrines have been promulgated among the multitude is a strong argument for a speedy and effectual Reform. That government is attacked is a reason for making the foundations of government broader, and deeper, and more solid. That property is attacked, is a reason for binding together all proprietors in the firmest union. That the agitation of the question of Reform has enabled worthless demagogues to propagate their notions with some success, is a reason for speedily settling the question in the only way in which it can be settled. It is difficult, Sir, to conceive any spectacle more alarming than that which presents itself to us, when we look at the two extreme parties in this country—a narrow oligarchy above—an infuriated multitude below,—on the one side the vices engendered by power; on the other side the vices engendered by distress; the one party blindly averse to improvement, the other party blindly clamouring for destruction—the one party ascribing to political abuses the sanctity of property, the other party crying out against property as a political abuse. Both these parties are alike ignorant of their true interest. God forbid that the State should ever be at the mercy of either, or should ever experience the calamities which must result from a collision between them! I anticipate no such horrible event. For, between those two parties stands a third party, infinitely more powerful than both the others put together, attacked by both, vilified by both, but destined, I trust, to save both from the fatal effects of their own folly. To that party I have never ceased, through all the vicissitudes of public affairs, to look with confidence, and with a good hope. I speak of that great party which zealously and steadily supported the first Reform Bill, and which will, I have no doubt, support the second Reform Bill with equal steadiness, and equal zeal. That party is the middle class of England, with the flower of the aristocracy at its head, and the flower of the working classes bringing up its rear. That great party has taken its immovable stand between the enemies of all order, and the enemies of all liberty. It will have Reform: it will not have Revolution: it will destroy political abuses—it will not suffer the rights of property to be assailed—it will preserve, in spite of themselves, those who are assailing it, from the right and from the left, with contradictory accusations—it will be a daysman between them—it will lay its hand upon them both—it will not suffer them to tear each other in pieces. While that great party continues unbroken, as it now is unbroken, I shall not relinquish the hope that this great contest may be conducted, by lawful means, to a happy termination. But, of this I am assured, that, by means, lawful or unlawful, to a termination, happy or unhappy, this contest must speedily come. All that I know of the history of past times—all the observations that I have been able to make on the present state of the country—have convinced me, that the time has arrived, when a great concession must be made to the democracy of England—that the question, whether the change be in itself good or bad, has become a question of secondary importance—that, good or bad, the thing must be done—that a law as strong as the laws of attraction and motion has decreed it. I well know that history, when we look at it in small portions, may be so construed as to mean any thing—that it may be interpreted in as many ways as a Delphic oracle. "The French Revolution," says one expositor, "was the effect of concession." "Not so," cries another, "the French Revolution was produced by the obstinacy of an arbitrary government." "If the French nobles," says the first, "had refused to sit with the *tiers état*, they would never have been driven from their country." "They would never have been driven from their country," answers the other, "if they had agreed to the reforms proposed by M. Turgot." These controversies can never be brought to any decisive test, or to any satisfactory conclusion. But, as I believe that history, when we look at it in small fragments, proves any thing, or nothing, so I believe that it is full of useful and precious instruction when we contemplate it in large portions—when we take in, at one view, the whole life-time of great societies. I believe that it is possible to obtain some insight into the law which regulates the growth of communities, and some knowledge of the effects which that growth produces. The history of England, in particular, is the history of a government constantly giving way—sometimes peaceably, sometimes after a violent struggle—but constantly giving way before a nation which has been constantly advancing. The forest-laws—the law of villenage—the oppressive power of the Roman Catholic Church—the power, scarcely less oppressive, which, for some time after the Reformation, was exercised by the Protestant Establishment—the prerogatives of the Crown—the censorship of the Press—successively yielded. The abuses of the Representative system are now yielding to the same irresistible force. It was impossible for the Stuarts—and it would have been impossible for them if they had possessed all the energy of Richelieu, and all the craft of Mazarin,—to govern England as it had been governed by the Tudors. It was impossible for the princes of the House of Hanover to govern England as it had been governed by the Stuarts. And so it is impossible that England should be any longer governed as it was governed under the four first princes of the House of Hanover. I say impossible. I believe that over the great changes of the moral world we possess as little power as over the great changes of the physical world. We can no more prevent time from changing the distribution of property and of intelligence—we can no more prevent property and intelligence from aspiring to political power—than we can change the courses of the seasons and of the tides. In peace or in tumult—by means of old institutions, where those institutions are flexible—over the ruins of old institutions, where those institutions oppose an unbending resistance, the great march of society proceeds, and must proceed. The feeble efforts of individuals to bear back are lost and swept away in the mighty rush with which the species goes onward. Those who appear to lead the movement are, in fact, only whirled along before it; those who attempt to resist it, are beaten down and crushed beneath it. It is because rulers do not pay sufficient attention to the stages of this great movement—because they underrate its force—because they are ignorant of its law, that so many violent and fearful revolutions have changed the face of society. We have heard it said a hundred times during these discussions—we have heard it said repeatedly, in the course of this very debate, that the people of England are more free than ever they were—that the Government is more democratic than ever it was; and this is urged as an argument against Reform. I admit the fact; but I deny the inference. It is a principle never to be forgotten, in discussions like this, that it is not by absolute, but by relative misgovernment that nations are roused to madness. It is not sufficient to look merely at the form of government. We must look also to the state of the public mind. The worst tyrant that ever had his neck wrung in modern Europe might have passed for a paragon of clemency in Persia or Morocco. Our Indian subjects submit patiently to a monopoly of salt. We tried a stamp duty—a duty so light as to be scarcely perceptible—on the fierce breed of the old Puritans; and we lost an empire. The Government of Louis 16th was certainly a much better and milder government than that of Louis 14th; yet Louis 14th was admired, and even loved, by his people. Louis 16th died on the scaffold. Why? Because, though the government had made many steps in the career of improvement, it had not advanced so rapidly as the nation. Look at our own history. The liberties of the people were at least as much respected by Charles 1st, as by Henry 8th—by James 2nd, as by Edward 6th. But did this save the crown of James 2nd? Did this save the head of Charles 1st? Every person who knows the history of our civil dissensions, knows that all those arguments which are now employed by the opponents of the Reform Bill, might have been employed, and were actually employed, by the unfortunate Stuarts. The reasoning of Charles, and of all his apologists, runs thus:—"What new grievance does the nation suffer? What has the King done more than what Henry did—more than what Elizabeth did? Did the people ever enjoy more freedom that at present—did they ever enjoy so much freedom?" But what would a wise and honest counsellor—if Charles had been so happy as to possess such a counsellor—have replied to arguments like these? He would have said, "Sir, I acknowledge that the people were never more free than under your government. I acknowledge that those who talk of restoring the old Constitution of England use an improper expression. I acknowledge that there has been a constant improvement during those very years, in which many persons imagine that there has been a constant deterioration. But though there has been no change in the government for the worse, there has been a change in the public mind, which produces exactly the same effect which would be produced by a change in the government for the worse. Perhaps this change in the public mind is to be regretted. But no matter; you cannot reverse it. You cannot undo all that eighty eventful years have done. You cannot transform the Englishmen of 1640 into the Englishmen of 1560. It may be that the submissive loyalty of our fathers was preferable to that inquiring, censuring, resisting spirit which is now abroad. It may be, that the times when men paid their benevolences cheerfully were better times than these, when a gentleman goes before the Exchequer Chamber to resist an assessment of 20s. And so it may be, that infancy is a happier time than manhood, and manhood than old age. But God has decreed that old age shall succeed to manhood, and manhood to infancy. Even so have societies their law of growth. As their strength becomes greater—as their experience becomes more extensive, you can no longer confine them within the swaddling-bands, or lull them in the cradles, or amuse them with the rattles, or terrify them with the bugbears of their infancy. I do not say, that they are better or happier than they were; but this I say;—they are different from what they were: you cannot again make them what they were, and you cannot safely treat them as if they continued to be what they were." This was the advice which a wise and honest Minister would have given to Charles 1st. These were the principles on which that unhappy prince should have acted. But no. He would govern—I do not say ill—I do not say tyrannically; I say only this, he would govern the men of the seventeenth century as if they had been the men of the sixteenth century; and therefore it was, that all his talents and all his virtues did not save him from unpopularity—from civil war—from a prison—from a bar—from a scaffold. These things are written for our instruction. Another great intellectual revolution has taken place; our lot has been cast on a time analogous, in many respects, to the time which immediately preceded the meeting of the Long Parliament. There is a change in society. There must be a corresponding change in the government. We are not—we cannot, in the nature of things, be—what our fathers were. We are no more like the men of the American war, or the men of the gagging bill; than the men who cried "privilege" round the coach of Charles 1st were like the men who changed their religion once a year, at the bidding of Henry 8th. That there is such a change, I can no more doubt than I can doubt that we have more power-looms, more steam-engines, more gas-lights, than our ancestors. That there is such a change, the Minister will surely find—if ever such a Minister should arise—who shall attempt to fit the yoke of Mr. Pitt to the necks of the Englishmen of the nineteenth century. What then can you do to bring back those times when the constitution of this House was an object of veneration to the people? Even as much as Strafford and Laud could do to bring back the days of the Tudors—as much as Bonner and Gardiner could do to bring back the days of Hildebrand—as much as Villèle and Polignac could do to bring back the days of Louis 14th. You may make the change tedious; you may make it violent; you may—God in his mercy forbid!—you may make it bloody; but avert it you cannot. Agitations of the public mind, so deep and so long continued as those which we have witnessed, do not end in nothing. In peace or in convulsion; by the law, or in spite of the law; through the Parliament, or over the Parliament, reform must be carried. Therefore, be content to guide that movement which you cannot stop. Fling wide the gates to that force which else will enter through the breach. Then will it still be, as it has hitherto been, the peculiar glory of our Constitution that, though not exempt from the decay which is wrought by the vicissitudes of fortune, and the lapse of time, in all the proudest works of human power and wisdom, it yet contains within it the means of self-reparation. Then will England add to her manifold titles of glory this the noblest and the purest of all—that every blessing which other nations have been forced to seek, and have too often sought in vain, by means of violent and bloody revolutions, she will have attained by a peaceful and a lawful Reform.

ON THE ANATOMY BILL.*

FEBRUARY 27, 1832.

SIR, I cannot, even at this late hour of the night, refrain from saying two or three words. Most of the observations of the hon. member for Preston I pass by, as undeserving of any answer, before an audience like this. But on one part of his speech, I must make a few remarks. We are, says he, making a law to benefit the rich, at the expense of the poor. Sir, the fact is the direct reverse of this. This is a bill which tends especially to the benefit of the poor. What are the evils against which we are attempting to make provision? Two especially; that is to say, the practice of Burking and bad surgery. Now to both these the poor alone are exposed. What man, in our rank of life, runs the smallest risk of being Burked? That a man has property, that he has connexions, that he is likely to be missed and sought for, are circumstances which secure him against the Burker. It is curious to observe the difference between murders of this kind and other murders. An ordinary murderer hides the body, and disposes of the property. Bishop and Williams dig holes and bury the property, and expose the body to sale. The more wretched, the more lonely, any human being may be, the more desirable prey is he to these wretches. It is the man, the mere naked man that they pursue. Again, as to bad surgery; this is, of all evils, the evil by which the rich suffer least, and the poor most. If we could do all that in the opinion of the member for Preston ought to be done,—if we could prevent disinterment,—if we could

* Hansard, 3d Series, vol. x. 1832, p. 842–3.

prevent dissection,—if we could destroy the English school of anatomy,—if we could force every student of the medical science to go to the expense of a foreign education, on whom would the bad consequences fall? On the rich? Not at all. As long as there is in France, in Italy, in Germany, a single surgeon of eminent skill, a single surgeon who is, to use the phrase of the member for Preston, addicted to dissection, that surgeon will be in attendance whenever an English nobleman is about to undergo a critical operation. The higher orders in England will always be able to procure the best medical assistance. Who suffers by the bad state of the Russian school of surgery? The Emperor Nicholas?—By no means. But the poor dispersed over the country. If the education of a surgeon should become very expensive, if the fees of surgeons should rise, if the supply of regular surgeons should diminish, the sufferers would be, not the rich, but the poor in our country villages, who would again be left to mountebanks, and barbers, and old women; to charms and quack medicines. The hon. Gentleman talks of sacrificing the interests of humanity to the interests of science, as if this were a question about the squaring of the circle, or the transit of Venus. This is not a mere question of science—it is not the unprofitable exercise of an ingenious mind—it is a question of care and pain. It is a question of life and death. Does the hon. Gentleman know from what cruel sufferings the improvement of surgical science has rescued our species? I will tell him one story, the first that comes into my head. He may have heard of Leopold, Duke of Austria, the same who imprisoned our Richard Cœur-de-Lion. Leopold's horse fell under him, and crushed his leg. The surgeons said that the limb must be amputated; but none of them knew how to amputate it. Leopold, in his agony, laid a hatchet on his thigh, and ordered his servant to strike with a mallet. The leg was cut off, and he died of the gush of blood. Such was the end of that powerful prince. Why, there is not now a bricklayer who falls from a ladder in England, who cannot obtain surgical assistance, infinitely superior to that which the sovereign of Austria could command in the twelfth century. I think this a bill which tends to the good of the people, and which tends especially to the good of the poor. Therefore I support it. If it is unpopular, I am sorry for it. But I shall cheerfully take my share of its unpopularity. For such, I am convinced, ought to be the conduct of one whose object it is, not to flatter the people, but to serve them.

ON PARLIAMENTARY REFORM.*

FEBRUARY 28, 1832.

The Bill for England, Committee, 17th Day.

He felt unwilling to occupy the time of the House upon this subject, after the observations which he had thought it his duty to make in the course of the last Session. But the extreme solicitude he felt on account of the importance of the question, and of the peculiar circumstances under which they were called on to discuss it, compelled him to make a few observations on the subject. In that, as in every other place, the first grand object in the discussion of these questions was, to clear the ground, and settle upon whom lay the burthen of proof. It was his opinion, that the burden of proof in this instance lay upon the Opposition. He considered that he was speaking to a House of Reformers—there might be one or two exceptions; but the great body on that and on the other side of the House had, he believed, agreed that some change in the Representation must take place. He did not assert that every individual in that House entertained that opinion; but he could not avoid taking it for granted, that the great majority of the Opposition did; for he was warranted in saying, that, in a great majority of the speeches they had delivered, they had admitted the necessity of some change. If he did not entertain the opinion he now expressed as to their sentiments, he must put aside all the addresses sent up from the country by the noblemen and gentlemen who, in their different counties, had opposed this

* Hansard, 3d Series, vol. x. 1832, p. 926–933.

measure of Reform, but all of whom had said, that some change was necessary—that some Reform must take place—and that some large bodies of people must have representatives given to them. If the fact was as he had stated, they on the side of the House on which he sat proposed that, as part of the large communities entitled to Representation, the metropolitan districts should be represented. If enfranchisement ought to be part of the Reform that the times required, and that Gentlemen opposite admitted to be necessary, it was for those Gentlemen to shew why the places now proposed should not partake of the advantages of enfranchisement. He was aware that they had no precise standard by which to determine what were the towns that should receive Representatives. He should use the word importance, to constitute that standard; for though it was possible to raise quibbles upon it, none could possibly deny, that, if they were compelled to bestow representation on one of two places, they would rather bestow it upon a town like Manchester than upon a petty village, and their choice would be guided by the greater importance of the place selected. If they took the amount of population as the standard of importance—if they adopted that of the number of 10*l.* houses—if they took the amount of the assessed taxes—if they took the wealth—if they adopted intelligence as their criterion—indeed, estimate it as they might, let them take any combination of arithmetical figures that they pleased—let them multiply or divide—let them subtract or add—let them adopt the course pointed out by Lieutenant Drummond, or that of the hon. Member who proposed to decide the question by the square root of population and taxes—in short, let them take whatever course of arithmetic they pleased, there was none from which these metropolitan districts would not come marked with the proofs of a most undoubted importance. If they took population, wealth, and intelligence, as the standard by which to measure their decision, fifty would be a more proper number of Representatives than eight to give to these districts. That was a fact recognised by the hon. and learned Gentleman himself. It was admitted by all hon. Members that, in all these elements of fitness for the formation of a constituency, the metropolitan districts stood higher than any other. If so, it was for those who wished to withhold the enfranchisement to give the reason why it should be withheld. The noble Lord had offered some reasons for refusing the Members to these districts, which reasons the hon. and learned Gentleman had most elaborately exerted himself to upset. What, said the hon. and learned Gentleman, will you let loose 150,000 voters—will you give the rights of franchise to such an immense body? Yes, said the noble Lord, I will add Marylebone to Westminster—I will give the Tower Hamlets and Finsbury to the City, and Lambeth to Southwark. Yes, they who had talked so much of swamping constituencies—who had exclaimed so loudly against such a course—who affected so much dread of a large constituency—actually proposed to swamp Westminster with Marylebone; to swamp the City with Finsbury and the Tower Hamlets; and to swamp Southwark with Lambeth; and that, too, although at the same time they described the present constituencies of each of these places as sufficiently numerous. What, were they not afraid of the unhealthful state of the metropolis—of the agitation excited by elections among such very large constituencies? No, they seemed to be afraid of none of these things when they made the proposal. Of what, then, were they afraid? Of eight Members. Simply of eight Members—that must be the cause of their fear. But the fear was still more remarkable, for the noble Lord proposed to add two Members to Middlesex; so that it might be said, that the noble Lord feared six members—a number not so great as was returned by some individual Peers under the present system to that House. The only argument against giving Representatives to the metropolitan districts was, that the Members would be called to a very strict account by their constituents; that they would not speak their own sense, but merely the fluctuating sense of those who sent them as their Representatives. But that argument applied as strongly to the instances of Members returned by individuals. He did not understand the grounds on which those who represented the submission of Members to be called to account by a numerous constituency as a disgrace, while they thought it a point of honour to submit to the same strictness of account to an individual. He did not understand that spirit of honour that could lick the heels of an oligarchy, while it spurned at the wishes of the people. He did not understand that point of honour which made a man boast that he had gone out of his seat because he had voted in a particular manner against the wish of one man, his patron, while he taunted another Member for quitting his seat solely because he had offended 12,000 persons. But supposing this strictness of calling to account to be an evil, was that evil confined to the metropolitan districts? Certainly not. During the discussion on the Catholic Claims there were many Gentlemen who disguised their opinion—who compromised their real wishes and feelings—for fear of offending their constituents. He did not understand on what ground they were more afraid on the subject of the influence to be exercised by the constituency in the metropolitan districts than in other large towns. He knew an instance of an individual who declared that there were many Gentlemen who said on that occasion, that they could not vote for the Catholic Question, if they wished to retain their seats. That, however, was not the evil of popular Representation alone. It was the fault of all Representations, individual and numerous. To suppose otherwise would be to manifest an ignorance of human nature. But the great argument really was, in plain words, a dread of the preponderance of the people. There might be some evil in that; but if it was an evil, it was one which this Bill would not increase. It had always been found that a great city exercised an influence over the empire of which it formed a part, but that influence was not connected with the number of Representatives it possessed. It might, indeed, exist without the city having any Representative at all, and was nowhere so great as under arbitrary and despotic Governments. It was unnecessary to remind the House that at Rome the despotic emperors, while they exercised the most unbounded, and the most brutal tyranny over the people, yet thought it necessary to conciliate the populace with expensive shows. At Madrid, under their tyrannical government, the mob often compelled their despot king to promise the dismissal of an obnoxious Minister; they had done so in the reign of Charles II. and again in that of Charles III. They had risen in the streets; surrounded the palace of the king; compelled him to appear on the balcony, and to promise them all they demanded. That had nothing to do with the share which the people of Madrid had in the Cortes. If there was any country in which the people exercised a morbid influence over the government, it was in Turkey, in despotic Turkey—even there, where reigned the most absolute, the most unmitigated despotism, the most iron-handed tyranny, the Sultan was often forced to sacrifice his ministers, and obey the will of the people living in the neighbourhood of the Seraglio. That was an influence which nothing could take away but an earthquake like that of Lisbon. That species of influence would always be possessed by London, and nothing would remove it but such a fierce and dreadful calamity, as that which in a great degree overwhelmed this great city in 1666. But did the noble Lord propose to take away that influence? The noble Lord knew it was impossible. From all time the City of London had been of great importance in the struggles of party and of the people; and it had generally, by the force of its power, decided those struggles; but it would be absurd to think of making a law to regulate a power which was only to be dreaded when all law was at an end. As long as the rule of law continued, the power of London would only consist of the number of votes it had in that

House. When law was at an end, the power of London would consist of 1,500,000 persons, and of that power there was nothing to deprive it. As long as regular Government existed, the metropolis was, in fact, weak; but when the course of regular Government was disturbed, the metropolis possessed, and could employ, a vast and overwhelming force. But the noble Lord proposed that which would, in fact, increase the danger, for he would refuse to the metropolis all votes whatever. Without recurring to the speeches of any democratic orator, he could show the danger of this refusal, by proving the advantage of the concession. He would refer to the speech which Mr. Burke delivered on the question of conciliation with America. In that speech it was said by Mr. Burke, after referring to the dissensions that had existed in Wales, "A complete and not ill-proportioned Representation by counties and boroughs was bestowed upon Wales by Act of Parliament. From that moment, as by a charm, the tumults subsided, obedience was restored, peace, order, and civilization followed in the train of liberty—when the day-star of the English Constitution had arisen in their hearts, all was harmony within and without—

"Simul alba nautis
Stella refulsit,
Defluit saxis agitatus humor:
Concidunt venti, fugiuntque nubes:
Et minax (quòd sic voluere) ponto
Unda recumbit."

He had mentioned Madrid and Constantinople; but London differed from those cities in this respect, that the population of London had never assembled round the palace of the Sovereign, demanding the punishment of an obnoxious Minister. He repeated it—the population of London had never done this, at least in his memory. He had, indeed, seen the people assemble round their Sovereign, with the warmest expressions of a sincere attachment. The people of London were orderly; but exactly as he believed them to be more orderly than the people of Madrid or Constantinople, because they had better modes of expressing their opinions, so did he believe, that the people of represented London would be more quiet than the people of unrepresented London. The cause of all commotions in States had been, that the natural and artificial powers did not correspond with each other. That had been the case with the governments of Greece and Italy. It was no new principle—it had been laid down by Aristotle—it had been maintained and exemplified by Machiavel. Its effects in the earlier ages were well known. In the last century it had produced the French Revolution; in this the cry for Reform. The danger was in struggling to resist that alteration which had been rendered necessary by the altered circumstances of the times. That danger this Bill was intended to rectify. It gave to the people a place in the government like that which they must have in society; and was it not a most monstrous argument to say, that, because a great natural power existed, it should have no political power associated with it? Was it for them to create dissension where none had yet appeared? This Bill was meant to be a great deed of reconciliation; would they deprive it of that character; would they make it produce heart-burnings instead of peace, dissensions instead of reconciliation and harmony of feeling? It was the object of the Government to frame this measure so as to be final—as final as any human measure could be. Would they be the first to deprive it of that character—would they make it short-lived? Was it to be the first business of the Reformed House of Commons to discuss a new measure of Reform? The hon. Gentlemen opposite had frequently predicted that this settlement of the Reform Question would not be permanent; and they were taking the greatest pains to accomplish their prediction. He agreed with them in their dislike and dread of change, as change, and he was prepared to bear with many anomalies, many practical grievances, rather than venture heedlessly on political alterations; but when a change had become absolutely necessary, as undoubtedly it had at present, then his opinion was that it should be full and effectual. It was dangerous to change often. The Constitution was more injured by being frequently tampered with than by a great revolution. If no Members were now given to the metropolitan districts, they would be demanded with clamour, and by that very people of whom the noble Marquis was so much afraid, in the first Session of the next Parliament. If Gentlemen believed, as they professed to believe, that the new Parliament would be more democratically inclined than the present, they must expect that it would not resist the demand, and that the alteration would be larger. The question, then, was, whether they should pass the Reform Bill, not without anomalies, for no measure could be without them, but in such a state as was sure to engender dislike and discontent in a large and influential body of voters. Ought they to frame it so as to outrage the feelings of those it professed to conciliate, and continue the abuses it proposed to destroy? He would support the proposition to give Members to the metropolitan districts, not only because Members ought to be given, but because the majority of that House were now on their trial before the country, and it was for them now to prove whether they were sincere or not; whether the pledge they had given in last October—to support the principle and the leading details of the Bill—was now to be redeemed. The question was not only whether the metropolitan districts should have eight Members or none, but whether they would carry the Bill or compromise it; compromise that to which they had pledged themselves, in order to gratify those, who, finding it impossible to throw out the Bill, resolved to fritter it away. He called on them, for God's sake, to be firm. The hon. Gentlemen who sat in that House for Ireland, would not suffer those who, in the last Parliament, had deprived them of five Members, to flatter them into the belief that, by voting against this proposition, they would secure even a single additional Member for their country. But all the hon. Gentlemen who heard him, whatever district of the United Kingdom they were connected with, on this occasion owed a solemn duty to their country; as they performed that duty, the confidence which they had justly earned would be confirmed or lost; and, on this occasion, it was perfectly and completely true, that he who was not with them, was against them.

ON PARLIAMENTARY REFORM.*

MARCH 19, 1832.

On the Bill for England—third Reading.

Mr. Macaulay said, it was unnecessary for him to declare that he fully concurred in the feeling which the House had expressed at the speech of the hon. and learned Gentleman [Mr. Pemberton] who had just sat down, and if that hon. and learned Gentleman thought it necessary to apologize to the House, on account of having once before delivered a speech which, like that just concluded, met with the most enthusiastic reception, how much more necessary was it for him to offer some apology for again trespassing on the time of the House. He could not, however, suffer this occasion—the third reading of the Reform Bill—to pass over without coming forward once more to vindicate the principles he professed. The noble Lord who opened the debate, in a speech distinguished, like everything which fell from him, by the greatest ingenuity and ability, told the house that the first great evil of this bill was, that it pronounced an absolute condemnation upon our ancestors; and he asked whether we were prepared utterly to condemn all which they had done. He certainly was not prepared to take any such course; but, at the same time, he must say, that the men of the present day were better enabled to decide political questions than their ancestors. Government was not a matter of *à priori* reasoning, and must always be determined by experiment, and it was the essence of every experimental science that it should be progressive.

* Hansard, 3d Series, vol. xi. 1832, p. 450–463.

Moreover, it was essential that every experiment concerning Government should be founded on the special and peculiar circumstances which called for it. Arguments, therefore, that were unanswerable a thousand years ago, would be very defective if applied to the present day; and he would venture to say, that there was no Gentleman in this House who would not be ashamed to be guided by the wisdom of our ancestors, if he were about to make an experiment on any other subject than that of Government. Take chemistry, botany, surgery, or any science, for example, in which ingenuity and invention were necessary, and there was no man in that House who would reject improvements in those sciences because they did not comport with the wisdom of our forefathers, or who would say that the present age, instead of being vastly superior to those times, was, in fact, very inferior. And why was that? Because these sciences depended on observation and experiment. Every age had greater opportunity for experiment than that which preceded it; and every age must, therefore, be considered as wiser than its predecessor. Like the other sciences he had mentioned, the science of Government was essentially an experimental science—that is, its conclusions were so wholly the creatures of experience, and its application so dependent upon ever-changing circumstances, that nought could be predicated of them of universal applicability. Political doctrines were not like the axioms and definitions of the geometer—of intrinsic truth, wholly uninfluenced by time and place; their worth and force depended on experience, and were necessarily as changing as the circumstances on which all experience was founded. This truth had been happily expressed by Lord Plunkett, with that noble person's characteristic force and stern precision of language. It was observed by him, that history not read in a philosophical manner was merely an old almanack. Another extraordinary doctrine had been advanced with respect to the payment of debts by nations, and their manner of discharging the duties which devolve upon them. But he appealed to experience—was it not a fact, that, among all the democratic revolutions which had been witnessed, payment of no national debt had been refused on the ground assigned in this argument. There had been instances, both in monarchies and democracies, of the payment of debts being refused on account of the difficulty or impossibility of paying them; but no such course had been pursued as that which was stated by the noble Lord. Look to France—look to the different changes which had taken place in the representative system of that country—look to the changes of 1815, of 1817, of 1821, and of 1831, which were all constituted on entirely different principles, and yet, at this moment, the national credit was preserved. The only instance that he knew of a government refusing to discharge a debt on the ground that it was contracted by an illegitimate authority, was not the case of a democracy, but of a monarchy, where the government refused to pay a debt contracted under that very constitution which the king had sworn to maintain. The noble Lord also said, that the classes of men who ought not to be admitted into this House would be admitted by the Bill, and that those whom it would be desirable to admit would never be returned under this measure. He would again only refer to experience, and ask, whether that was the case in large towns which now possess the franchise? The noble Lord said, that the eldest sons of Peers would find great difficulty in obtaining seats in that House. Let him look over the lists of the sons of Peers returned for counties at the present time. Let the noble Lord look to Bedfordshire, Buckinghamshire, Dorsetshire, Northamptonshire, Northumberland, Lincolnshire, Westmoreland, Devonshire, Oxfordshire, and Cheshire; and he would find that there were at present but few sons of Peers returned as the Representatives of the people. The noble Lord was decidedly inaccurate in one of his statements; the noble Lord said, that, in the county of Northumberland this prejudice existed to a very great extent, and to that cause he attributed the circumstance of his noble friend, the under Secretary for the Colonies, being unsuccessful in the election of 1826. The noble Lord forgot that it was the eldest son of a Peer who contested the election with him, and was returned in opposition to him. The noble Lord had not proved his statement, which appeared to proceed entirely upon assumption. There was, however, another class of men, who, according to the noble Lord, would be excluded by the operation of this Bill—those Members who had been returned by the oligarchy of this House. The noble Lord thought it a hard case that they should be excluded, but the reason for their exclusion was a proper one, for they were not sent there by the people. The noble Lord also stated, that we had long enjoyed the blessings and protection of good Government, repeating that the system had practically worked well, and that the nation was, in fact, in a state of the greatest happiness and prosperity. Indeed, the hon. member for Oxford said, that we had attained such a state of prosperity, that we ought not to hazard it by making an experiment. If this argument proceeded on facts, he would admit that it was unanswerable. The happiness of nations might be influenced by causes unconnected with their political institutions; but, on the whole, there could be no doubt that the happiness of a people was the best test of the form of Government under which they lived. If it were proved that the House was about to destroy that constitution under which the people of England had long enjoyed so great a measure of happiness as that which the hon. Gentleman described, it would be acting the part of madmen. But he denied that the condition of the people of England was one of unmixed prosperity; and he denied that the Bill was a measure of unmixed destruction. When he heard it said, over and over again, that the English were the happiest people under the sun—when he heard this laid down as an undeniable proposition, which it would be unnecessary to prove, and absurd to deny—he could not but feel astonished at such an argument. From the first acquaintance he had had with political affairs, he had heard, from all sides and from all parties, statements of the distressed situation of the people. Speech after speech from the Throne, parliamentary address after parliamentary address, had admitted the existence of great distress, expressing a vain hope that it would be but temporary. He scarcely remembered the time in which some great interest had not been complaining. It was certain that the people of this country were by no means in a prosperous condition. The hon. Baronet, the member for Oakhampton, himself, has distinctly told us, that all the cry for Reform originated in the severe distress of the people, and the indifference of the House to their complaints. The hon. member for Aldborough, too, frequently, in glowing and energetic terms, set forth the miserable state of our commercial and manufacturing classes, and distinctly attributed their distress to the legislative measures pursued by successive Parliaments. When the question of the currency, the renewal of the corn-laws, or the state of trade came before the House, then the country was described in a condition of the deepest distress, plunged into a state of absolute misery, a cloud was over us, our present condition was bad, but our future prospects were alarming. When the Reform Bill was under discussion, all our miseries vanished at once, the sun broke out, the clouds cleared away, the sky was bright, and we were the happiest people on the face of the earth! If hon. Gentlemen wanted a large issue of small notes, our condition was again gloomy, but when the case of Gatton or Old Sarum was noticed, then we laboured under no other imperfections than the unfaithfulness of our own hearts. Was it fair for hon. Gentlemen to describe the country as in a state of the greatest misery, when they complained of the political economists, and to speak of our people as the happiest under Heaven when they wished to attack the Reformers? For different opponents they had different weapons. The Reformers of our commercial code, they slew with the national distress, and with the national prosperity they sought to annihilate the Reformers of the Constitution. The real situation of the country was midway between their extremes. There was much truth in both descriptions, but, at the same time, there was much fiction. He would, however, give his opponents their choice. If they ascribed to the institutions of the country the national greatness, let them also ascribe to those institutions all the evils the nation endured. If it was the Constitution which had improved the public credit, which had extended our trade—if it was the Constitution which had converted the barbarous hordes who once infested the Scottish borders into the finest peasantry in the world—if the Constitution had improved our machinery—if we owe to the Constitution the important factories of Manchester, and the gigantic docks of Liverpool—we were bound, by strict reason and justice, to ascribe to the Constitution, on the other hand, the heavy burthen of taxation under which the people labour, and against which they had to struggle, the frequent stagnation of trade, commerce, and manufactures, and the dreadful and deplorable situation of those parts of the country in which the rate of wages was scarcely sufficient for the support of animal life, in which the labourer, starved and wretched as he is, considers the parochial rates as a fund, not for his occasional relief, but for his daily maintenance; in which men may be met harnessed to cars like beasts of burthen, and in which the far-spreading light of midnight fires, and the outrages of incendiaries, have but too often indicated wretchedness and despair, starvation and daring recklessness. Hon. Gentlemen opposite generally content themselves with pursuing the very convenient course of contemplating only one side of the picture; they dwelt very fully on all the outward signs of our national prosperity, and they concluded, therefore, that the existing system must work most beneficially. There were also violent Reformers who had adopted a course directly the reverse, and who could see nothing in the present state of the country, but causes for apprehension and dismay. He could not agree in either of those extreme opinions.

He saw great cause for rejoicing, but also great cause for apprehension and dread. We had vast resources, but we had to bear great burthens. We had magnificent institutions, but they were surrounded by the most appalling misery, and heart-breaking famine and wretchedness. If he was to adopt the lesson of hon. Gentlemen opposite—if he was to judge of the system by its practical working—if he was to look at the condition of society, and pronounce upon the merits of our Constitution, he should be irresistibly led to this conclusion, as he saw great good alloyed by great evil, so in the Constitution there must be sound and just principles defaced by great corruptions. It was not difficult to ascertain which parts of the Constitution were the source of prosperity; nor would it be difficult to get rid of those corruptions to which we must attribute our distresses. The protection which the laws give to the liberty and property of the subject is a great advantage undoubtedly, and the mere existence of a House of Commons in which, however defective its Constitution, there have always been some Members chosen by the people, and zealous for their service, in which the smallest minority has some weight, and grievances, if not redressed, can at least be exposed, is, undoubtedly, some security for every other advantage. To these circumstances we owe our prosperity—and it was proposed, by the measure then under discussion, to give additional protection to the subject and make the House of Commons more useful to the people. The distress which the country had suffered, and of which it had so bitterly complained, he must attribute to an unthrifty squandering of the public money—to the injudicious measures of Government—to the negligence of that House—to defects in the Representative system, which had made the House more the council of the Government than the defender of the people—to laws deservedly unpopular, more easily adopted than they could have been under the eye of a reformed Parliament—to laws made for the benefit of particular classes at the expense of the people generally—in short, he attributed the distress to Ministers who had not yet been controlled by Parliament, and to Parliament who had not before its eyes the fear of the people. The noble Lord who moved the Amendment, had argued that in no instance had that House been reluctant to "back" Ministers in measures of public economy. What! the House of Commons merely backing Government who might be disposed to cut down useless expenditure of the public money—the House of Commons whose duty it was to force every Government to effect every reduction of the public expenditure compatible with the public service. Was that a description or justification of the House of Commons? The Commons ought to go before the Government in measures of economy, and force it to be wise. A reformed House of Commons would do it. But the utmost praise bestowed on it by the noble Lord—the negative praise of not being a greater spendthrift than the Government—was upon the House of Commons the bitterest satire. Those who supported the Bill were charged with loving democracy; for his part he had no idea that any species of Government was universally applicable. There was no universal form which could be assured of good Government. He would not make institutions for all ages and all nations. He gave his assent to the Bill because he thought it was adapted to this country at present, but he should think it unsuitable, because too democratic, for Hindostan, and because not democratic enough for New York. He had no more idea that a Government could be called good, which was not in unison with the feelings, habits, and opinions of the people governed, than that a coat could be called good which was not suited to the size or shape of the person for whom it was intended. A coat that does not fit is a bad coat, though it has been cut to suit the Apollo Belvidere. He did not support the present Bill because he thought that democratic institutions were best for all ages and for all countries, but because he thought that a more democratic constitution than that which now existed in this country, and in our age, would produce good Government; and because he believed that, under the present system of Representation, we would soon have no Government at all. He had never declared war with anomalies—he had never, to quote the words of the noble Lord opposite, confounded anomalies with abuses—he had never lifted up his hand against any anomaly, unless he saw in it a cause of misgovernment. He did not, therefore, support the Bill because it removed anomalies, but because it eradicated real abuses, and averted dangers, not imaginary or remote, but palpable and near. That, he conceived, would be the practi[illegible] result of the Reform Bill. Some men sacrificed practical law to general doctrines; they spoke with rapture of the beautiful machinery of the Constitution, but would not look to its practical working, nor take into consideration existing circumstances. The Representative system, as it at present existed, was said to be good. Be it so; but it was good in vain, unless it suited the state of society for which it was intended. No Members of this House had advocated such arguments more strongly than the present opponents of this measure, when the propriety of giving liberal institutions to other countries had been under discussion. Whenever an attempt had been made to introduce into other countries our best institutions—whenever it had been proposed to give Spain or Naples the freedom of the Press, or the security of the Habeas Corpus Act, how often had it been said, that it was folly to legislate for those countries as if they were England—that what we considered tyrannical the Spaniards and the Neapolitans cherished as a privilege. How often has it been said, that it was absurd to force upon a people institutions which, however good in themselves, that people despise! Was this argument to be used only on one side, and to be invalid when applied to the other? When Spain or Naples was a question, hon. Gentlemen opposite reminded the House that governments should be accommodated to the wishes of the people—that popular institutions could not be useful nor stable, unless they harmonized with public feeling and public opinion. But if this argument be good when applied to one description of institutions, was it not equally good when applied to another? Can hon. Gentlemen mention a greater blessing than the Habeas Corpus Act, or the trial by jury? No man would deny that it would have been absurd to apply these institutions to nations which did not value them. Would Gentlemen, however, say, that the existence of Old Sarum and Gatton was consistent with the feelings and wishes of the people? That was the true answer to those arguments which had been urged on former occasions, and which had been so eloquently advanced to-night by the noble Lord who opened this debate on the subject of prescription. Prescription was certainly advantageous to a Government, because it was very probable that a Government founded on prescription would possess a greater share of public respect than one which was born yesterday; but if a Government did not possess the public respect, it was in no way the better for prescription. A man would rather have the measles than the cholera (to make use of a homely illustration), because he would be less likely to die of the one than of the other; but if he must die of the measles, why he might as well have the cholera. If a government did not possess the public respect, it might as well be a Representative system of yesterday as of centuries back. In fact, there never was a great change which took away so little of what was really valuable as this did—which took away so little of what we love and respect, or which took away so little of what was connected with our feelings and entwined around our affections. The Reformation and the Revolution of 1688, and the first revolution in France, shocked the prejudices of great masses of people. Glorious as they were, and calculated to promote the public good, they were certainly effected at the expense of long-cherished feelings, deep-rooted affections, and close-entwined associations; but what was there of all that in the present Bill? Did it propose to touch any one thing which the people esteemed, respected, or revered? Did it take from the Constitution anything but those which Mr. Burke called its shameful parts? Did it endanger the Government of the country? It was high time that some such measure as this should be introduced to preserve it, that the unpopular and worse parts of the Constitution should be separated from the good, or they would all perish together. But, however forcible the claims of prescription might be, the argument could not be justly used by the noble Lord, who had distinctly declared himself to be a Reformer. It was an argument which no Gentleman had a right to advance, who was disposed to agree to even the most moderate Reform, because the smallest possible change equally destroyed the claim of prescription as the most extensive and important alteration. Prescription might, like honour, be compared to Prince Rupert's drops, "one part cracked, the whole does fly." He appealed to the hon. Gentlemen opposite, whether they had not, in the debate on the question respecting the propriety of giving Members to Manchester, Leeds, and Sheffield, asserted, that if they once began to change, there would be no end to it. But they had now departed from their own principle; they admitted the necessity of some change, and all the arguments on the score of prescription must be at an end. The arguments urged against this Bill would apply with equal force against any plan of Reform whatever. A large majority of the Opposition called themselves Moderate Reformers; but the objections which they offered to the present Bill could be applied to any measure of practical reform. They talked of anomalies: could any plan of reform be devised in which anomalies would not exist? All reform must consist of disfranchisement and enfranchisement. To effect these objects lines must be drawn somewhere, and distinctions made, which would inevitably create anomalies, unless some uniform system were established, and at variance with, and sweeping away, the whole of our present institutions. They might take population, or assessed taxes, or whatever test they pleased, but there would always, as they had already seen, be mathematicians ready to prove that their mode of computation would produce anomalies. The most symmetrical system of Representation was that of the United States—yet, even in that, it would be easy to point out anomalies. It, therefore, became moderate Reformers, who objected to the Bill on the ground of anomalies, to consider whether any plan of moderate Reform could be produced in which there would not be anomalies. Those who support any plan of Reform must admit one of two things; either that the present system did not work well—or that, working well, it ought to be changed, in deference to what must be considered unreasonable clamour, to which they were prepared to bend. Any plan would also be open to the objection of not being final; and none more so than a very niggardly one. Of every plan of Reform, it might be said, that it was the first step to revolution. It would always afford an opportunity of making allusions to the scenes of the French revolution; to the guillotine—to heads carried upon pikes, and all the horrors of that eventful period. All these topics, however, it would be recollected, were brought into requisition when the only question before the House was, whether Manchester, Leeds, and Birmingham should have representatives. Most of the hon. Members opposite called themselves Reformers; and he was entitled to demand their plan of Reform, in order that the House and country might see whether the objections which they had raised be applicable to the Ministerial plan alone, or be objections to which any plan of Reform must be liable, and such, therefore, as no person who called himself a Reformer was entitled to employ. That something must be done was admitted on all hands; While the Ministerial Bill was the only plan of Reform which had been proposed. The hon. Member who had just sat down said that, at the last election, people were compelled to vote in favour of candidates who supported the Reform Bill, because there was no other plan left before the country. They had no choice—it was this plan or none. He had a right, under these circumstances, to call on the leaders of the hon. Members opposite to let the country know what their plan was; and he was entitled, in particular, to make this appeal to the right hon. member for Tamworth. The hon. Baronet stood at the head of a great party; he had filled a high situation in the state, and might possibly fill a still higher, and these were circumstances which not only gave him (Mr. Macaulay) a right, but made it his duty, to make observations freely, but respectfully, on the public conduct of the right hon. Baronet. After thirteen months of discussion on the question of Reform, all that the House knew of the opinion of one of its most distinguished Members was, that he was opposed to the Ministerial plan of Reform. He had, indeed, declared, that, though he would not himself have brought forward, yet he would have assented to, a measure of moderate Reform. What the plan of Reform was to which the right hon. Baronet would have assented—on what grounds he would have given his support to a measure which he thought unnecessary—and what were the reasons which made him to hesitate to bring forward such a plan himself, he had not yet explained to the House. The question of Reform might be a question which divided men's opinions, but with respect to the importance of the question all were agreed; and he could not understand, on looking to the high character and station of the right hon. Gentleman, how he could shrink from the responsibility of proposing such a measure as, in his opinion, would satisfy the country, and be less injurious in its effects than the Ministerial proposition. Yet all that the right hon. Gentleman had as yet said was, that he disliked the plan proposed by Government, and that there was a something which would have met with his assent, but that Ministers had not hit upon that something. But let the right hon. baronet observe the state of the public mind, the excitement which prevailed on the subject, and the delight with which the Ministerial plan of Reform had been received by the people; and then let him ask himself whether he was prepared to bear the responsibility of the consequences which would follow its rejection. But the right hon. Baronet would doubtless say, "that is no affair of mine: the excitement is your own." [*Cheers.*] He supposed, from that cheer, that the answer was considered satisfactory by the hon. Gentlemen opposite. The next generation would judge them. When the dearest interests of the empire were at stake, the world would hold them responsible, not only for the evil which they had done, but for the good which they had omitted to do. History would not hold such men guiltless if they did not take enlarged views of the state of society; if they did not rise to great occasions; and if, when the public good required them to speak out, for fear of compromising themselves, they held their tongues, or spoke in such a way as not to be understood. If any persons were to be held responsible for the public excitement, the late Ministers had more to answer for than the present. But the great question was, not "what person is to blame," but "what is now to be done?" That was the question before the House and the country; and that was the question which he thought he had a right to ask the right hon. Baronet opposite. The right hon. Baronet possessed pre-eminent talent for debate; but the country had a right to expect from him something of a higher character. The country had a right to call on him for his opinion of the principles upon which Reform ought to be founded, and of the extent to which concession should be made to the public wish at such a crisis as the present. He asked the right hon. Baronet whether he should wish it to go down to posterity that he, in the most eventful period of British history, when the dearest interests of the empire were at stake—that he, being one of the most distinguished members of the House of Commons, brought some sound, and many specious objections against everything proposed by others—hinted in general terms that something might be done, but never could be induced to explain what that something was? Did the right hon. Baronet suppose that he could ever again conduct the affairs of the Government on Anti-reform principles? It would be madness for any Government, pledged to no Reform, to attempt to go on with the present House of Commons. They must dissolve the Parliament, and appeal to the people in a moment of fearful excitement; and they would then find that they had committed the same error which Charles committed when he dissolved the Short Parliament, and exchanged it for the Long Parliament. But supposing that such a Government gained more by the elections than could possibly be expected, and supposing that they should obtain a majority in the House of Commons, still, he asked, what would be the case out of doors? The agitation which prevailed in the year 1817 and in 1819, at the time of Queen Caroline's return to England, and during the latter period of the Duke of Wellington's administration, would seem peace and tranquillity in comparison with the disorder and excitement which would immediately spread throughout the country. Tumults, seditions, agitators without end, would arise. Agitators they had at present; but were they disposed to try what would be their power under a Government hostile to Reform? It was impossible to keep them down by a strong hand, and, if they would not have liberty, they must have licentiousness. Measures of coercion and security would be of no avail. Charles tried them against Hampden, and failed: James employed them against the Bishops, and failed. It was the same with Mr. Pitt, when he prosecuted Hardy and Horne Tooke; and the same with Lord Castlereagh, when he passed the Six Acts in 1819; and the same would be found by any Government which attempted to smother the complaints of the people of England without redressing their grievances. There was only this simple alternative—Reform, or anarchy. About the result he had no fear, for he placed the fullest reliance in his Majesty's Ministers. If he required any other pledges from them than those which he found in their character, he found them in their position. To abandon their country would be to abandon themselves. They had done that which changed the character of our institutions. They had taken no slight step—no step that could be easily retraced, on the 1st of March, 1831. Before them was glory—behind them was disgrace. For himself, he believed that their virtues, abilities, and firmness would be found equal to the momentous occasion, and that their names would to the latest period be inseparably associated with the noblest measure that ever restored to health a corrupt Government, and bound together the hearts of a divided people.

ON THE RESIGNATION OF MINISTERS.*

May 10, 1832.

In the course of the last eighteen months, they had often been on the verge of anarchy; but, until this crisis, he had never known what it was to be once anxious on the subject of political affairs. If ever there was a time which called for the firmness, honesty, wisdom, or energy, of a political assembly—if ever there was a question in which the interest of the community was involved, that time was the present—that question was the question of his noble friend. Amidst all his anxiety, however, there was ample cause for joy. He remembered with delight the noble conduct which that House had pursued from the day they first met in that place up to the present moment; and he anticipated with confidence that the majority would adhere to that noble line of conduct which was indispensable to their own honour, and the safety of the commonweal. It was pleasing to reflect that they had still leaders to whom they could look up with confidence and pride, that those leaders were deserving of the support which they had given them, and who had fallen, indeed, but it was with unblemished honour. Amidst the dark events by which they were surrounded, there was this consolation—their sincerity as Statesmen had been put to the test, and it was not found wanting. By the voice of the people they were brought into power—by that voice they were supported in power—and they retired from power rather than betray the people who trusted them. They would thus carry with them to their retirement—and very brief he trusted it would be—the proud

* Hansard, 3d Series, vol. xii. p. 849–857.

satisfaction that their conduct was fully appreciated by the people. He did not feel bound, on the present occasion, to enter into any discussion on the subject of Reform, but he should address himself at once to the particular Motion before the House. [He was sure that the right hon. Baronet opposite must, on a little reflection, see that he was wrong in asserting that that House had no right to interfere with the prerogative of the King in the choice of his Ministers. It appeared to him that there was nothing more in accordance with the principles of the Constitution—nothing for which there could not be found more numerous examples in the best times of our history—than the course which was now proposed to be adopted by the House, namely, the respectfully offering its suggestions to the Sovereign as to the choice of his Ministers. The appointment of his Ministers undoubtedly belonged to the Sovereign, but it was a clear constitutional doctrine, to which he did not know a single exception, that, with respect to every prerogative of the King, that House had the right respectfully to offer its advice and its suggestions to the Sovereign. That was a position, he was sure, which a person of the constitutional knowledge of the right hon. Baronet would not feel disposed to dispute, and he was equally sure that it would not be denied that, under certain circumstances, that House had a right to offer its advice to the Sovereign as to the persons whom it judged fit to fill the offices of his Ministers, as it had often suggested to the King the names of persons fit to fill offices in the Church, or fit, on account of their services in the army or navy, to fill any public offices under the Crown. He, therefore, laid down this as a position that would not be controverted, that the House had a right, with respect to the prerogative of the Sovereign in the choice of his Ministers, as with regard to all the other prerogatives of the Crown, to offer its respectful advice. He undoubtedly did understand the present Resolution as a recommendation to his Majesty to retain his present Ministers. He could not see how it could be otherwise understood, for he could not discover any other materials from which such a Ministry as that which they recommended to his Majesty could be formed. "But," said the hon. member for Thetford, "the Ministers had voluntarily retired from office, and the House, in adopting such a Resolution as this, would be advising his Majesty to force office on men who would not undertake it." Surely such a sophism was unworthy of the acute mind of that hon. Member. When we advise the King to take back his Ministers, we also advise him to take back their advice with them. That was what he (Mr. Macaulay) meant by the vote which he would give on this Motion, and he was sure it was on such an understanding that it would be supported by a majority of that House. Now, as to the objection raised to the creation of Peers, it amounted, if he understood it right, to this—that a creation of Peers, for the purpose of carrying a measure, even of the most vital importance, went to destroy the authority and weight of the House of Lords, and was, therefore, indefensible upon any principle of the Constitution. He conceived that the prerogative vested in the Crown, of creating Peers, for the purpose of carrying any public question, was a valuable and useful power, the existence of which was absolutely necessary, in order, on important occasions, to obviate great and pressing inconveniences. He believed it would be found that the exercise of such a power was in accordance with the principles of the Constitution, as laid down by the greatest constitutional writers on all sides and of all parties. A reference to Swift, on the one side, to Walpole and Steele on the other, and to De Lolme as a middle and impartial authority, would satisfactorily bear out that assertion, and would prove that the Constitution did not recognize any branch of the Legislature existing as the House of Lords would exist if this prerogative were not vested in the Crown, with uncontrolled and irresponsible power. They knew that kings had fallen upon erroneous courses, and what had happened in the case of an hereditary monarchy might happen in the case of an hereditary nobility. We had had a James II., and it was not beyond the range of possibility that we might have a House of Lords full of high spirit, imbued with prejudices that could not be overcome; and, unfortunately, opposed to the wishes and feelings of the people, and was there to be no means of remedying such a state of things? The Constitution afforded the means of dealing with a factious and perverse opposition on the part of the House of Commons, for the King could dissolve the Parliament, and appeal to the people, at a time when he might think that appeal would stand the best chance of success. Again, that House had a check upon the King, for it could refuse the supplies; and was there to be no check at all upon the House of Lords? Was there anything in the Constitution of that illustrious assembly—the House of Lords—which exempted it from the necessity of some similar controlling check? If that power, which was subject to abuse from Kings and Commons, could never be abused by Dukes or Earls, the best course was, to leave the whole Government in the hands of so pure, wise, and virtuous an assembly, to abolish the Monarchy, and to dissolve themselves. But, if this were not the case, was it not monstrous to imagine that the House of Lords should be exempt from some check like that to which both King and Commons are subject? Were there no check, the only appeal of the people could be to physical force; but, fortunately, the Constitution affords the means required, by conferring on the King the prerogative of making Peers. He admitted that there was some danger that the power might be abused; but of two dangers, he thought it proper to choose the least; and when they remembered that the Ministers who advised the creation of Peers would be responsible for that advice, he thought it a power not much likely to be abused. Unless some one could bring in a Peerage Bill much less liable to objection than the Peerage Bill of Lord Sunderland, he thought the King's prerogative a useful one, and one which, at this period, he was called upon to exert. As to impeachment, which had been spoken of, who would venture to impeach the Ministers for a step absolutely essential to the welfare of the kingdom? This exercise of the Royal prerogative might be necessary, too, for the preservation of the very existence of the other estates of the realm, and justified on grounds of the purest public policy. Let them suppose a case in which the two Houses were placed in direct and immediate collision by an uniform and continued difference of opinion on every question. Suppose the House of Lords was to be for war, and the House of Commons for peace—suppose the House of Commons to be for one Ministry, and the House of Lords for another—suppose, too, the struggles consequent on these differences of opinion to be continued—suppose that they lasted throughout an entire Session of Parliament—suppose that they were found so inveterate as to be incurable even by a dissolution of the House of Commons—why, what, he would ask, must be the consequence of such a state of things? That the whole machinery of Government must be stopped unless his Majesty exercised his prerogative by giving one of the parties a predominance. The Government must in such a case stand still, or new Peers must be created. But, then, it is urged against this creation, the monstrous anomaly of which you would be guilty by concurring in the creation of Peers merely to give one party an ascendancy over the other on a particular question. He would ask them to look a little more narrowly into that question. He thought he should be able to show that it was a course just, reasonable, and perfectly defensible on all principles of law and of equity. If the objections were so strong to the creation of a large number of Peers in one day, were there none to the creation of more than two hundred in less than half of a century? Suppose that one party holding power for nearly fifty years ennobled, from time to time, nearly two hundred of its own supporters, while all others were passed by; suppose all the Peers for that period to be chosen from one faction, while all rank was denied to the other; was there anything so monstrously unconstitutional in that other party setting themselves right in the political balance, and resuming that station in the House of Lords to which they were entitled when they obtained the ascendancy? If it was unconstitutional for the Whigs, when they obtained power, to resume that balance of influence in the House of Lords, of which the long tenure of office by their adversaries had deprived them, then the inevitable result must be, that the possession of political ascendancy for thirty or forty years would be a possession for ever. It was no longer a question of public opinion or political rectitude, but it must be a question of whether one party or the other had been longest in office; of whether Mr. Pitt or Mr. Fox held the Premiership in 1800; or Lord Grey or Lord Liverpool presided over the Cabinet in 1820. The upholding of such doctrines was not to be tolerated even for an instant. It would make the present generation the mere slaves of the past, and be utterly inconsistent with the first principles of politics. But the matter might be placed on still stronger grounds than that. Suppose this party, holding power so long, to have adhered to principles tending one way, while public opinion was constantly and rapidly verging towards the other; suppose the party which possessed a majority in the House of Lords to be devoted to a course of policy directly contrary to the feelings and wishes of the nation; suppose, in fact, the House of Lords and the nation to have been during the whole of that period moving in diverging directions; supposing, as the result, an overwhelming majority in favour of the one course in the House of Commons, and an equally overwhelming majority in favour of a different course in the House of Lords; he did not mean to say that this state of things was decidedly injurious to the Crown or to the country, or that it might not arise out of the working of the Constitution; but, then, he would ask them in such a case to look at the situation of the Lords. The House of Lords was not strictly a representative body, nor did he contend that it should be so; but it must, nevertheless, be mixed up a little with the other classes of the country, and have some connection and affinity with the general interests of that people from whom they derived their wealth and importance. Under such circumstances as he had attempted to describe, to add to the number of the House of Lords out of the great mass of the intelligence and respectability of the country would not impair, but, on the contrary, extend their influence—would not swamp, but, on the contrary, support their power and independence. This was his view of the condition in which they were placed, and he saw no other course left for them to adopt than by a large addition to the numbers of the House of Lords from the supporters of that party so long excluded from power, to place the Aristocracy in harmony with the other institutions of the State. It appeared to him that everything was in favour of this creation—the letter of the law and the strongest reasons of public policy. The power of the King to exercise his prerogative for the purpose was undoubted; and the letter of the law was in harmony with the letter of the highest law of all—the safety of the State. He, therefore, for once concurred most cordially in the Motion of the noble Lord, and concurred with him also in the expressions of regret for the retirement of those who had supported the Reform Bill, and in his desire that none should be looked for as their successors who were not prepared to give that Bill their unqualified concurrence. If that Government, which had supported the Reform Bill with so much zeal and so much sincerity, did not return to office, then he would say the Bill was lost to the country. Lost, he would say, because he could not conjecture how those who would then have the management of it, could, even in a mutilated form (for mutilated it would be), consent that it should be carried. That the hon. Members who sat on the benches opposite should attempt to carry such a Bill seemed to him utterly impossible; and, although one or two expressions which fell from them might bear the interpretation of such an intention, he could not believe they were spoken in earnest. He would not go back to the history of East Retford in 1829 and 1830. He would take a much later period. He would speak of those who abandoned office not eighteen months ago—who resigned their places because they were hostile to all Reform whatever. He would speak of those who, from the 1st of March, when the first Bill was introduced, down to the final dismissal of the second Bill to the House of Lords, attacked all its provisions with the most inveterate hostility; who stigmatized all disfranchisement as robbery, and all enfranchisement as usurpation; and who bellowed Universal Suffrage as a means of terror into the ears of the rich, and declaimed about 10*l.* Aristocracy to the poor. It was of these hon. Members and their party he spoke; and he could not think it possible that they would so descend as to give their support and countenance to the Reform Bill. He believed they had too much honesty; he believed they had too strong a sense of shame. The inconsistency of the act would be too glaring—the time was too short—the memory of their former professions was too recent—the motive would be too obvious. He could not trust himself to believe that the party of which he spoke could entertain an idea of supporting the Reform Bill. The party, then, that—if they accepted office—could carry the Reform Bill, would not carry it; and there remained only that other party which might be disposed to attempt it, but who were much too powerless and insignificant to form an Administration. He did not mean to designate those attached to that party offensively, but the House probably understood that he alluded to those who were commonly known by the name of the "waverers." From that party, he apprehended, it was utterly impossible to select a number of men who could conduct the public business of the House of Commons. The case, then, stood thus: those who might support the Bill could not form a Government; and those who could form a Government could not support the Bill with any regard to their public character, or with any respect to political consistency, unless with the introduction of most extensive amendments. The Bill he regarded, therefore, as lost; and, on the whole, he thought it better it should be lost than suffer mutilation in the hands of its enemies, and be drained of that which they called its venom, but which he considered its life-blood. The Members of his side of the House had been accused of making prophecies which they accomplished themselves, and no one had been more subjected to these accusations than he had. They had been accused of prophesying the agitation which they endeavoured to excite. The fault of that argument was, that it might be used at all times, with the same success, whenever a deliberative assembly was warned of the dangers which awaited its decisions. It was the duty, however, of those who believed such dangers existed to speak out, and to speak boldly. If they spoke for the purpose of exciting discontent, they were guilty of a great crime; but his conscience acquitted him of any such intention. He knew that he was as anxious as any man for the preservation of order and the security of property. He knew that he was prepared to contend as strongly against the errors of the people as to argue for their rights; and he would, at all times, rather be the victim of their injustice than its instrument. The time, however, might come when those who derided the warning would be sensible of its value—when those who laughed at the danger might witness the evils they could no longer avert—when those who despised all advice might feel themselves bereft of all relief. The time might come when the candid but unpretending counsel of a Cordelia would be found preferable to the bold but crafty recommendations of a Goneril. Let the Legislature depend on those who boldly declared their opinions as to the danger of rejecting Reform, rather than upon the smooth-tongued Conservatives; the former, he contended, were the only true Conservatives. He would not cry "peace, peace," when "there was no peace." As to those who might attempt to play the part of a Polignac Ministry in England, and endeavour to carry on the affairs of the State without public confidence, nay, in direct opposition to the sentiments of the people, he told those individuals that they had to do with a people more firm and determined than the French, and he warned them to take care how they ventured on the attempt. Why, the ink was scarcely yet dry of the protests which noble Lords had entered against the Reform Bill. Their speeches were yet ringing in the people's ears, in which they denounced the measure, and would they attempt to take office? In attempting to administer the Government they were so eager to grasp, they must either shamelessly desert the whole of their former protestations, or go in direct opposition to the wishes of the majority of that House. And, even if they could succeed in overcoming the majority of that House, they would still have dangers before them from which Mr. Pitt would have shrunk, and even an Earl of Strafford have hesitated to encounter. They would go forth to the contest with public opinion without arms either offensive or defensive. If they had recourse to force they would find it vain—if they attempted gagging Bills they would be derided; in short, they would, in taking office, present a most miserable exhibition of impotent ambition, and appear as if they wished to show to the world a melancholy example of little men bringing a great empire to destruction. In this perilous hour he would call on the House of Commons to remember the high mission with which they stood charged—to remember the important privileges with which they were invested. Now, at the hour when a paltry faction, elated by a momentary triumph, were, on the one hand, preparing to destroy all the hopes of the people, and the enemies of social order, on the other hand, were rejoicing in the prospect of anarchy and confusion—now, at this eventful hour, he implored them to rise in the grandeur of their hearts, and save a Sovereign misled by evil counsel—save a nobility insensible to their own welfare or true interests—save the country, of which they were the guardians, from a disastrous convulsion, and save, he would say, the hive of industry, the mart of the whole world, the centre of civilization—from confusion and anarchy. Their vote of that night would, he trusted, revive industry, and restore confidence. It would place out of all possibility of danger the public peace; it would stay political dissensions, and, by averting the calamities with which they were threatened, preserve the authority of the law, and uphold the Majesty of the Crown.

ON SLAVERY IN THE COLONIES.*

MAY 24, 1832.

AFTER the very extensive view of this subject which has been taken by my hon. friend, I shall not attempt to take a general survey of the subjects of Negro Slavery, but merely confine myself to the question of the decrease of the negro population, the only point of all my hon. friend's argument that the member for Dumfries has ventured to dispute. The hon. Member has not contented himself with charging my hon. friend with a mis-statement, but has actually gone the length of accusing him of having knowingly and wilfully brought forward a system which he was, in his own mind, convinced was incorrect. I beg, however, to say, that I am, in my own mind, most entirely convinced, that the argument of my hon. friend is impregnable. I first say, that this decrease, which the hon. Gentleman attributes to the inequality of the sexes, is to be found in many islands where the females exceeded the males in number in the year 1817. I next say, that in St. Christopher's, which is the island selected by the hon. Member himself, the women, in 1817, exceeded the men in numbers. To be sure, the hon. Gentleman has talked about the sexes approximating in 1825 and 1826; but if this means anything it means that the women diminished in number, for it cannot be otherwise explained. It is true that, in Barbadoes, the black population has increased, which circumstance the hon. Gentleman may attribute to what he calls the approximation of the sexes, if he pleases, but which I attribute to the cultivation of sugar being little practised in that island. But, Sir, there are some colonies in

* Hansard, 3d Series, vol. xiii. p. 52–53.

which the number of the men exceeds that of the women, such, for instance, are Berbice, Demerara, and Trinidad; and there we find, not only that there is a total decrease, but even a decrease in the number of the females. I say, that this fact reduces the whole matter to irresistible demonstration; for if he be correct, and if the men exceed the women, the worst that could happen would be, that the islands would be in as bad a situation as if the men were reduced to the number of the women, and the two sexes made equal. But if we look to those colonies, we shall find that there is a decrease in the women as well as in the men; and, therefore, again I say, that it is clear to demonstration, that the decrease in the slave-population cannot arise from this ill-assortment of the sexes, as argued by the hon. Gentleman. But the hon. Gentleman seems to think that he has done enough when he has made out, as he supposes, that no decrease has taken place; but I contend that, not only should there be no decrease, but that there should be a most rapid and striking increase. The negro population in the West Indies are placed in a situation admirably suited to their nature and disposition; the produce of the land is all-prolific—the bright and vivid sky is favourable to their African constitutions—they have a great extent of rich virgin soil ready to pour forth its gifts, with but little labour, into their hands. This, therefore, ought, to them, to be the golden age of existence; it ought to be their age of easy life, smiling children, and happy wives; it ought to be their age of high wages, full meals, light work, early marriages, and numerous families. But is it so? Alas, Sir, no; a blight is on them, and they drag on a weary, burthensome existence, darkened by despair, and uncheered by a single ray of hope. Let us look at the result of the same advantages in other countries. How is it in New South Wales? There the population is made up of convicts and prostitutes; and yet, in spite of that deterioration—in spite of the inequality of the sexes—we see that colony daily increasing, with every probability of these convicts becoming the patriarchs of a mighty empire. We all know the origin of the United States; we all know that they were originally peopled by the refuse of European society. And how is it with them? The population there has gone on swelling and swelling, like an irresistible torrent; the people have multiplied, till at length, in whole tribes, they have poured themselves across the mountains of Alleghany, the streams of Ohio, and the plains of the Arkansas. Year after year the woods and the forests, the fortresses of nature, have been receding before the advancing tide of human beings: and, year after year, mankind has shown, by its multiplication, that, under favourable circumstances, its tendency is to fulfil the immutable law of nature. Why, then, does not the same rule apply to those colonies? Why is all America teeming with life, and why are the West Indies becoming desolate? Sir, that our colonies should decrease in so rapid a manner is to me one of the most appalling facts in the history of the world. In the worst governed state of Europe—in the worst managed condition of society—the people still increase. Look, for instance, at the miserable population of Ireland—at the oppressed serfs of Russia—look even at the slave-population of America, or that of our own colonies where sugar is not cultivated. In the Bermudas and the Bahamas, where no sugar is manufactured, the population goes on increasing; but when we come to the sugar islands, the ordinary law of nature is inverted, and, in proportion to the exuberance of the soil, is the curse of suffering and of death. In these islands, which are subject to one eternal reign of terror, human life flickers and goes out like a candle in a mephitic atmosphere. What the Spaniards did on the continent for gold, we are doing in the islands for sugar. Let me remind the House of what Mr. Fox said on this subject. No one will deny that, perhaps, of all our statesmen, Mr. Fox was the most ardent for political liberty, and yet his observation on this question was, that all political liberty was but as a mere nothing compared with personal liberty. I shall give my best support to the Motion of my hon. friend. I shall do so, because I feel that this continued waste of life, without example and without parallel, is a foul blot to this country, and because I hope that the adoption of this Resolution may remove it.

ON THE RUSSIAN-DUTCH LOAN.*

JULY 12, 1832.

He could have wished that the conduct to be pursued by the gallant Officer who had last addressed the House, were to be the direct reverse to that he had announced himself it would be, and that, on the vote of censure upon the Government, he should vote against them; and in that respecting the violation of national faith, he should be with them. It was of little importance by whom the affairs of the country were administered, but it was of

* Hansard, 3d Series, vol. xiv. p. 293–300.

Note. Lord Althorp, in moving for a Committee of the House, thus stated this question:—The House was aware, that in 1815 a treaty had been entered into between the king of the Netherlands, England, and Russia, and that, previously, a treaty had been concluded between Great Britain and the king of the Netherlands, to take upon themselves the payment of a certain portion of a loan due from the emperor of Russia. It was not now necessary to enter into that question—to inquire whether this arrangement was right or wrong; it was sufficient to consider if the treaty was binding in equity and honour upon this country. The agreement concluded was, that the Netherlands and Great Britain should undertake to pay the interest of a loan due from the emperor of Russia, at five per cent., together with a Sinking Fund of one per cent., until the whole loan was extinguished. In case of the separation between Belgium and Holland, it was provided that the obligation of the king of the Netherlands and Great Britain ceased. This was the letter of the treaty. The separation had taken place. The question was, if it were such as was contemplated by the treaty, and if this country was absolved, in justice and honour, from paying its portion of the debt. He thought not. The separation was not such a separation as was contemplated by the Treaty, which was exclusively one effected by foreign force.

the deepest moment that the national honour should be preserved inviolate. Consideriug, that upon this subject hung the national faith and honour of England, he confessed it did in the highest degree astonish him, that hon. Members should think of introducing topics which had not the slightest relation to such a subject. If we were bound by the solemn obligations of a mutual compact, of what importance to us was the general conduct of the Monarch with whom that compact might have been contracted? Were we at full liberty to enter into as many treaties as we please with all the Monarchs of the world, and yet keep faith only with those who proved to be merciful, liberal, and constitutional rulers? We entered into treaties with the Burmese and Siamese governments, and were we to require of them that they should conform their respective principles of government to that which we conceived might be suitable and becoming as between them and their subjects? The only argument on that side of the House was the necessity of keeping faith; and how had the hon. and gallant Member met that argument? Why, the hon. and gallant Member talked as if we paid tribute to Russia, at the moment it was attacking Poland. On what ground else did he speak of economy? To exercise economy in a case of this description, the payment must be optional, for he had not yet heard anybody rise in the House and say, that economy was to be preserved at the expense of national honour. If the common-sense interpretation of the treaty called upon this country for its execution, the hon. and gallant Member might as well call upon them to economize by a reduction of the Three per Cents, or a non-payment of Exchequer Bills. The question which they were then engaged in debating, naturally divided itself into two parts. The first was, whether or not the country was bound, by the most obvious principles of public faith, to continue these payments; secondly, did Government act illegally in continuing them without obtaining a new Act of Parliament for the purpose? All the hon. Members who spoke upon the other side, pro fessed to pursue the object of keeping these questions perfectly distinct; and yet it strangely enough happened, that there was not one amongst them who did not mix both these topics; and that confusion of those questions was strikingly conspicuous where Vattel was referred to. Referring to the Treaty of 1815, he must admit, that if they examined the letter of that treaty, they would find, that the proviso had arisen, and that we were absolved from the payment of the debt. Yes, according to the letter of the treaty we were absolved. According to the letter we might be absolved; but were they now to be told for the first time, that the foreign policy of this great and renowned country was to be governed by such pettifogging rules of construction as were enunciated from the other side? Principles such as those were never meant, in any age or country, to be applied to the construction of compacts affecting the peace or the fate of nations. Reference, for the purposes of present argument, had been made to the opinions of jurists; but he knew enough of jurists to know, that they were the most convenient authorities that could in any case be referred to for the purposes of such a debate as the present. In the early ages of the Church the Fathers were frequently quoted, and many of them so frequently to serve opposite ends, that it became a proverb, that you might apply to the Fathers and obtain their authority in support of either side of almost any question. If they adopted the rule of literal construction, there must be an end of all that had heretofore been considered the faith of treaties. Hon. Members on the other side had spoken much and emphatically of the authorities which they had quoted in support of their respective opinions; but he would call their attention to one authority which few amongst them would be disposed to dispute—he meant the authority of the Duke of Wellington. One of the great conventions to which he was a party bore date in the same year with that which they were then discussing. It related to the entrance of the Allied Armies into Paris in the year 1815. By that Convention it was strictly stipulated, that all public property, other than military stores, should be respected; and it was further agreed, that if any doubt should arise respecting the construction of any part of that Convention, it should be construed favourably to the city of Paris, yet all the pictures of the Louvre were removed. The people of France held up the letter of the treaty, and insisted that the works of art, of which Napoleon had despoiled the nations of Europe, should still remain within the French capital; but they were restored to their original possessors, and the British nation and all Europe approved the act, for it was understood at the time of signing the Convention, that the pictures at the Louvre were to be restored. There was an understanding that an exception had been made in respect of them particularly. He was aware it might be alleged that the rules of construction required, that when any exception whatever was specified, none other could be introduced or added; but let the House only look to the circumstances of 1815 —look to that very Convention in which the Duke of Wellington himself was concerned. The treaties entered into at the period when what was called the Settlement of Europe had been effected, were directed to objects which could not, from their very nature, be long maintained; but was the pecuniary part of those treaties to be therefore set at nought by a people calling themselves free, liberal, and enlightened? The treaties of that period could certainly accomplish no object of a permanent kind, for these Governments thought but of other Governments, and nothing of the nations. In all their partitions they looked to making up compact states—they looked to nothing beyond the convenient frontiers which an acquaintance with the state supplied—they attended not to the national characters, habits, feelings, religion, morals of the several nations whose fates they presumed to decide; and what better proof could be supplied of that than that very plausible but hollow union of Holland and Belgium? But though, in those various points of policy, England had failed, that failure, so far from furnishing an argument in support of breach of pecuniary faith, had quite an opposite tendency. He said nothing of the policy of that union, but it was a great and primary object of the then Ministry of this country to form it, and it would be an eternal disgrace to the present Ministers, who differed as to that measure, if they refused to fulfil the stipulations of their predecessors. It was well known, that Russia was averse from the union between Holland and Belgium; and as a means of reconciling the Court of St. Petersburg, the payment of the Russian debt due in Holland was guaranteed by England [*cries of* "*no*"]. He certainly understood, and believed he could show from good authority, that Russia was opposed to that union—it was stated at the time—he could show it had been recorded—it had been stated in that House, that, in 1815, Russia was averse from the union; the Treaty was concluded under that view, and with the express object and intention of inducing Russia to accede to it; and, in order to prevent Russia having an interest in disturbing that union, the payments were made to depend upon its continuance. The period fixed for the determination of those payments was the dissolution of the union, not because there was any natural connexion between the two, but because it was from Russia that danger was chiefly apprehended. If looked at in that view, the treaty was intelligible: in any other it had no meaning. The hon. member for Thetford said, that these payments were due, not to Russia but to Holland, and that England could only contemplate paying them as long as Holland had the ability to pay her share to Russia. But, if that were the contingency of our payments, it might have been as well made to depend on the fall of the next meteoric stone, or the drying up of the Mediterranean. If the principle were that Russia should not receive the money in consequence of a separation which she could not prevent, or that England should be exonerated from the payment in consequence of a separation which she had promoted, the treaty in which such a principle was embodied would be the most extraordinary that ever was made. If he understood the spirit of those treaties rightly, it was, that if there were the slightest reason to believe that Russia, by direct or indirect means, had produced a separation between Holland and Belgium—if she had been inclined to lag behind, and to make no exertion to prevent it—if she had favoured that separation—if she had thrown any obstruction in the way of any efforts we might have been inclined to make for the purpose of preventing that separation—then the circumstances contemplated by the proviso had arisen, and we were relieved from the payment of the money. But was that the present state of affairs? Was it not notorious, that since 1815 the two countries had, so to speak, interchanged their parts with reference to this question. In 1815 we were for the union and Russia was against it; in 1831 Russia was decidedly opposed to the separation. He would not say that England either caused, or was desirous of, that separation. He did not mean to say, that England desired that the people of Belgium should be discontented with the government of Holland, nor that the Belgians should have risen against the king of Holland. He did say, however, that while the king of Holland continued to be, virtually, the king of that country, hostilities took place; the resistance of the Belgians was successful; and Belgium was separated, to be again united, in all probability, by the European powers only. England was desirous that the separation should be recognized, and it became necessary that the new independent state of Belgium should be invited to enter into the great European family. In the mean time, the circumstances of Russia had changed in a directly opposite direction. In the first place, as every Gentleman knew, a matrimonial alliance had, since 1815, very closely united the Courts of Petersburg and the House of Orange; but, above all, they could not help feeling, that the circumstances under which the Belgian revolution took place, were such as could not be contemplated with pleasure by a government, distinguished by its jealousy of all popular institutions arising out of the people. The forcible expulsion of the troops of the government and the Sovereign, and a democratic council being called to the government of the country, the question between a republic and a hereditary monarchy put to the vote, and a Sovereign invited and elected by the people themselves, on certain constitutional terms—these were the characteristics of the Belgian revolution ; and these were things which it could not be supposed the Russian government would contemplate with pleasure. It appeared to him, therefore, that the two countries had entirely changed their former parts; that this recognition was now effected by the great Powers of Europe, and that the independence of the state of Belgium had not been effected in that way which would absolve us from our obligations. It had been effected, not by the interference of Russia, but in conformity with the wishes of England, and in spite of a strong reluctance on the part of Russia. He could not but think, then, that we were still bound to fulfil our obligations. There was a case he would mention to the House, which appeared nearly parallel to the present. He remembered to have read, long ago, in one of the old jurists—he could not recollect where, but it was not necessary to mention the authority, for its great similarity to the present case would carry its own argument along with it—the writer, according to a common practice, as many hon. Gentlemen knew, with the jurists, put a supposed case. There were two States before the invention of fire-arms. Certain circumstances induced one State to agree to pay the other an annual subsidy of 1000 ducats; the other state stipulating in return, that whenever the state paying this money was invaded, they would send to their assistance 1,000 pikemen ; and the treaty contained a stipulation that, if this number and the force were not sent within three days after such an invasion, then the payment of the annual subsidy should cease and be discontinued. Fire-arms were subsequently invented, and came into general use; an invasion took place, the party invaded sent to the other state, not for pikemen, but for musqueteers—"For the love of heaven send us some musqueteers; pikemen are of no use now" A battalion of musqueteers immediately marched to the assistance of the distressed state, and the invasion was repelled. Afterwards, when the subsidy was demanded, the answer was,—"Look to the terms of the treaty; it declares that you shall send 1,000 pikemen, and that, if you do not send such a force, in number and arms, as herein stipulated, payment of our annual subsidy shall thereupon cease." Why, what would be the language of the Power cheated in this way?—Would it not say, "You are taking advantage of your own wrong; circumstances have changed; military tactics have altered; we have conformed to that alteration; by doing so we have saved you, and this is the return you give us for what we have done?" These cases were analogous. In 1815 we were desirous of the union; in 1832 we were desirous to promote a separation; and with what face could the British Ministers stand up and say to the Russians, "You did not frustrate my wishes with respect to Belgium, you did not plunge all Europe into war to support your own views, and I will now take advantage of the separation which I promoted, and which you might have prevented, but did not, in order to evade payments which literally, though not according to the spirit of the treaty, were made to depend upon the continuance of the union." He had no difficulty, then, upon grounds such as these, broadly and roundly to assert, that his Majesty's Government had deserved well of the country, and, therefore, he paid but little attention to the taunts, coming from the other side, about the difficulty that Members might have in facing their constituents, after voting in favour of a continuance of those payments. For his part, he should have no difficulty in defending such a vote before any constituent body in the empire; for the people of England had long shown that they knew and felt there was a fixed identity in the state—that public and private morals were the same—that honesty was the best policy—and they believed that to pay what they owed was the truest economy—that the state could not be guilty of a breach of faith in one instance without bringing suspicion on all its engagements, and thus reducing itself to a situation at once disgraceful and perilous, putting to hazard that peace throughout Europe now happily so long preserved—a peace, in the continuance of which every artisan, every ploughman, every shopkeeper, in the land knew that he was deeply interested; and he need not say, that to preserve peace, public faith must be maintained inviolably. Upon these principles, Members of Parliament might go before the people of England—upon these principles, Members of Parliament might be willing to act, and content to suffer.

ON THE AFFAIRS OF THE COUNTRY.*

FEBRUARY 6, 1833.

On the Address in Answer to the King's Speech—The Irish Question.

Last night he had formed the intention of not taking part in the present debate; but circumstances which had this evening arisen determined him to adopt an opposite course, and to say a few words in reply to the attack which had been made upon him by his hon. friend, the member for Lincoln [Sir E. L. Bulwer]; at the same time that he felt that he should quite as well discharge the duty which he owed to himself, and much better consult what was due to the House, by postponing the defence of his own personal consistency until after he had more directly addressed himself to the question which mainly occupied the attention of the House. His hon. friend, so ingenious in the construction of an argument, and so successful in making a point, was sometimes not always aware of the effect of the words which he used. His hon. friend told the House that the Government proposed coercion, while the hon. and learned member for Dublin [O'Connell] recommended redress. When called upon to choose between both, the hon. member for Lincoln declared that he could not hesitate; but he was sure that, upon reflection, his hon. friend would see that he and the hon. and learned member for Dublin did not attach the same meaning to the words which the one was the first to use, and that the other had but too readily adopted. The hon. and learned member for Dublin meant Repeal of the Union—to that

* Hansard, 3d Series, vol. xv. p. 250–264.

his hon. friend was averse. When they were told that the question of the Union of Ireland was not to be sneered down till after the most complete investigation, till after the fullest inquiry, and after the gravest debate, he could not help putting the question, whose fault was it that they had no full and formal debate upon the subject? Why was it that the question had not been fully agitated? Had not his Majesty's Government given the challenge, and was it not fully in the recollection of the House, that the hon. and learned member for Dublin had addressed them for two or three hours—he forgot how long, for no one could consider the time long while that Gentleman continued speaking; but had he not spoken for two or three hours, without opening the question of the Union in a manner that could be grappled with, or indeed fairly encountered at all? This was the more remarkable, as that hon. and learned Member had last night placed fourteen notices on the book, and not one of them related to the subject of the Legislative Union between Great Britain and Ireland. The hon. and learned Member had permitted judgment to go against him by default. Hon. Members at that side of the House (the Ministerial) had called upon the hon. and learned Member to proceed, but he had declined the invitation—he shrunk back—he skulked away from the opportunity of giving effect in that House to the doctrines which he had promulgated elsewhere with so much vehemence, and accompanied with so much of personal invective and objurgation. If ever there was an occasion which naturally led to a discussion of the question of Repeal, it was the Amendment moved by the hon. and learned Member; but he had not only then neglected to take advantage of the opportunity offered to him, but instead of making any approach towards joining issue upon it, he had delivered one of the most evasive speeches that had ever been uttered within the walls of Parliament. From the beginning to the end he had most carefully and studiously avoided meeting the question of Repeal. He should be the last man in the world to deny that that speech was very able and eloquent, but though the most ample opportunity had been afforded the hon. and learned Member by the occasion which then presented itself, to press upon the attention of the House the question of Repeal; yet he had cautiously abstained from improving that opportunity, and had not accepted the challenge of those who stood strong in their defence of the Legislative Union, the Repeal of which was supposed by the hon. and learned member for Dublin to be the panacea for all the evils with which Ireland was afflicted. It was not for lack of argument that Ministers did not discuss the Question. They were strong in irresistible arguments, and feared not on any occasion to meet the advocates of Repeal. They were told, indeed, to wait till they had examined the petitions of the Irish people; but no Gentleman who took an interest in the affairs of the country had neglected already to make himself master of it in all its bearings. He was prepared to discuss the question of Repeal inch by inch, and to show, that so far from being likely to remedy the social and political grievances of Ireland, it would have the effect of aggravating every one of the causes of discontent at present in operation. If the advocates of Repeal wished to separate the Crowns of England and Ireland—if they desired to establish an Hibernian Republic, their arguments might be considered rational and consistent; but the hon. and learned Gentleman required a separation of the Legislatures of the two countries, and the identity of their Crowns. The hon. and learned Member required two independent Legislatures (for if the Legislatures were not independent, the separation was a mockery), and one Executive. Could it be then that a mind so acute and informed as his, could be unconscious that such conclusions were opposed to the first principles of the science of Government? When a Union of the Crowns was spoken of, he took it for granted that no such Union was meant as that which subsisted between Great Britain and Hanover, in which the Crown appertained to the same Royal Personage, but in which the Ministers by whom the Executive authority was actually exercised were perfectly distinct: a Union of that sort, so far as he knew, had never been advocated; and he entertained not the slightest doubt, that could such a Union ever be called into existence, the first question asked would be, what was the use of continuing it—what purpose could it serve to either country? Let the House only contemplate for a moment what was the nature of the Union subsisting between this country and Hanover. Hanover was a member of the Germanic Diet, and might send its contingency to the aid of a war carried on against the Allies of England, or against England herself. Did they contemplate any Union of that sort for Ireland with this country? If they did, let them say so at once—let them declare candidly, did they, or did they not, desire two Legislatures and one Executive, connected as England and Hanover were, for he professed himself unable to understand, and he felt assured, from the nature of the proposition, that no man in his senses could imagine that he understood any other scheme by which the business of Government in both countries could be carried on with the Legislatures separated and the Crown united. But the hon. and learned Member said, that he thought it would be a great calamity if the two countries were to be separated, and were not to have the same King, meaning obviously, the same Executive Government. The hon. and learned Gentleman then meant simply by the Repeal of the Union, two independent Legislatures under one Executive. Was such a state of things possible? If the Executive Power were really quite distinct from the Legislative Power, they might easily have two Legislatures under one Executive just as they had two Chancellors, and two Courts of King's Bench. But be the theory of the Constitution what it might, no man acquainted with the working of that Constitution, could for a moment imagine a total separation of the Legislative from the Executive? It would be a political anomaly, or rather a political impossibility. For himself he was disposed to rest the question upon this issue—Had or had not the Legislature a most powerful influence upon the Executive? Could the Crown pursue war, or conclude peace, without the consent, and sanction, and support of the Legislature? War, peace, and all the functions of the Executive, were, in some degree, dependent upon the Legislature, and the Legislature exerted a considerable share of power in every part of the duties assigned to the Executive. The King might choose his own Ministers; but he could not maintain them in office after Parliament had become hostile to them. The conduct of negotiations was intrusted to the Monarch, he appointed Ambassadors; but the King could not pursue any line of foreign policy in opposition to the views and feelings of the Parliament. The Repealers might, therefore, be refuted out of their own mouths. They said, that the Executive Power ought to be one: but the Legislature had a share of Executive Power. Therefore, by the confession of the Repealers themselves, the Legislature ought to be one. Now the futility of such an opinion could be at once exposed by a most simple, obvious, and familiar illustration. Suppose the one Legislature voted an Address in favour of peace, and the other declared for war, what would ensue? Did they suppose that there were to be at all foreign states with which we maintained diplomatic relations two Ambassadors—one for England and the other for Ireland? And yet it was impossible to avoid arriving at that conclusion if a distinction were established between the Legislative, and therefore, of necessity, between the Executive powers of the two countries. And what would be the next step? Negotiations might be carried on with foreign states, and the Legislature of this country express the highest approbation of the manner in which they might have been conducted—might declare its confidence in, and offer its thanks to the diplomatic agent employed; while the Legislature of the other State might resolve upon his impeachment. Not ten—not five years would elapse before occasions must present themselves, out of which causes of irreconcileable dispute must arise. Not one year could the two countries exist under the same Imperial Executive. The supposition was monstrous and absurd, and all history showed that the plan would be utterly impracticable. It had been supposed that parallel cases should be referred to; but when those came to be examined, it would, in every instance, be seen, that a similarity of circumstances did not prevail; and that where they did, the case but strengthened the position for which he was contending. Take the case of Ireland herself during the short period in which she possessed an independent Parliament. It was only during eighteen years that there did exist in the British empire two independent and co-equal Legislatures; and though the circumstances under which they so existed rendered collision exceedingly difficult—for during the whole of that period, as was well known to all who heard him, the Irish Houses were managed by that Parliamentary corruption which no one could desire to see renewed, and the Irish people were overawed by a large military force—yet, for all that, so filled was the system with the seeds of disunion, that six years did not elapse from the declaration of independence till occasion for a difference of opinion arose. In the year 1788, George 3rd was incapacitated by illness from the exercise of the powers appertaining to the Kingly office, and according to the Constitution, the privilege devolved upon Parliament of making provision for the discharge of those high and important functions. What occurred? The Parliament of England offered the Regency to the Prince of Wales with extensive restrictions—the Parliament of Ireland offered him the same powers without any restrictions whatever. Surely if they possessed the right and the power to make such offer respecting the conditions upon which the Royal functions were to be exercised, they possessed as fully and could as freely exercise the privilege of selecting the individual to whom the appointment might be offered, and with quite as strong a claim of right constitute the Duke of York Regent, as extend the powers of the office when vested in the Prince of Wales. They might have chosen their own Regent, and might have invested him with such powers as they thought proper; and had George 3rd continued for the remainder of his life incapable of the duties of Monarch, England and Ireland would have been for thirty-two years with a divided Executive, without departing one iota from the principles of the Constitution. This would have been the unavoidable consequence; yet it was loudly deprecated in the very same breath which sent forth a warm recommendation to call into life and activity the causes from which that consequence must necessarily flow. Were he to pursue the argument further, he could occupy the attention of the House with nothing more than reciting such a series of monstrous results, as certainly never before ensued, and which were probably never yet contemplated in reference to any public measure. Not only was all argument opposed to it *à priori*, but all history would show the scheme to be founded upon a gross and pernicious fallacy. They might have again a legislature in Dublin and in London as they had before 1782, but all that the former would have to do, would be to obey the decrees of the latter under a mock form of independence. He admitted that some cases bore the appearances of divided legislatures and united Crowns, but those appearances were to the utmost degree deceptive, and the more closely they were examined the more clearly did that character develope itself. Such was the case, for example, in the co-existent parliaments of France, Burgundy, and Brittany; and, equally so, in those mockeries of the names of Parliament with which the House of Austria still amused the people of Hungary and the Tyrol. In all these cases there was no such thing as an independent legislature; all the power lay in the hands of the Crown; the Parliament was a mere pageant—a mockery—or means of riveting the fetters of the conquered. In fact, if history had one lesson which stood out more emphatically than another,

—it was that which, indeed, reason would strike out for itself, the impossibility of two independent legislatures co-existing under the same executive head. It was not easy to get at the precise plan of Repeal contemplated by the learned Member for Dublin. He had not himself developed it, and it was only to be guessed at by some partial revelations. Among a number of statements of the learned Gentleman on this head, which he had read in the public Journals, the most precise plan was one proposing a kind of federal union of a local legislature sitting in Dublin, with an imperial legislature in London. But did the learned Gentleman deceive himself so much as to suppose, that by this plan he evaded the difficulties of two independent legislatures? Supposing, as in the latter case, that there should spring up some difference of opinion or conduct between the two legislatures—the domestic and the imperial—who was to decide between them? Where was the paramount authority to declare, "you are right," and "you are wrong; you therefore must yield, &c.;" for on the supposition of the learned Gentleman, they were both to be independent and supreme. A dispute between the House of Commons and the House of Lords was bad enough; yet in that case the Crown possessed a constitutional power, which in practice had prevented collisions between the hereditary and the representative branches of the Legislature; it could dissolve the one,—it could add to the numbers of the other. They all knew that both expedients were had recourse to in the reign of Anne, in 1704 and 1712; in the one instance (the Aylesbury affair) the Queen dissolved the House of Commons; in the other (the question of the peace of Utrecht) she created a number of Peers. But who was to arbitrate between two independent Legislatures elected by two different nations? The federal union of a domestic and an imperial legislature, did not meet the difficulty which, indeed, the greatest federal republic in the world was at this moment exhibiting on a large scale. That republic—the most famed in the world—agreed to its present constitution in a great convention, over which the genius of Washington presided, and in which the most able statesmen of the day assisted. At that memorable convention, the different states of which the republic was composed agreed to a form of union, similar to that contemplated by the hon. and learned Gentleman; and yet, after more than half a century's trial, the constitution of the United States had found no other arbiter between a local and an imperial legislature, but physical force. The hon. and learned gentleman's plan for separating the legislatures of the two countries, and at the same time continuing the union of the Crowns, was, therefore, worse than a complete and total separation—that complete and total separation which the hon. and learned Gentleman said he should regard as a calamity; but which would be no calamity compared with that which he proposed to put upon us. If, on a fair trial, it were found that the two countries could not be made to co-exist in the same empire—could not be made harmoniously to combine in one course of mutual support and prosperity—in God's name let them be wholly separated. He did not wish to see them, like those strange twin beings lately exhibited in this city, connected by an unnatural tie, which made each the plague of the existence of the other—each in the other's way; more slow of motion, because they had more legs; more helpless, because they had more hands; partaking of no common aliment, sympathizing only in disease and helplessness, and each being perpetually subject to perish by the dissolution of the other. And, now, in what character was it that the hon. and learned Gentleman came forward? He said that he appeared as the last advocate of his own country—as the man who stood between the empire and civil war. But if they admitted that the Repeal of the Union was to save us from this calamity, what argument had the hon. and learned Member advanced in favour of that proposition? He had recounted many grievances; and he was not the man to speak lightly of those grievances—they were, undoubtedly, numerous, extensive, and of long standing; but when he heard the hon. and learned Gentleman go through that melancholy list of evils, many of which, unquestionably, required a speedy remedy —a remedy which he trusted soon to see applied—(at least so far as any remedy might be within the gift of the Legislature), when he heard the hon. and learned gentleman go through that melancholy list, he detected one alone which, as it seemed to him, the Repeal of the Union could, even in the hon. and learned Gentleman's own opinion, tend to remove. What was the nature of the evils to which the hon. and learned Gentleman alluded—were they such as did not exist previous to the Union? Certainly not; and he had yet to learn that the Repeal of the Union would be a remedy for grievances which existed long before that Union took place, and which grievances, he would confidently venture to add, a Repeal of that Union would but aggravate. The learned Gentleman, in his *post hoc* and *propter hoc* distinctions, seemed to reverse the well-known logic of the Goodwin Sands *versus* Tenterden Steeple. The steeple was the cause of the sands, said the rustic logicians, because it existed before they encroached upon the coast; but the learned Gentleman reversed the reasoning, and said, because the Union took place long after the existence of certain grievances, therefore it must be the cause of them. Some of the grievances which he thus ascribed to the Act of Union were not peculiar to Ireland, or to any form of government. For what did they reform the House of Commons? Was it not on the same grounds upon which the hon. and learned Member now came forward and asked for a Repeal of the Union? Was not the removal of many of them—undeserving sinecurists, political judges, corrupt magistrates, for example—one of the great objects of the Reform Bill? Surely, the removal of the remaining Irish grievances did not in all fairness require a domestic legislature in Ireland. Besides, see to what the argument tended; if local abuses in Ireland required a local legislature to remedy them, why should not every other part of the empire, also complaining of grievances, be allowed its domestic legislature? They all remembered what complaints were made a few years since with respect to the Welsh Judges; but did anybody, therefore, dream that Wales should be separated from England, and that it should have a domestic legislature of its own? In the same way he never heard it said that a domestic legislature should be established in Cornwall because there were several local grievances in that county which required a remedy. Nay, to come nearer his political home—Leeds—he could assure the House, that a large majority of his constituents complained loudly of the grievances imposed upon them by its corporation; but not a hint had been thrown out that the best remedy would be the establishing a nice federal independent domestic legislature in the West Riding of Yorkshire. And yet, if the learned Gentleman's project were good for anything, it must be capable of being applied to Wales, and Cornwall, and Yorkshire, and every county in England, as well as to Ireland. He would go further (perhaps the learned Gentleman would say much further), and maintain that the clearest ground which could be guessed at, as the basis of his repeal scheme, would apply *à fortiori* to a separation of the legislatures of the north and the south of Ireland. If a rooted difference of religion, and the existence of the worst consequences of that difference, would justify the separation of the English and Irish legislatures, the same difference, and, still more, the same baleful consequences, would warrant the separation of Protestant Ulster from Catholic Munster. If, as the learned gentleman had often declared, it was impossible for a Catholic prosecutor or prosecuted to obtain even the semblance of justice from an Orange juryman, and that such a state of things would be a justification of a Repeal of the Legislative Union between England and Ireland (though the fact was notorious that no such conduct would, under any circumstances, be manifested towards any British subject in England), why then the same reasoning, that only a domestic legislature could remedy a domestic grievance, would in a tenfold degree apply in favour of one domestic legislature in Dublin, and another in Derry, or some other large town in the north of Ireland. All the arguments which the hon. and learned Gentleman had advanced in favour of his favourite scheme of Repeal seemed invalid. In making these observations, he had, in a great measure, vindicated himself from the charge of inconsistency brought against him by his hon. friend, the member for Lincoln. It was very easy for hon. Gentlemen to come forward with a speech made by another, upon the Reform Bill, to read a few sentences from it, and to say: "this binds you to support a Repeal of the Union." It was hardly fair to take such a course, because every expression uttered in the House ought to be construed only in reference to the occasion upon which it had been used. No man knew better than a practised writer like the hon. member for Lincoln, that the whole force or wisdom of words depended on their application; that nothing was easier than to write a theory on either side of a subject, either all panegyric or all vituperation; and that the wisdom or folly of the theory depended solely on its application. For example, were he to defend Thistlewood in the tone and language which he should, or at least ought to employ, if he were the advocate of a Lord William Russell, or an Algernon Sydney, it would be plain that he should be employing words, to say the least, inappositely. The whole test of the propriety is the application—the appositeness of the expressions at the time; and by these considerations he ought, in fairness, to have been judged by his hon. friend, the member for Lincoln. He believed the Reform Bill to be a remedy which might be easily applied for the removal of the greater portion of the evils complained of by the hon. and learned member for Dublin. He believed that the project for the Repeal of the Union was a mere delusion; nay more, he believed that, in the manner in which it was proposed, it was an impossibility. He believed also that if it were practicable, there was no part of the empire to which it would be so fatally ruinous as to Ireland itself. The expressions which he used on the occasion alluded to by the hon. member for Lincoln, and which he did not shrink from, imputed much, perhaps nine-tenths, of the grievances and ills which afflicted the country previous to the passing of the Reform Bill, to the misgovernment consequent upon a withholding of that beneficial measure. But it should be recollected, in applying his language to the case of Ireland, that he did not, therefore, argue that the breaches of the law to which these consequences of misgovernment led, should go unpunished. When he said that in his mind the burnings and destruction of agricultural produce, which disgraced so many portions of England, were mainly owing to the then Ministers turning a deaf ear to the people's cry for Reform, he did not at the same time contend, that the incendiaries and the lawless disturbers of social order should not be hanged or otherwise punished. Then, though he earnestly deplored the probable results of rejecting the Reform Bill, he did not assert that the outrages and excesses committed under the name of that rejection should pass with impunity—that for the Bristol rioters, for example, the sword of justice should not be unsheathed—but he would defend the consistency of his language, on that and the present occasion, out of the mouth of the learned member for Dublin himself. That learned Gentleman told the House yesterday, that the coercers might goad by their harsh policy, some of the least prudent, least thinking multitude, into a general war against property and order, but that then he should be found in the ranks of the Executive in resisting the outrages, and punishing the guilty. The learned Gentleman, it was true, said that he would thus join the ranks of the Government as the lesser of two great evils—that while he aided it, he would abuse and execrate it as the parent source of all the mischief—but still he would be found in its ranks. If, therefore, the learned Gentleman did not deem himself inconsistent, when aiding in the case he put to check the lawless consequences of grievances which he called upon the Houes to remedy, he was at least as little obnoxious to a similar charge by his hon. friend, the member for Lincoln. The hon. Gentleman and he agreed in ascribing to misgovernment the real parentage of the grievances which had led, or might lead, to acts inconsistent with social order; and both of them agreed, that while the grievances should be remedied, the violation of the law should be punished. The only difference between them was one of time—that was, when the law should be enforced against its transgressors. He agreed with the learned Gentleman, that Ireland presented many grievances which demanded a remedy from the Legislature. He, for one, would do his best to redress those grievances. He would go further, and declare he would not belong, for a moment, to any Government to which that redress should be a matter of unnecessary delay. But because he was thus ready to redress the grievances of Ireland, was he, in the mean time, to see the law outraged—nay, despised by a furious and misguided multitude? Talk of the distribution of Church property in a country in which no property was respected, and were they to be told that, to enforce the law against the robber, and the murderer, and the incendiary, was to drive an injured people into civil war? Did they who talked thus wildly recollect the present deplorable state of Ireland? Did they recollect that, in one county alone, according to the authority of the right hon. Secretary for Ireland, not less than sixty murders, or attempts at murder, had been perpetrated in comparatively a few weeks, and not less than 600 burglaries, or attempts at burglary? Why this was far worse than civil war. A loss of life and property equal to the sacking of three or four towns. Civil war, indeed! he declared solemnly that he would rather live in the midst of any civil wars he had ever read of, than live in some parts of Ireland at this time. Much rather would he have lived on the line of the Pretender's march at Carlisle or at Preston, than now live in some of the districts of Ireland in which burglary and murder were the nightly occupations. In point of fact, to threaten civil war was only to threaten that which was now suffered, for Ireland was in a state of civil war. And yet, to endeavour to put an end to such a disgraceful scene of anarchy and strife was, forsooth, "brutally" to coerce Ireland. He repeated that the civil war had long since begun, and, if not checked, must end in the ruin of the empire. In the course of the remarks with which he had thus troubled the House, he had avoided all allusion to those irritating topics connected with the vituperations which the hon. and learned member for Dublin had, more than once, thought it fitting to pour out against the party now in office. That party would spare itself the task of reproaching him with conduct, to say the least, savouring of ingratitude. The hon. and learned Gentleman might be assured that his abuse was not a bit more stinging to those against whom it was directed, than that which was so lavishly bestowed upon them by those who so long withheld from him and his Catholic brethren their political rights, and who were now allied with him in hostility against those very persons who were ever the earnest and uncompromising advocates of those rights. He might be assured that the high-minded men who braved the "no Popery" cry in all its fury, were not likely to be scared by a cry for the Repeal of the Union. As attached to that party known by the name of "the Whigs," it was not for him to speak of their claims upon the favour of an enlightened public. The time would come, when history would do them justice, and would show, among other things not unworthy of commendation, how much they had done and suffered for Ireland; it would show that, in 1807, they left office because they could not knock off the political fetters of their Catholic fellow-subjects; and that, for the same sacred cause, they remained upwards of twenty years out of office, though more than once it was within their grasp, braving at the same time the frowns of the court and the hisses of the multitude. Yes, for the Catholics they renounced power and place, without obtaining in return the poor reward of a fleeting popularity. These were men, in those days of "no Popery" triumph, who might, by uttering one little word against the Catholics—nay, in some places, by merely not saying a little word in favour of them, have been returned by numerous constituencies to a seat in the Legislature; but who, sooner than utter that little word, contrary to their well-founded convictions of right and justice, were not only excluded from Parliament, but from all those places of honour and trust which are coveted by every high-minded English gentleman! The Whigs retired from public life, but their honour was unsullied. The clamour, therefore, which the hon. and learned member for Dublin was endeavouring to excite against Earl Grey's Government could not be of much moment, compared with that which Earl Grey had already withstood in order to place the learned Gentleman where he sat. Though a comparatively young member of the Whig party, he could take it upon him to speak their sentiments on this head. He therefore could tell the hon. and learned Gentleman that the same spirit and moral courage which sustained the Whigs when out of office, in their conflict with bad laws, would sustain them in office in their conflict with the enemies of good laws. They were not deterred by clamour from making the learned Gentleman not less than a British subject; he might be assured they would never suffer him to be more. In saying this, he believed that he was speaking the sentiments of many thousands. He was proud to say that he stood there, for the first time, the Representative of a new, a great, and a flourishing community, who conceived that, at the present time, the service of the people was not incompatible with that of the Crown; and who had sent him there, charged (as the words of his Majesty's writ expressed it), "to do and consent to such things as should be proposed in the great council of the kingdom." In their name, therefore, he hereby gave his full assent to that part of the Address wherein the House declared its resolution to maintain, by the help of God, the connexion between England and Ireland inviolate, and to intrust to the Sovereign such powers as might be necessary for the security of property, for the maintenance of order, and for preserving, entire, the integrity of the empire.

THE DISTURBANCES (IRELAND) BILL.*

FEB. 28, 1833.

He confessed, that the apprehensions entertained by the hon. and learned Gentleman who had just sat down [Mr. Sheil] did not appear to him to be in any degree well-grounded, nor did he think that the speech of that hon. and learned Gentleman, however much it had been cheered at that side of the House, would at all weaken the lasting impression made by the admirable address delivered by his right hon. friend (Mr. Stanley) yesterday evening. That speech had produced an impression which he was convinced would not easily be removed from the minds of those who heard it. The hon. and learned Gentleman had told them, that that speech, great as he admitted it to be, owed much of its force to the prepossessions of the majority in that House. According to the hon. and learned Gentleman, it would appear that English members were eager to find an excuse for exposing Ireland to the operation of this measure. For himself and for those who concurred with him in opinion as to the necessity of the measure, he begged most distinctly and positively to repudiate the charge. That Englishmen were anxious for some excuse to put their fellow-subjects of Ireland out of the pale of the Constitution was, he must, in justice to himself and other English members, say, altogether unfounded. For his own part, he had never risen in that House under more painful feelings than those which now oppressed him. He had never thought, that it would have become necessary for him to stand up and defend the suspension of the *Habeas Corpus* Act,

* Hansard, 3d series, Vol. xv. p. 1326–1337.

and the suspension of the trial by jury. But on what grounds did he defend that course? Before he went to those grounds, he would begin by saying, that he entertained no feelings with respect to the rights and liberties, and prosperity of England, which he did not hold as fully and as strongly in regard to those of Ireland. He thought there was no situation in the life of a public man more painful than that in which he found himself, under the necessity of supporting the suspension of the *Habeas Corpus* Act, and even the temporary abolition of the trial by jury. These were sacred portions of our Constitution, older than Parliament itself—their origin was lost in the darkness of ancient times, they were beyond the Heptarchy; they formed parts of the great charter of British liberties; they were those great bulwarks of freedom for which our ancestors had bravely and successfully struggled—to preserve which kings had been deposed, dynasties had been changed—for which a noble army of martyrs had bled. He touched those sacred bulwarks with trembling and awe. Never ought they to be touched or disturbed but in case of the greatest necessity; but that necessity once made out, he would not stop to inquire, how far or how short he was to go beyond them. He would not—having once admitted the principle—enter into the details, for they must be granted, in order that the application of the principle might not be in vain. He could imagine nothing worse than the enactment of a measure which, being unconstitutional, should, at the same time, be ineffectual, which, while it went beyond the law, did not afford any security for the briefness of its own duration. In departing from the law, he would rather err on the side of vigour than of lenity. He would therefore adopt a strong measure, that its duration might be short, and that it might be less liable to be drawn into a precedent. When once, therefore, he had made up his mind that a suspension of the *Habeas Corpus* and of the trial by jury had become necessary, it was to him of little importance to go into discussion as to details, and in that feeling he would not inquire which would be the best substitute for the trial by jury—the trial by one judge, or by three barristers, or by courts-martial—for though he was not without an opinion as to which was the best, he would not stop to choose between them, but as he had mentioned them, he must say that, in his opinion, any of them would be preferable to that substitute suggested by the hon. and learned Gentleman who had just addressed the House. That the hon. and learned Gentleman seemed to think, that the trials under the Bill before them ought to be by a jury, but a jury chosen from the aristocracy. Now, it seemed to be generally admitted, at least he had not yet heard any hon. member who controverted the opinion, that the very worst hands to which the administration of strong measures like the present could be confided, were the local gentry or magistracy. Yet, to something like this, to a sort of special jury of the aristocracy, would the hon. and learned member confide the administration of these strong measures. He would have a jury of the Protestant gentry to try the Catholic peasantry. Could anything be more likely to create irritation, when the passions and prejudices and superstitions of the great mass of the people would be opposed to it? Was that the course which the hon. and learned member would adopt? But how, then, could a jury of the aristocracy be formed, without incurring the objection that seemed so generally to prevail as to the unfitness of the local gentry to administer strong measures? Let him, without going further into details, which, he repeated, he looked upon as of minor importance, if the necessity for the principle was made out—let him ask, was that necessity proved to exist? He thought it was. The question of that recessity was divided into two great parts. There was predial agitation and political agitation. Was any doubt entertained of the existence of the former? Could anything be more appalling than the details which were received, and some of which the House had heard, as to the meetings and outrages of the peasantry? Well, but it was said, "put a stop to that," and he thought he had heard it said, let it be enacted that any man in the disturbed districts who was found from his home after eight o'clock at night, should be liable to the punishment, not only of a misdemeanour, but a felony. ["No, no," *from Mr. O'Connell.*] If his ears had not deceived him, that was said, and there were many near him who were under the same impression. But, perhaps, there had been some words said very like them in sound, though differing in sense, as in another case, which must still be fresh in the recollection of the House. He thought that something of the kind was said at the time when a threat was intimated of vengeance to be taken for Ireland by the mob of St. Giles's. To him it appeared to be incontrovertibly proved, that predial agitation existed, and it was closely connected with political agitation. He did not rest on the anecdotes which he had heard on the subject, though some of them were of great importance as showing the opinions of the great mass of the people. He did not take this proof from the ballads on which the hon. and learned Gentleman (Mr. Sheil) had commented; yet, from circumstances such as these, trifling as they might at first appear, the signs of the times might often be collected. Such things were, as Lord Bacon said, like straws which, thrown up, showed which way the wind blew. Taking the whole of what he had heard, he could not refuse his belief to the facts, nor could he avoid coming to the conclusion, that there was a close connexion between predial and political agitation. A likeness existed both in feature and in principle, and the principle of each was evidently one and the same—that of preventing peaceable inhabitants from being loyal to their King, and obeying the laws of their country. Both were founded on intimidation. The Whitefeet threatened, and put their own threat into execution; the political agitators also held out their threats, and in doing so usurped a power which no subject had a right to. There was an active and a passive resistance to the law. That the active was unlawful no man would pretend to deny; that the passive resistance—that which directed or recommended men not to deal with other men of certain political opinions—not to buy from or sell to them, was also unlawful; he would assert; and he was satisfied that the hon. and learned member for Dublin would not stake his legal reputation on the assertion that it was otherwise. But there were other modes of intimidation. What were those district courts which were recommended, and to which men were told to refer their differences? What were those but so many sources of intimidation, by which those who should refuse to conform to them were to be held up to public odium? What was that organization of an unarmed body, which might be armed? Were not all these so many means of intimidation? They had heard in that House of declarations against the Whitefeet, of disavowals of their acts; no doubt, most, if not all, of their acts were such as no man had yet the hardihood to defend. But was there no use in keeping up excitement just below crime, and amongst those who were just above the vilest criminals? Was such agitation not of some benefit to those who made a profit of it, and could they be otherwise than desirous that it should be kept up just below that point where it excited the disgust and the horror of all reasonable men? Some men turned agitation into a lucrative trade, and it was of use to those who could turn it to a profitable account. But why, he would ask, declaim so strongly against the predial agitation by the Whitefeet and others, when they who so declaimed, kept up an agitation, of a different kind as to the means it was true, but much alike in the tendency? Suppose one of those Whitefeet brought before an association of agitators of a different kind, and asked to account for his conduct, what would be his natural answer? "You," he would say, "agitate, so do I; you pursue one course, I another; you intimidate, so do I; but though the execution of my threats is more immediate, it is not more certain than that of yours in the result. You speak of your unarmed volunteers, so have I mine;

mostly unarmed, but I have my arms under lock and key, to be delivered for use as occasion may require. I have as much right to act against the law in my way as you have in yours." What was the difference between this active and passive resistance? Why, the active resister of the law was exposed to great personal risk, from which the cunning of the passive resister might screen him. In this respect the difference between them was, he admitted, great, but in a moral point of view, were they not both the same? The active resister might well ask, "Who gave you the right to draw the line, and to say where passive resistance should end, and where the active should begin? Who made you Judges over your fellow-countrymen? What right have you to determine on taking up arms, and forming yourselves into what you call a national guard? You say you have grievances to redress. So have we. We have woods to cut down, cultivated grounds to uncultify, houses and farm-yards to burn down, stewards and landlords to dismiss; and we do this with the same right that you have to take upon you to cure your own wrongs." The Whitefeet might be disavowed by the agitators and pacificators, but that the acts of the one had a connexion with the agitation of the other he thought no man who paid any attention to what was passing in Ireland could for a moment entertain a doubt. But suppose, for a moment, that no such connexion existed, still he would contend, that political agitation was a proper subject for legislative interference. It was, as it had been seen, a usurpation of the power of law, a self-appointed association, sitting to try causes—not merely a civil, but also a criminal tribunal, where men were denounced for holding certain political opinions, and the terror of those denunciations obliged those who gave an honest vote to move about with pistols in their pockets for the protection of their lives. What did such an association want? A story was told of a king of Scotland, who, meeting a border robber, was so struck by the number of his followers and the splendor of their appearance, that he exclaimed, "What wants that knave which beseems a king?" So he said, what wanted the Volunteers? Not power—not terror—they wanted nothing but responsibility to make them a government. He would as soon trust to them, as soon be under their domination, as of those ancient secret societies of Germany, who sent their spies abroad, and despatched their assassins to the right hand and to the left. History scarcely supplied a parallel of a similar association. The present Volunteers compared themselves to the Volunteers of 1782, and to the Unions of England. Nothing could be more grossly incorrect than the comparison—nothing more unlike than the two things. He knew of no body to which they could be compared—at least no existing society. The only one that he could recollect was one which, by its applications, had usurped all the powers of Government, and which, through the medium of its dictators, spread tyranny over the unhappy country in which it existed. He meant, as might be easily seen, the Jacobin Club of the first French revolution. That club was long under the control of a man who was the idol of the people, but who, after plunging his country into the abyss of ruin, miserably perished. It was to that club, and to that only, that the present political associations in Ireland could be assimilated. In their organization, in their conduct, there was a resemblance between the Jacobin Club and the Irish Volunteers. Let anybody read the debates and speeches of both societies, and the closest application would be found in his comparison. A member of this Irish association declares that he will stand upon a mine, to the train of which the match is about to be applied, if the great leader of that association commands it. So, among the Jacobins, were found those who would drink poison rather than disobey the wishes of their chiefs, or separate themselves from their political fortunes. Since those associations followed the career chalked out to them by the Jacobins—since they imitated them in even minute details—should the present Government imitate that weak administration of France, which shut its eyes upon the designs of those Jacobins—allowed them to wax powerful, and at last to dictate to all without control? He hoped not, and that it would be taught by experience, and destroy the evil in its bud. He would ask a Reformed Parliament, freely chosen by the electors of the greatest nation of the world, whether it was to see such power assumed by any body of men—he would ask them as freemen, whether they could sanction the existence of such associations? In former times there were brave men who had resisted the tyranny of the Stuarts; but when they saw a fresh tyranny springing up, they naturally enough asked; "Have we slain the lion in order to be devoured by the wolf?" So he asked, "Had they beaten down parliamentary corruption, only to make way for the rule of clubs?" He belonged to that party which had carried Reform, in order to avoid revolution. But that party had not fought the battle against the proudest aristocracy in the world, in order that an oligarchy which had since sprung up should rule in its stead, an oligarchy which had no title to power but the lenity of the Government and its own audacity. Were they prepared to surrender Ireland to the domination of such a party? It was said that this measure would destroy liberty in Ireland. Where was that liberty? He remembered in Mr. Matthews's very amusing description of American peculiarities, the exclamation of the Kentucky man, who cried out, "Pretty liberty, when a man cannot wallop his own nigger." He might say of the sort of liberty enjoyed in Ireland, "Pretty liberty, where a man cannot enjoy or express his own opinion—pretty liberty, where a man is not secure of his property or life—where he is constantly obliged to go about armed, to protect himself from the violence of those who will not allow him to think and judge for himself—where he is called upon to resort to those self-constituted courts of arbitration rather than to the ordinary tribunals of the land—a liberty that prevents buying or selling—a liberty that flourishes in the midst of conspiracies—a liberty whose *insignia* are plunder and assassination." That was the liberty Ireland was to be bereft of! Never was that word more profaned—never was that sacred word of liberty more foully abused, than it was at present in Ireland. The history of Europe gave but one example of such profanation of the word Liberty—that was, when over the doors of the execrable Jacobin Club were emblazoned the words, "Liberty or Death." The Government were defending real liberty, when they asked for those coercive measures so much decried. What were the *Habeas Corpus* and Trial by Jury intended for? Why, to be the means, not the ends, of protecting life and property; they were valuable, because they secured life—because they secured property—because they protected order—and they became worthless the instant they afforded protection to villains and depredators. Allusion had been made to former measures of this kind. He would say, that there never was a measure which stood on such grounds as this, and for which such a necessity existed. No Ministry had ever yet applied for such measures who stood upon the same grounds as the present Ministers. The present Ministers had the confidence of the nation, and would not abuse it. They asked for great powers to be granted them; but, at the same time, they felt that they were responsible to a Reformed Parliament for the use they made of those powers. Besides, they asked for those powers, in order to be able to apply to Ireland those measures of redress which they knew she was entitled to. It had been argued, last night, by the hon. member for Lincoln (Mr. E. L. Bulwer), that, with them, it was "to-day, concession—to-morrow, coercion. A quick alternation of kicks and kindness—coaxing with the hand, and spurring with the heel." Such an accusation did not come well and consistently from that hon. Member, as he would confess, if he recollected his words on the Address to the Throne; he said then, "If you ask for coercive powers, why do you not, at the same time, hold out measures of redress ?"—That was the very thing Government did; it agreed with the hon. Member's first thoughts, which, in his humble opinion, were better than his second thoughts. The Government, in asking for those measures, gave a strong proof of consistency—a strong proof that it acted upon the principles of Reform. It was a proof that it still advocated the same principles as when it recommended Reform. It was determined to provide a remedy in time, so that it might not be compelled to legislate in the midst of such scenes as were acted at Nottingham and Bristol. They had recommended Reform as a remedy, and they were determined it should not be abused. Two different diseases existed in Ireland, and they had different remedies for the grievances complained of, and for the system of outrage. To the latter, which was a temporary paroxysm, would be applied temporary remedies—to the former, which were founded upon deeply-rooted discontent, would be applied an efficacious, speedy, and yet permanent cure. At all events, the present Government, in asking for coercive powers, were only following the example of the Administrations that went before them. He considered, that the present state of Ireland might be aptly compared to the state of the Highlands of Scotland eighty years ago. At that period there existed in the Highlands two species of agitation—predial and political agitation. The one carried on under the influence of Lord Lovat, resembled the political associations of Ireland at the present day. The other, the principle of which was burnings, robbery, and murder, was conducted by the noted Rob Roy. The means of the two were different, yet they were closely connected. The Government of that day broke up the connexion, which was more honest than the present, for that was kept up by family ties, the present by intimidation; but the Government broke it up by the enactment of salutary laws, and at the same time it improved the condition of the Highlanders by making roads and bridges, and otherwise facilitating intercourse to every part of the country. And what is now the consequence, he would ask, of having then had recourse to means of coercion? Let the Highlanders be asked: there would not be found one among them who did not bless the severity used towards them at the period mentioned, and the salutary wisdom that dictated that severity. He had no desire whatsoever to disguise the appalling features of the present measure. Though it were nothing but a mere experiment (if an experiment, it was at least *experimentum in corpore vili*), though its features were still more hideous, yet it was less appalling than the state of things in Ireland. It asked for courts-martial; but could any thing that would result from them, by any possibility, be half so despotic and arbitrary as what might be expected from the New National Guards already organized and prepared to extend their sway? Looking at the courts-martial in their worst light, were they so bad as the courts which were now opened to try men for their political opinions; and having passed sentence of denunciation against them, to hand them over to the peasantry, with the request that they might be dealt with as leniently as possible? See how the two systems would operate—that of the proposed measure, and the one which at present prevailed. This would tend to prevent illegal assemblages at night; that which now prevailed tended only to encourage the midnight assassin. This would authorize domiciliary visits, in order to find out who were engaged in these outrages; the other made those visits only to punish the innocent. He knew which species of visits he should prefer; and he emphatically declared, that let the measure be stigmatized as it might; let it be branded as an Algerine Act, he preferred it to a Kilkenny Act. He would far rather live in Algiers, in its most despotic day, than he would live in the county of Kilkenny at the present time. There was last year as ample a suspension of the laws in some parts of Ireland as was now demanded; and yet the powers it gave were not abused. The cause of that suspension was, to prevent an evil at which even agitation trembled—the further propagation of cholera. Now, if it were given him to choose, and to say which he should prefer—that dreadful pestilence, such as it prevailed in Russia or India, or this moral pestilence, under which there was no security for property or life, under which men were exposed to the visits of the midnight assassin, and to the noonday murderer, to having their houses burned by night, and to be shot as they fled from the fearful conflagration—if, he repeated, it were given him to make a choice between those two evils, he would choose the former; for he would say with the Hebrew king, "Let me fall into the hands of God, not into those of men." He had thus stated his opinion freely and candidly of this measure; but he could assure the House that, in what he said, he was in no degree influenced by his official connexion with the Government. He did not expect any credit on this score from the hon. and learned Gentleman opposite. He would admit, that there were many cases in which a man might give up his own opinion out of respect or attachment to political friends, or from connexions with Government; but the suspension of the *Habeas Corpus* Act was not one of those cases in which such a sacrifice of opinion could be honestly made. He could appeal to many of his hon. friends near him, who would bear testimony to the fact that he had come down on an early night of the Session, when the measure of Church Reform was to be introduced, prepared, in spite of his attachment to those who formed the Administration, and in spite of his own connexion with Government, to separate himself from that Government, if he should not find that the measure to be proposed was of a nature which the country had a right to expect. But as he was then ready to part from Ministers if he could not concur with them, so now he was ready to lend them all the feeble aid in his power, being firmly convinced that the course which they proposed was the right one. He should have no fear of meeting his constituents in consequence of his vote on this occasion. He knew their zeal for liberty; but he also knew that it was zeal with knowledge. While they would oppose any unnecessary inroad on the rights of any portion of their fellow-subjects, they would, though they regretted its necessity, not object to a measure which, while it temporarily suspended the Constitution, did so only that it might not be wholly endangered by anarchy. He would willingly render them an account of his conduct, satisfied that they were too sincerely attached to true liberty, and too enlightened, not to distinguish between it and that unbridled license which could end only in the worst of slavery. Whatever might be the result of the opinions he had expressed, he would abide by them. He had made up his mind on the subject. He might become the victim of popular injustice, but he would never condescend to be its flatterer.

CHURCH REFORM, IRELAND.*

APRIL 1, 1833.

In Committee on the plan for regulating the temporalities of the Church of Ireland.

He had two species of opposition to contend against—that of those hon. Gentlemen who did not conceive the Bill went far enough, and that of those who either considered that it went too far, or of those who believed that such a measure never should have been entered upon at all. Now, with respect to the first, he was glad, at least, to learn from the hon. and learned Member opposite, that the Bill was satisfactory so far as it went, and that it would not have, in fact, been equally judicious, if at present it did go further. On this opinion of the hon. and learned Gentleman he was willing to rest his defence of the Ministers for having gone no further. He was heartily glad that the hon. and learned member for Tipperary had withdrawn his notice of Motion, which stood upon the books; and he wished sincerely that that hon. and learned Gentleman's example might prevail with others, and induce them in like manner to withdraw the Motions they had announced. He conceived that it was a matter of extreme importance that this measure should be carried; and he felt that the difficulty of carrying it would be most considerably increased if it were made stronger. He consequently should, if it were necessary, feel no difficulty in moving the previous question, should the hon. Member not consent to withdraw his Amendment.

* Hansard, 3d Series, vol. xvi. p. 1383–1393.

He had now, however, to approach the other species of opposition against which he had to contend, and which was much the more formidable of the two—namely, that the Bill went too far, or rather, that it proceeded on an erroneous principle. Among those who had supported this view of the subject, the hon. and learned member for Dover had contended, that if his Majesty should give his sanction to this measure, it would be given in direct violation of his Coronation Oath. The hon. and learned Member also said, that this measure was a violation of the rights of the Church, and of the rights of property. The argument respecting the Coronation Oath was urged when the questions of the Catholic Emancipation and the repeal of the Test and Corporation Acts were before the House, and he had thought that that argument had been so completely refuted on those occasions, that it would not have been brought forward again. He was, however, prepared to show that the objection had no force. It was perfectly clear, from the words of the oath, that they could not bear the construction the hon. and learned Member had put upon them. What was the oath?—that the King would maintain for the Church "all such rights as do, or by law shall appertain to the Church." The whole force of the passage rested on the word "shall." In another part of the oath his Majesty says, "We declare to govern all our people according to the Statutes agreed to in Parliament;" but surely that did not mean that his Majesty swore to govern by the Statutes actually in existence at the moment he came to the Throne. Certainly not; for if that were the sense of the passage, every Act of Parliament to which the Sovereign gave his consent, in the course of his reign, would be an act of perjury upon his part. How much less, then, was there any doubt of the wording with respect to the rights and privileges of the Church! The fact was, the passage was introduced into the oath for the purpose of guarding the Church against such acts as those which James 2nd exercised as head of the Church. The present measure contemplated no interference of that kind with the Church, and it was perfectly clear to him, that the oath had not the smallest reference to the conduct of the King in his legislative capacity, and did not bar him from giving his assent to any measure agreed to by both Houses of Parliament. Allusion had been made to the articles of the Union as if they prevented any change in the established Church of Ireland. The words of the 5th article of the Union were, that "the doctrine, discipline, worship and government of the Church are to be maintained in both countries unchanged." If this measure were passed, all those things would be unchanged. No alteration was to be made in the Articles, the Book of Common Prayer was untouched, and the discipline would still be episcopal, the Archbishops and Bishops would retain all their authority, and the doctrine and discipline would be unaltered. Would it be said, that the union of certain sees in Ireland made any difference in the doctrine, discipline, worship, or government of the Church? He should suppose not. If so, all the fundamental principles of the government of the Church of England were compromised by the junction between the sees of Lichfield and Coventry. Nor were they destroying the Church of Ireland by arrangements contained in the Bill for a different distribution of church property. Such arrangements had been frequently made by the Legislature. The present case was a parallel to the case of London after the fire. The number of parishes then destroyed was eighty-seven, and soon afterwards an Act passed by which they were consolidated, and reduced to fifty-one, and a commutation of tithes for a fixed money-payment was also ordained. Indeed local Acts of a similar description were continually passed, and every one of them was as much the destruction of the Church of England as this Bill would be, were it to become a law to-morrow. It had next been asserted that the rights of property had been attacked by this Bill; this, he maintained, was an assertion; if it could be proved, he would give up the Bill. The right of property was of immense importance. To preserve that, Kings, and Parliaments, and Coronation Oaths, all existed. For that alone, law was made. Admitting the momentous nature of this consideration, he denied, that the rights of property had been attacked by the framers of the Bill. No necessity existed which should induce Ministers to infringe on those sacred rights. On the contrary, Ministers felt bound to defend to the utmost the institution of property, believing, as they did, that it was to that institution mankind were indebted for the origin and the progress of civilization—believing that it was in consequence of that institution that we were not now, like our rude ancestors, naked and painted bodies, savages feeding upon acorns and sheltering ourselves in caves. They felt, however, at the same time, that in the institution of property there were many anomalies and evils; and yet these anomalies and evils were not only willingly, but cheerfully borne by the many, in consideration of the manifold blessings which the institution of property conferred upon society at large. He would admit, too, that the anomalies in the distribution of the property of the Church of Ireland were not greater than in the distribution of lay property in other countries. It was an anomaly, that a young man who had never served the commonwealth either with head or hand should hold possession of half a county, while other men who had deserved well of the State in arts and arms, were left without an acre; and yet this was cheerfully endured by all, rather than derange the settled order of things. This was as great an anomaly as existed between the Revenues of the Archbishop of Armagh and the poorest working curate. But, as mankind found no argument in the former for attacking all property, so the latter could apply no inducement to attack the property of the Irish Church. But, the more sacred he regarded the right of property, the more care did it require that the right should not be enfeebled and contaminated by abuses. It was by protecting the abuses with which it was mingled that the institution itself was brought into disrepute. The House had heard from an eloquent voice, which, alas! they would never hear again, some opinions upon the subject of the institution of property, to which he entirely subscribed. He alluded to his excellent and accomplished friend, the late Sir James Mackintosh, who in one of the discussions on the Reform Bill, while he supported in the strongest way the institution of property, denied it was fortified by the abuses which had accumulated around it. He said: "Of all doctrines which threaten the principle of property, none more dangerous was ever promulgated, than that which confounds it with political privilege. None of the disciples of St. Simon, or of the followers of the ingenious and benevolent Owen, have struck so deadly a blow at property, as those who would reduce it to the level of the elective rights of Gatton and Old Sarum. Property, the nourisher of mankind, the incentive of industry, the cement of human society, will be in a perilous condition, if the people be taught to identify it with political abuses, and to deal with it as being involved in their impending fate." He entirely concurred in those observations, and objected strongly to those who cried out that the institution of property was endangered by removing any of the abuses that had gathered about it. He believed the Government were most anxious to preserve the institution of property; but he thought that the best and truest friends of the institution of property had little reason to be obliged to those who talked of Old Sarum as being property, and vested rights existing in it; and of the anomalies and abuses of the Irish Church being sacred property. He wished to have it understood, at the same time, that he allowed an incumbent had a right of property in his benefice, but not of the same species with the right to landed property. The incumbent was a proprietor, but he was also a public functionary; and his rights in the former capacity were controlled by his duties in the latter. He held this property, as subject not only to the existing regulations, but also to such as the Legislature might choose hereafter to impose. The hon. Gentlemen opposite must allow that, unless they were prepared to charge a number of former Parliaments with spoliation, and many of the noblest characters whose names graced our history with having encouraged schemes of robbery, there was nothing in this Bill which could authorise the allegations which had been thrown out against it. It was not a spoliation of individuals; it was not a confiscation of property. It did not legalize rapine and plunder. If that were its character, what must the Act of Supremacy have been? That Act deprived Clergymen who took orders under previous circumstances, of their benefices. It was true they were not married, for that was not permitted; but they might have incurred debts, and involved themselves in pecuniary obligations. Yet, without any regard to their possible situation, the Parliament passed an Act of expulsion against any clergyman who refused to acknowledge the supremacy of Queen Elizabeth. He was aware that few clergymen were affected by that Act, because the great majority took the oath; but one instance of a clergyman expelled was as complete an illustration of the principle as a hundred. That Act was passed when the opinions of men were loose and unsettled, but nevertheless that House would not condemn an Act by which the Reformation was firmly established in England. Again, at the time of the Restoration, when the Act of Uniformity was passed, the Prayer Book was altered. It was changed from that which it had been in the reigns of James I. and Charles I.; and those clergymen who might conscientiously object to the new Prayer Book, were liable to be turned out of their benefices. The Clergymen were all told, that if they did not before a fixed day—and that day was St. Bartholomew—notify their assent to the new Prayer Books, they would be ejected from the Church. The consequence was, that several thousands of the clergy were obliged to abandon their livings, and the Church lost several distinguished men. He admitted, that the authority of many exemplary and excellent individuals was given, to add weight to the principles of this Act; and that it received the sanction of Sheldon, of Juxon, and of other equally celebrated men. That Act was either one of direct spoliation, or else there was an absolute distinction between Church property and other property; since the proprietors of benefices were deprived of their property, for refusing to conform to certain prescribed regulations which were not enforced until long after they were in possession of their benefices. He would not dwell on the changes at the Revolution, but he would come to an Act passed in our own time, introduced by one who could not be accused of any wish to lessen the right to church property—the late Mr. Perceval—and followed up and perfected by Lord Harrowby. According to the principles laid down to-night, this must have been as complete a spoliation of property as ever was committed. It provided, that all non-resident clergymen should, under certain circumstances, pay a salary to a curate, proceeding upon a graduated scale, almost similar to that recommended in the measure now before the House. That was as much a violation of the incumbent's right of property as was contemplated by the present Bill. The right hon. member for Tamworth said, on a former debate, that if the Legislature imposed a tax on absentees, it would be neither more nor less than an act of confiscation. He said, that such a proceeding would be utterly inconsistent with the preservation of the rights of property. But, in the Bill he had just alluded to, and which was introduced by one who was a leader of the high Church party, within the last thirty years, there was either a recognition of the difference between Church property and other property; or else it was a positive confiscation of property. His own opinion of church property was, that it was a sort of mixed property—that it was something more than salary, and something less than an estate; and no man could deny, after the cases he had quoted, that the Legislature had a right to deal with it. In one sense it might be compared to the half-pay of our army and navy. No man would say, that the total abolition of that half-pay would not be a grievous spoliation. Yet, though it was admitted to be the property of the individual, no man would deny the right of the State to regulate it in any manner it pleased. Such power had repeatedly been exercised, in changes and regulations respecting it, both in respect of the amount, and of the administration of the fund from whence it was paid, when the benefit of the service had seemed to require it. If the good of the Church, and the well-being of the community, could be promoted by a new distribution of Church property, was there any reason why the Legislature should not make it—provided that existing interests were honestly and liberally considered? He admitted that this measure would take something from the clergy; but in no case would it take such an amount as to reduce any of them to distress. The money to be taken from them was to be applied to purposes beneficial to the clergy themselves, and to the security of the Church in Ireland, by removing some portion of that odium, which was entertained to an alarming extent against the Establishment in that country. He did not expect to hear any hon. member of that House contend, that not filling up a vacant bishopric was a spoliation, or a violation of property. How could it? There could be no robbery where there was no person to be robbed, and there could be no injury where there was no one to be injured. The bishopric of Waterford, for instance, was vacant, and it was not the intention of Government to fill up the vacancy. To whom was the injury done here? Not to the bishop—for there was none; not to his predecessor, for he was dead; nor to any of the 10,000 persons from whom a selection might be made, not one of whom would probably consider his chance of the appointment worth a sovereign. There was, then, no injury to any, unless it could be shown that those who had been under the spiritual care of the preceding bishop were to be left without future spiritual instruction; but if adequate provision were to be made on that head, there could be no injury to any party, but there would be a direct and positive good in the application of the revenues of that see to other Church purposes which required them. He had heard with astonishment the argument of the hon. and learned member for the University of Dublin, who maintained, "that the whole property of the Church, even for the purpose of distribution, was beyond the control of Parliament, and that no Parliament could sanction any measure of this kind without being guilty of sacrilege." He denied the truth of the proposition of the hon. and learned Gentleman. Parliament had the same power to alter and remodel, as to frame; and the Church of England had no rights, except under the Act of the Legislature. Did the hon. and learned Member say, that the unity of the Church would be destroyed by the diminution of ten Bishops in Ireland, when the whole doctrine, and discipline, and worship, continued the same? Or did he mean to say, that that unity was to be kept up only by its temporalities remaining in the same hands? Did he mean to renew the doctrine of those who once held, that the gold was to be preferred to the temple which sanctified it? Had the clergy of England been as inflexible in doctrine as some of their Bishops at the period of some of the changes of doctrine and worship to which he had already alluded, would not the whole of the Church property of the country have changed hands? What would then have been said of the identity of the Church? What would the hon. Baronet, the member for the University of Oxford, say to a revision of the wills of those pious men by which the colleges which he represented had been so liberally founded, and so munificently endowed? If he contended that any interference with Church property was spoliation, as no doubt he would contend, what would he say, on referring back to the wills and donations of some of the pious founders of the colleges of Oxford? William of Wyckham; Chicheley, the opponent of the Lollards; Flemming, the enemy of Wickliffe; Cardinal Wolsey, a candidate for the Papal Throne; Sir Thomas Pope, the follower of Mary and the teacher of Elizabeth—would have burned off their hands before they left bequests which they conceived were likely to be used against the religion they professed. If any one had told any of those pious founders, that mass would soon cease to be celebrated in the chapels which they had built, and that the refectories and chambers of the halls and colleges which they had endowed, would no longer be occupied by those who acknowledged the jurisdiction of the Bishop of Rome in England, they would much rather have left their money for the education of laymen without religion than have it used for the dissemination of doctrines which they considered as atrocious heresy. He would support the measure because he thought it would tend to the peace of Ireland—to the preservation of property there—to the real benefit of the clergy. It was the beginning of a series of judicious measures of reform, which would greatly promote the interests of religion and of the Established Church. He looked upon it also as one which would be for the interest of the people of England. But, before he concluded, he was anxious to remark that one of the objections urged against the Bill, was that by reducing the number of Bishops they left no room for the expansive force of Protestantism—no machinery by which the affairs of an Enlarged Church might be administered. Ireland was about half the size of England, and she was to have half the number of Bishops which England had. If Protestantism should expand, it would have the machinery necessary for such expansion; but he owned that he did not anticipate any such expansion, with all its wealth, and power, and learning. It had not been deficient in these aids—it had not lacked the aid of whatever they could give of penal laws in its favour; and yet the Protestants of Ireland at the present day were not a fourth of the population, and of that small number more than the half did not belong to the

Established Church. Compare the expansive power of Protestantism in Ireland for the last century and a half with that which existed in the 16th century. The spirit—the restless and over-mastering spirit—of Protestantism was much changed. That spirit which displayed itself in so eminent a degree in the 16th century, which bore it along triumphantly against Popes and Cæsars, and General Councils, and Princes, and Prelates—which enabled it to subdue conquerors and armies—made it proof against inquisitions, and dungeons, and racks, and slow fires—had fled. The heart and mind of man, supported by the enthusiasm of a pure faith, had then triumphed over all opposition against all. Within a brief period Protestantism had spread from the Vistula to the Danube; from the Pyrenees to the Frozen Ocean. The same person who heard Luther preach his first sermon against indulgences, might, without enjoying a life protracted to a great number of years, have observed Protestantism expanding itself, and established in England, Scotland, Ireland, Holland, Sweden, Denmark, Norway, the North of Germany, a part of Switzerland, and struggling in France, not for toleration, but for supremacy. But, as a Protestant, he regretted to say, that Protestantism had made comparatively little progress during the three last centuries. It remained, on the Continent, where it had reached in the days of Philip and Mary, or rather it had receded within the marks to which it had then extended. And what had already arrested its course in Ireland? Was it that the doctrines were less pure, or was it, that from the constitution of the human mind, as men became more and more enlightened, they were less and less capable of perceiving the pure truth? Was it that the Protestant Church in Ireland had not been supported by wealth, and dignity, and power, and by the aid of favouring and penal laws? Certainly not. How then was it? If he were a Roman Catholic, he might say, because the Catholic faith was strong in its strength, and founded on the immortality of truth; but, being a Protestant, he must look for some other reason, and inquire if they had not incumbered the Establishment by worse than superfluous helps, and whether in succeeding to the wealth and pomp of the religion of Rome, Protestantism had not become tainted with something of the languor of the old religion ? Had the progress of vigorous and sound thought been arrested by that fatal languor which accounted for the want of success of a great general of antiquity, who declared he had lost more at Capua than he gained at Cannæ ? How was it that the spirit of Protestantism had died out where it had been raised to honour and wealth, when it had formerly extended itself, in spite of opposition, over all the kingdoms of Europe ? He would not however pursue that painful theme. For himself, at least, he must say, that he did not conceive that there could be any marvellous advantage to the cause of Protestantism, by the retention of the sees which the Bill proposed to dispense with hereafter. If Protestantism depended upon sees, there would not be a Presbyterian in Ulster, nor a Catholic in Connaught. It was time that they should try new councils, and that they should remove the grievances of the Dissenters, and restore peace to Ireland, and its just and proper powers to the Protestant Church.

THE EAST-INDIA COMPANY'S CHARTER BILL.*

JULY 10, 1833.

HAVING, while this measure was in preparation, enjoyed the fullest and kindest confidence of my right hon. friend, agreeing with him completely in all those views which on a former occasion he so luminously and eloquently developed, having shared his anxieties, and feeling that, in some degree, I share his responsibility, I am naturally desirous to obtain the attention of the House while I attempt to defend the principles of this Bill. I wish that I could promise to be very brief; but the subject is so extensive that I will only promise to condense what I have to say as much as I can.

I rejoice, Sir, that I am completely dispensed, by the turn which our debates have taken, from the necessity of saying anything in favour of one part of our measure—the opening of the China trade. No voice, I believe, has yet been raised in Parliament to support the monopoly. On that subject all public men of all parties seem to be agreed. The resolution proposed by the Ministers has received the unanimous assent of both Houses, and the approbation of the whole kingdom. I will not, therefore, Sir, detain the House by vindicating a measure which no gentleman has yet ventured to attack, but will proceed to call your attention to those effects which this great commercial revolution necessarily produced on the system of Indian government and finance.

The China Trade is to be opened: reason requires this—public opinion requires it. The Government of the Duke of Wellington

* Hansard, 3d Series, vol. xix. p. 503–536.

felt the necessity as strongly as the Government of Lord Grey. No Minister, Whig or Tory, could have been found to propose a renewal of the monopoly; no parliament, reformed or unreformed, would have listened to such a proposal.—But though the opening of the trade was a matter concerning which the public had long made up its mind, the political consequences which necessarily follow from the opening of the trade, seem to me to be even now little understood. The language which I have heard in almost every circle where the subject was discussed was this: "Take away the monopoly, and leave the government of India to the Company:" a very short and convenient way of settling one of the most complicated questions that ever a Legislature had to consider. The hon. member for Sheffield, though not disposed to retain the Company as an organ of government, has repeatedly used language which proves that he shares in the general misconception. The fact is, that the abolition of the monopoly rendered it absolutely necessary to make a fundamental change in the constitution of that great Corporation.

The Company had united in itself two characters; the character of trader and the character of sovereign. Between the trader and the sovereign there was a long and complicated account, almost every item of which furnished matter for litigation. While the monopoly continued, indeed, litigation was averted. The effect of the monopoly was, to satisfy the claims both of commerce and of territory, at the expense of a third party—the English people; to secure on the one hand funds for the dividend of the stock-holder, and on the other hand, funds for the government of the Indian Empire, by means of a heavy tax on the tea consumed in this country. But when the third party would no longer bear this charge, all the great financial questions which had, at the cost of that third party, been kept in abeyance, were opened in an instant. The connexion between the Company in its mercantile capacity, and the same Company in its political capacity, was dissolved. The sovereign and the trader, from partners, became litigants. Even if the Company were permitted, as has been suggested, to govern India and at the same time to trade with China, it would make no advances from the profits of its Chinese trade for the support of its Indian government. It was in consideration of its exclusive privilege, that it had hitherto been required to make those advances;—it was by the exclusive privilege that it had been enabled to make them. When that privilege was taken away, it would be unreasonable in the Legislature to impose such an obligation, and impossible for the Company to fulfil it. The whole system of loans from commerce to territory, and repayments from territory to commerce, must cease. Each party must rest altogether on its own resources. It was, therefore, absolutely necessary to ascertain what resources each party possessed, to bring the long and intricate account between them to a close, and to assign to each a fair portion of assets and liabilities. There was vast property. How much of that property was applicable to purposes of state? How much was applicable to a dividend? There were debts to the amount of many millions. Which of these were the debts of the government that ruled at Calcutta? Which of the great mercantile house that brought tea at Canton? Were the creditors to look to the land revenues of India for their money; or were they entitled to put executions into the warehouses behind Bishopsgate-street?

There were two ways of settling these questions—adjudication, and compromise. The difficulties of adjudication were great—I think insuperable. Whatever acuteness and diligence could do, has been done. One person in particular whose talents and industry peculiarly fitted him for such investigations, and of whom I can never think without regret, Mr. Villiers, devoted himself to the examination with an ardour and a perseverance which, I believe, shortened a life most valuable to his country and to his friends. The assistance of the most skilful accountants has been called in. But the difficulties are such as no accountant, however skilful, could possibly remove. The difficulties are not arithmetical, but political. They arise from the constitution of the Company, from the long and intimate union of the commercial and imperial characters in one body. Suppose that a gentleman who is the treasurer of a charity, were to mix up the money which he receives on account of the charity with his own private rents and dividends, to pay the whole into his bank to his own private account, to draw it out again by checks in exactly the same form when he wants it for his private expenses, and when he wants it for the purposes of his public trust. Suppose that he were to continue to act thus till he was himself ignorant whether he were in advance or in arrear; and suppose that many years after his death a question were to arise whether his estate were in debt to the charity or the charity in debt to his estate. Such is the question which is now before us—with this important difference: that the accounts of an individual could not be in such a state unless he had been guilty of fraud, or of that *crassa negligentia* which is scarcely less culpable than fraud, and that the accounts of the Company were brought into this state by circumstances of a very peculiar kind—by circumstances unparalleled in the history of the world.

It is a mistake to suppose that the Company was a merely commercial body till the middle of the last century. Commerce was its object; but in order to enable it to pursue that object, it had been, like the other Indian Companies which were its rivals, like the Dutch India Company, like the French India Company, invested from a very early period with political functions. More than 120 years ago, it was in miniature precisely what it now is. It was intrusted with the very highest prerogatives of sovereignty. It had its forts and its white captains, and its black sepoys—it had its civil and criminal tribunals—it was authorised to proclaim Martial-law—it sent ambassadors to the native governments, and concluded treaties with them—it was Zemindar of several districts, and within those districts, like other Zemindars of the first class, it exercised the powers of a sovereign, even to the infliction of capital punishment on the Hindoos within its jurisdiction. It is incorrect, therefore, to say, that the Company was at first a mere trader, and has since become a sovereign. It was first a great trader and a petty prince. Its political functions at first attracted little notice, because they were merely auxiliary to its commercial functions. Soon, however, they became more and more important. The Zemindar became a great nabob, became sovereign of all India —the 200 sepoys became 200,000. This change was gradually wrought, and was not immediately comprehended. It was natural, that while the political functions of the Company were merely auxiliary to its commerce, its political accounts should be mixed up with its commercial accounts. It was equally natural, that when once this mode of keeping accounts had been commenced, it should go on; and the more so, as the change in the situation of the Company, though rapid, was not sudden. It is impossible to fix on any one day, or any one year, as the day or the year when the Company became a great potentate. It has been the fashion to fix on the year 1765, the year in which the Company received from the Mogul a Commission authorising them to administer the revenues of Bengal, Bahar, and Orissa, as the precise date of their sovereignty. I am utterly at a loss to understand why this period should be selected. Long before 1765 the Company had the reality of political power. Long before that year, they made a nabob of Arcot; they made and unmade nabobs of Bengal; they humbled the vizier of Oude; they braved the emperor of Hindostan himself. More than half the revenues of Bengal, as Lord Clive stated, were under one pretence or another administered by them. And after the grant, the Company was not, in form and name, an independent power. It was merely a minister of the Court of Delhi. Its coinage bore the name of Shah Alum. The inscription which, till the time of Lord Hastings, appeared on the seal of the Governor General, declared that great functionary to be the slave of the Mogul. Even to this day, we have never formally deposed the king of Delhi. The Company contents itself with being Mayor of the palace, while the *roi faineant* is suffered to play at being a sovereign. In fact, it was considered, both by Lord Clive and by Warren Hastings, as a point of policy to leave the character of the Company thus undefined, in order that the English might treat the princes in whose names they governed as realities or nonentities, just as might be most convenient.

Thus the transformation of the Company from a trading body, which possessed some sovereign prerogatives for the purposes of trade, into a sovereign body, the trade of which was auxiliary to its sovereignty, was effected by degrees, and under disguise. It is not strange, therefore, that its mercantile and political transactions should be entangled together in inextricable complication. The commercial investments had been purchased out of the revenues of the empire. The expenses of war and government had been defrayed out of the profits of the trade. Commerce and territory had contributed to the improvement of the same spot of land, to the repairs of the same building. Securities had been given in precisely the same form, for money which had been borrowed for purposes of State, and for money which had been borrowed for purposes of traffic. It is easy, indeed,—and this is a circumstance which has, I think, misled some Gentlemen,—it is easy to see what part of the assets of the Company appears in a commercial form, and what part appears in a political or territorial form. But this is not the question. Assets which are commercial in form, may be territorial as respects the right of property; assets which are territorial in form, may be commercial as respects the right of property. A chest of tea is not necessarily commercial property; it may have been bought out of the territorial revenue. A fort is not necessarily territorial property; it may stand on ground which the Company bought 100 years ago out of their commercial profits.

Adjudication, if by adjudication be meant decision according to some known rule of law, was out of the question. To leave matters like these to be determined by the ordinary maxims of our civil jurisprudence would have been the height of absurdity and injustice. For example, the home-bond debt of the Company, it is believed, was incurred partly for political, and partly for commercial purposes. But there is no evidence which would enable us to assign to each branch its proper share. The bonds all run in the same form; and a Court of Justice would, therefore, of course either lay the whole burthen on the proprietors, or lay the whole on the territory. We have legal opinions, very respectable legal opinions, to the effect, that in strictness of law, the territory is not responsible, and that the commercial assets are responsible for every farthing of the debts which were incurred for the government and defence of India. But, though this may be, and I believe, is law, it is, I am sure, neither reason nor justice. On the other hand, it is urged by the advocates of the Company, that some valuable portions of the territory are the property of that body in its commercial capacity; that Calcutta, for example, is their private estate, though they have, during many years, suffered its revenues to merge in the general revenues of their empire, that they hold the island of Bombay, in free and common socage, as of the Manor of East Greenwich. I will not pronounce any opinion on these points. I have considered them enough to see, that there is quite difficulty enough in them to exercise all the ingenuity of all the lawyers in the kingdom for twenty years. But the fact is, Sir, that the municipal law was not made for controversies of this description. The existence of such a body as this gigantic corporation—this political monster of two natures—subject in one hemisphere, sovereign in another—had never been contemplated by the Legislators or Judges of former ages. Nothing but grotesque absurdity and atrocious injustice could have been the effect, if the claims and liabilities of such a body had been settled according to the rules of Westminster Hall—if the maxims of conveyancers had been applied to the titles by which flourishing cities and provinces are held, or the maxims of the law-merchant to those promissory notes which are the securities for a great National Debt, raised for the purpose of exterminating the Pindarrees, and humbling the Burmese.

It was, as I have said, absolutely impossible to bring the question between commerce and territory to a satisfactory adjudication; and, I must add, that, even if the difficulties which I have mentioned could have been surmounted—even if there had been reason to hope that a satisfactory adjudication could have been obtained—I should still have wished to avoid that course. I think it desirable that the Company should continue to have a share in the government of India; and it would evidently have been impossible, pending a litigation between commerce and territory, to leave any political power to the Company. It would clearly have been the duty of those who were charged with the superintendence of India, to be the patrons of India throughout that momentous litigation, to scrutinize with the utmost severity, every claim which might be made on the Indian revenues, and to oppose, with energy and perseverance, every such claim, unless its justice were manifest. If the Company was to be engaged in a suit for many millions, in a suit which might last for many years, against the Indian territory, could we intrust the Company with the government of that territory? Could we put the plaintiff in the situation of *prochain ami* of the defendant? Could we appoint governors who would have had an interest opposed in the most direct manner to the interest of the governed, whose stock would have been raised in value by every decision which added to the burthens of their subjects, and depressed by every decision which diminished those burthens? It would be absurd to suppose that they would efficiently defend our Indian Empire against the claims which they were themselves bringing against it; and it would be equally absurd to give the government of the Indian empire at such a conjuncture to those who could not be trusted to defend it.

Seeing, then, that it was most difficult, if not wholly impossible, to resort to adjudication between commerce and territory—seeing, that if recourse were had to adjudication, it would be necessary to make a complete revolution in the whole constitution of India—the Government proposed a compromise. That compromise, with some modifications which did not, in the slightest degree, affect its principle, and which, while they gave satisfaction to the Company, will eventually lay no additional burthen on the territory, has been accepted. It has, like all other compromises, been loudly censured by violent partisans on both sides. It has been represented by some as far too favourable to the Company, and by others as most unjust to the Company. Sir, I own that we cannot prove that either of these accusations is unfounded. It is of the very essence of our case that we should not be able to show, that we have assigned, either to commerce or to territory, its precise due. For our principal reason for recommending a compromise was our full conviction that it was absolutely impossible to ascertain with precision what was due to commerce, and what was due to territory. It is not strange that some people should accuse us of robbing the Company, and others of conferring a vast boon on the Company, at the expense of India: for we have proposed a middle course, on the very ground that there was a chance of a result much more favourable to the Company than our arrangement, and a chance also of a result much less favourable. If the questions pending between the Company and India had been decided as the ardent supporters of the Company predicted, India would, if I calculate rightly, have paid eleven millions more than she will now have to pay. If those questions had been decided, as some violent enemies of the Company predicted, that great body would have been utterly ruined. The very meaning of compromise is, that each party gives up his chance of complete success, in order to be secured against the chance of utter failure. And as men of sanguine minds always overrate the chances in their own favour, every fair compromise is sure to be severely censured on both sides. I contend, that in a case so dark and complicated as this, the compromise which we recommend is sufficiently vindicated, if it cannot be proved to be unfair. We are not bound to prove it to be fair. For it would have been unnecessary for us to resort to compromise at all, if we had been in possession of evidence which would have enabled us to pronounce, with certainty, what claims were fair, and what were unfair. It seems to me that we have acted with due consideration for every party. The dividend which we give to the proprietors is precisely the same dividend which they have been receiving for forty years, and which they have expected to receive permanently. The price of their stock bears at present the same proportion to the price of other stock which it bore four or five years ago, before the anxiety and excitement which a negotiation for a renewal of their Charter naturally produces, had begun to operate. As to the territory on the other hand, it is true, that if the assets which are now in a commercial form, should not produce a fund sufficient to pay the debts and dividend of the Company, the territory must stand to the loss, and pay the difference. But in return for taking this risk, the territory obtains an immediate release from claims to the amount of many millions. I certainly do not believe that all those claims could have been substantiated; but I know that very able men think differently. And suppose that only one-fourth of the sum demanded had been awarded to the Company, India would have lost more than the largest sum which, as it seems to me, she can possibly lose under the arrangement.

In a pecuniary point of view, therefore, I conceive that we can defend the measure as it affects the territory. But to the territory, the pecuniary question is of secondary importance. If we have made a good pecuniary bargain for India, but a bad political bargain—if we have saved three or four millions to the finances of that country, and given to it, at the same time, pernicious institutions, we shall, indeed, have been practising a most ruinous parsimony. If, on the other hand, it shall be found that we have added fifty or a hundred thousand pounds a-year to the expenditure of an empire which yields a revenue of twenty millions, but that we have at the same time secured to that empire, as far as in us lies, the blessings of good government, we shall have no reason to be ashamed of our profusion. I hope and believe that India will have to pay nothing. But on the most unfavourable supposition that can be made, she will not have to pay so much to the Company, as she now pays annually to a single state pageant—to the titular Nabob of Bengal, for example, or the titular King of Delhi. What she pays to these nominal princes, who, while they did anything, did mischief, and who now do nothing, she may well submit to pay to her real rulers, if she receives from them, in return, efficient protection, and good legislation.

We come then to the great question. Is it desirable to retain the Company as an organ of government for India? I think that it is desirable. The question is, I acknowledge, beset with difficulties. We have to solve one of the hardest problems in politics. We are trying to make brick without straw—to bring a clean thing out of an unclean—to give a good government to a people to whom we cannot give a free government. In this country—in any neighbouring country—it is easy to frame securities against oppression. In Europe, you have the materials of good government every where ready to your hands. The people are every where perfectly competent to hold some share,—not in every country an equal share—but some share of political power. If the question were, what is the best mode of securing good government in Europe, the merest smatterer in politics would answer—representative institutions. In India, you cannot have representative institutions. Of all the innumerable speculators who have offered their suggestions on Indian politics, not a single one, as far as I know, however democratical his opinions may be, has ever maintained the possibility of giving, at the present time, such institutions to India. One gentleman, extremely well acquainted with the affairs of our Eastern Empire, a most valuable servant of the Company, and the author of a History of India, which, though certainly not free from faults, is, I think, on the whole, the greatest historical work which has appeared in our language since that of Gibbon—I mean Mr. Mill—was examined on this point. That gentleman is well known to be a very bold and uncompromising politician. He has written strongly—far too strongly, I think, in favour of pure democracy. He has gone so far as to maintain, that no nation which has not a representative legislature, chosen by universal suffrage, enjoys security against oppression. But when he was asked before the Committee of last year, whether he thought representative government practicable in India, his answer was—"utterly out of the question." This, then, is the state in which we are. We have to frame a good government for a country into which, by universal acknowledgment, we cannot introduce those institutions which all our habits—which all the reasonings of European philosophers—which all the history of our own part of the world would lead us to consider as the one great security for good government. We have to engraft on despotism those blessings which are the natural fruits of liberty. In these circumstances, Sir, it behoves us to be cautious, even to the verge of timidity. The light of political science and of history are withdrawn—we are walking in darkness—we do not distinctly see whither we are going. It is the wisdom of a man, so situated, to feel his way, and not to plant his foot till he is well assured that the ground before him is firm.

Some things, however, in the midst of this obscurity, I can see with clearness. I can see, for example, that it is desirable that the authority exercised in this country over the Indian government should be divided between two bodies—between a minister on a board appointed by the Crown, and some other body independent of the Crown. If India is to be a dependency of England—to be at war with our enemies—to be at peace with our allies—to be protected by the English navy from maritime aggression—to have a portion of the English army mixed with its sepoys—it plainly follows, that the King, to whom the Constitution gives the direction of foreign affairs, and the command of the military and naval forces, ought to have a share in the direction of the Indian government. Yet, on the other hand, that a revenue of twenty millions a year—an army of two hundred thousand men—a civil service abounding with lucrative situations—should be left to the disposal of the Crown without any check whatever, is what no minister, I conceive, would venture to propose. This House is indeed the check provided by the Constitution on the abuse of the Royal prerogative. But that this House is, or is likely ever to be, an efficient check on abuses practised in India, I altogether deny. We have, as I believe we all feel, quite business enough. If we were to undertake the task of looking into Indian affairs as we look into British affairs—if we were to have Indian budgets and Indian estimates—if we were to go into the Indian currency question and the Indian Bank Charter—if to our disputes about Belgium and Holland, Don Pedro and Don Miguel, were to be added disputes about the debts of the Guicowar and the disorders of Mysore, the ex-king of the Afghans and the Maha-rajah Runjeet Sing—if we were to have one night occupied by the embezzlements of the Benares mint, and another by the panic in the Calcutta money-market—if the questions of Suttee or no Suttee, Pilgrim tax or no Pilgrim tax, Ryotwary or Zemindary, half Batta or whole Batta, were to be debated at the same length at which we have debated Church reform and the assessed taxes, twenty-four hours a day and three hundred and sixty-five days a year would be too short a time for the discharge of our duties. The House, it is plain, has not the necessary time to settle these matters; nor has it the necessary knowledge, nor has it the motives to acquire that knowledge. The late change in its constitution has made it, I believe, a much more faithful representation of the English people. But it is far as ever from being a representation of the Indian people. A broken head in Cold Bath Fields produces a greater sensation among us than three pitched battles in India. A few weeks ago we had to decide on a claim brought by an individual against the revenues of India. If it had been an English question the walls would scarcely have held the Members who would have flocked to the division. It was an Indian question; and we could scarcely by dint of supplication make a House. Even when my right hon. friend, the President of the Board of Control, made his most able and interesting statement of the measures which he intended to propose for the government of a hundred millions of human beings, the attendance was not so large as I have seen it on a turnpike-bill or a railroad bill.

I then take these things as proved, that the Crown must have a certain authority over India, that there must be an efficient check on the authority of the Crown, and that the House of Commons is not an efficient check. We must then find some other body to perform that important office. We have such a body—the Company. Shall we discard it?

It is true that the power of the Company is an anomaly in politics. It is strange—very strange—that a Joint-stock society of traders—a society, the shares of which are daily passed from hand to hand—a society, the component parts of which are perpetually changing—a society, which, judging *à priori* from its constitution, we should have said was as little fitted for imperial functions as the Merchant Tailors' Company or the New River Company—should be intrusted with the sovereignty of a larger population, the disposal of a larger clear revenue, the command of a larger army, than are under the direct management of the

Executive Government of the United Kingdom. But what constitution can we give to our Indian Empire which shall not be strange—which shall not be anomalous? That Empire is itself the strangest of all political anomalies. That a handful of adventurers from an island in the Atlantic should have subjugated a vast country divided from the place of their birth by half the globe—a country which at no very distant period was merely the subject of fable to the nations of Europe—a country never before violated by the most renowned of Western Conquerors—a country which Trajan never entered—a country lying beyond the point where the phalanx of Alexander refused to proceed;—that we should govern a territory 10,000 miles from us—a territory larger and more populous than France, Spain, Italy, and Germany put together—a territory, the present clear revenue of which exceeds the present clear revenue of any state in the world, France excepted—a territory, inhabited by men, differing from us in race, colour, language, manners, morals, religion;—these are prodigies to which the world has seen nothing similar. Reason is confounded. We interrogate the past in vain. General rules are almost useless where the whole is one vast exception. The Company is an anomaly; but it is part of a system where every thing is anomaly. It is the strangest of all governments: but it is designed for the strangest of all Empires.

If we discard the Company, we must find a substitute: and, take what substitute we may, we shall find ourselves unable to give any reason for believing that the body which we have put in the room of the Company is likely to acquit itself of its duties better than the Company. Commissioners appointed by the King during pleasure would be no check on the Crown; Commissioners appointed by the King or by Parliament for life, would always be appointed by the political party which might be uppermost, and if a change of Administration took place, would harass the new Government with the most vexatious opposition. The plan suggested by the right honourable Gentleman the member for Montgomeryshire, is I think the very worst that I have ever heard. He would have Directors nominated every four years by the Crown. Is it not plain that these Directors would always be appointed from among the supporters of the Ministry for the time being—that their situations would depend on the permanence of that Ministry—that therefore all their power and patronage would be employed for the purpose of propping that Ministry, and, in case of a change, for the purpose of molesting those who might succeed to power—that they would be subservient while their friends were in, and factious when their friends were out? How would Lord Grey's Ministry have been situated if the whole body of Directors had been nominated by the Duke of Wellington in 1830? I mean no imputation on the Duke of Wellington. If the present Ministers had to nominate Directors for four years, they would, I have no doubt, nominate men who would give no small trouble to the Duke of Wellington if he were to return to office. What we want is a body independent of the Government, and no more than independent—not a tool of the Treasury—not a tool of the opposition. No new plan which I have heard proposed would give us such a body. The Company, strange as its constitution may be, is such a body. It is, as a corporation, neither Whig nor Tory, neither high-church nor low-church. It cannot be charged with having been for or against the Catholic Bill, for or against the Reform Bill. It has constantly acted with a view, not to English politics but to Indian politics. We have seen the country convulsed by faction. We have seen Ministers driven from office by this House—Parliament dissolved in anger—general elections of unprecedented turbulence—debates of unprecedented interest. We have seen the two branches of the Legislature placed in direct opposition to each other. We have seen the advisers of the Crown dismissed one day, and brought back the next day on the shoulders of the people. And amidst all these agitating events the Company has preserved strict and unsuspected neutrality. This is, I think, an inestimable advantage; and it is an advantage which we must altogether forego, if we consent to adopt any of the schemes which I have heard proposed on the other side of the House.

We must judge of the Indian government, as of all other governments, by its practical effects. According to the hon. member for Sheffield, India is ill governed; and the whole fault is with the Company. Innumerable accusations, great and small, are brought by him against their administration. They are fond of war. They are fond of dominion. The taxation is burthensome. The laws are undigested. The roads are rough. The post goes on foot. And for everything the Company is answerable. From the dethronement of the Mogul princes to the mishaps of Sir Charles Metcalfe's courier, every disaster that has taken place in the East during sixty years is laid to the charge of this unfortunate Corporation. And the inference is, that all the power which they possess ought to be taken out of their hands, and transferred at once to the Crown.

Now, Sir, it seems to me that for all the evils which the honourable Gentleman has so pathetically recounted, the Ministers of the Crown are as much to blame as the Company—nay, much more so. For the Board of Control could, without the consent of the Directors, have redressed those evils; and the Directors most certainly could not have redressed them without the consent of the Board of Control. Take the case of that frightful grievance which seems to have made the deepest impression on the mind of the hon. Gentleman—the slowness of the mail. Why, Sir, if my right hon. friend, the President of our Board, thought fit, he might direct me to write to the Court and require them to frame a dispatch on that subject. If the Court disobeyed, he might himself frame a dispatch ordering Lord William Bentinck to put the dawks all over Bengal on horseback. If the Court refused to send out this dispatch, the Board could apply to the King's Bench for a mandamus. If, on the other hand, the Directors wished to accelerate the journeys of the mail, and the Board were adverse to the project, the Directors could do nothing at all. For all measures of internal policy the servants of the King are at least as deeply responsible as the Company. For all measures of foreign policy the servants of the King, and they alone, are responsible. I was surprised to hear the hon. Gentleman accuse the Directors of insatiable ambition and rapacity, when he must know that no act of aggression on any native state can be committed by the Company without the sanction of the Board, and that, in fact, the Board has repeatedly approved of warlike measures, which were strenuously opposed by the Company. He must know, in particular, that, during the energetic and splendid Administration of the Marquess Wellesley, the Company was all for peace, and the Board all for conquest. If a line of conduct which the hon. Gentleman thinks unjustifiable, has been followed by the Ministers of the Crown in spite of the remonstrances of the Directors, this is surely a strange reason for turning off the Directors, and giving the whole power unchecked to the Crown.

The hon. Member tells us that India, under the present system, is not so rich and flourishing as she was 200 years ago. Really, Sir, I doubt whether we are in possession of sufficient data to enable us to form a judgment on that point. But the matter is of little importance. We ought to compare India under our Government, not with India under Acbar and his immediate successors, but with India as we found it. The calamities through which that country passed during the interval between the fall of the Mogul power and the establishment of the English supremacy were sufficient to throw the people back whole centuries. It would surely be unjust to say, that Alfred was a bad king because Britain, under his government, was not so rich or so civilized as in the time of the Romans.

In what state, then, did we find India? And what have we

made India? We found society throughout that vast country in a state to which history scarcely furnishes a parallel. The nearest parallel would perhaps be the state of Europe during the fifth century. The Mogul empire in the time of the successors of Aurungzebe, like the Roman empire in the time of the successors of Theodosius, was sinking under the vices of its internal administration, and under the assaults of barbarous invaders. At Delhi, as at Ravenna, there was a mock sovereign, a mere pageant immured in a gorgeous state prison. He was suffered to indulge in every sensual pleasure. He was adored with servile prostrations. He assumed and bestowed the most magnificent titles. But, in fact, he was a mere puppet in the hands of some ambitious subject. While the Honorii and Augustuli of the East, surrounded by their fawning eunuchs, revelled and dozed without knowing or caring what might pass beyond the walls of their palace gardens, the provinces had ceased to respect a government which could neither punish nor protect them. Society was a chaos. Its restless and shifting elements formed themselves every moment into some new combination, which the next moment dissolved. In the course of a single generation a hundred dynasties grew up, flourished, decayed, were extinguished, were forgotten. Every adventurer who could muster a troop of horse might aspire to a throne. Every palace was every year the scene of conspiracies, treasons, revolutions, parricides. Meanwhile a rapid succession of Alarics and Attilas passed over the defenceless empire. A Persian invader penetrated to Delhi, and carried back in triumph the most precious treasures of the House of Tamerlane. The Afghan soon followed, by the same track, to glean whatever the Persian had spared. The Jauts established themselves on the Jumna. The Seiks devastated Lahore. Every part of India, from Tanjore to the Himalayas, was laid under contribution by the Mahrattas. The people were ground down to the dust by the oppressor without and the oppressor within; by the robber from whom the Nabob was unable to protect them, by the Nabob who took whatever the robber had left to them. All the evils of despotism, and all the evils of anarchy, pressed at once on that miserable race. They knew nothing of government but its exactions. Desolation was in their imperial cities, and famine all along the banks of their broad and redundant rivers. It seemed that a few more years would suffice to efface all traces of the opulence and civilization of an earlier age.

Such was the state of India when the Company began to take part in the disputes of its ephemeral sovereigns. About eighty years have elapsed since we appeared as auxiliaries in a contest between two rival families for the sovereignty of a small corner of the Peninsula. From that moment commenced a great, a stupendous process—the reconstruction of a decomposed society. Two generations have passed away; and the process is complete. The scattered fragments of the empire of Aurungzebe have been united in an empire stronger and more closely knit together than that which Aurungzebe ruled. The power of the new sovereigns penetrates their dominions more completely, and is far more implicitly obeyed, than was that of the proudest princes of the Mogul dynasty.

It is true, that the early history of this great revolution is chequered with guilt and shame. It is true that the founders of our Indian empire too often abused the strength which they derived from superior energy and superior knowledge. It is true that with some of the highest qualities of the race from which they sprang, they combined some of the worst defects of the race over which they ruled. How should it have been otherwise? Born in humble stations, accustomed to earn a slender maintenance by obscure industry, they found themselves transformed in a few months from clerks drudging over desks, or captains in marching regiments, into statesmen and generals, with armies at their command, with the revenues of kingdoms at their disposal, with power to make and depose sovereigns at their pleasure. They were what it was natural that men should be who had been raised by so rapid an ascent to so dizzy an eminence, profuse and rapacious, imperious and corrupt.

It is true, then, that there was too much foundation for the representations of those satirists and dramatists who held up the character of the English Nabob to the derision and hatred of a former generation. It is true that some disgraceful intrigues, some unjust and cruel wars, some instances of odious perfidy and avarice stain the annals of our Eastern empire. It is true that the duties of government and legislation were long wholly neglected or carelessly performed. It is true that when the new rulers at length began to apply themselves in earnest to the discharge of their high functions, they committed the errors natural to rulers who were but imperfectly acquainted with the language and manners of their subjects. It is true that some measures, which were dictated by the purest and most benevolent feelings, have not been attended by the desired success. It is true that India suffers to this day from a heavy burthen of taxation, and from a defective system of law. It is true, I fear, that in those states which are connected with us by subsidiary alliance, all the evils of oriental despotism have too frequently shown themselves in their most loathsome and destructive form.

All this is true. Yet in the history and in the present state of our Indian empire I see ample reason for exultation and for a good hope.

I see that we have established order where we found confusion. I see that the petty dynasties which were generated by the corruption of the great Mahometan empire, and which, a century ago, kept all India in constant agitation, have been quelled by one overwhelming power. I see that the predatory tribes who, in the middle of the last century, passed annually over the harvests of India with the destructive rapidity of a hurricane, have quailed before the valour of a braver and sterner race—have been vanquished, scattered, hunted to their strongholds, and either exterminated by the English sword, or compelled to exchange the pursuits of rapine for those of industry.

I look back for many years; and I see scarcely a trace of the vices which blemished the splendid fame of the first conquerors of Bengal. I see peace studiously preserved. I see faith inviolably maintained towards feeble and dependent states. I see confidence gradually infused into the minds of suspicious neighbours. I see the horrors of war mitigated by the chivalrous and Christian spirit of Europe. I see examples of moderation and clemency, such as I should seek in vain in the annals of any other victorious and dominant nation. I see captive tyrants, whose treachery and cruelty might have excused a severe retribution, living in security, comfort, and dignity, under the protection of the government which they laboured to destroy.

I see a large body of civil and military functionaries resembling in nothing but capacity and valour those adventurers who seventy years ago came hither, laden with wealth and infamy, to parade before our fathers the plundered treasures of Bengal and Tanjore. I reflect with pride that to the doubtful splendour which surrounds the memory of Hastings and of Clive, we can oppose the spotless glory of Elphinstone and Monro. I observe with reverence and delight the honourable poverty which is the evidence of a rectitude firmly maintained amidst strong temptations. I rejoice to see my countrymen, after ruling millions of subjects, after commanding victorious armies, after dictating terms of peace at the gates of hostile capitals, after administering the revenues of great provinces, after judging the causes of wealthy Zemindars, after residing at the Courts of tributary Kings, return to their native land with no more than a decent competence.

I see a government anxiously bent on the public good. Even in its errors I recognise a paternal feeling towards the great people committed to its charge. I see toleration strictly maintained. Yet I see bloody and degrading superstitions gradually losing their power. I see the morality, the philosophy, the taste of Europe, beginning to produce a salutary effect on the hearts and understandings of our subjects. I see the public mind of India, that public mind which we found debased and contracted by the worst forms of political and religious tyranny, expanding itself to just and noble views of the ends of government and of the social duties of man.

I see evils: but I see the government actively employed in the work of remedying those evils. The taxation is heavy; but the work of retrenchment is unsparingly pursued. The mischiefs arising from the system of subsidiary alliance are great: but the rulers of India are fully aware of those mischiefs, and are engaged in guarding against them. Wherever they now interfere for the purpose of supporting a native government, they interfere also for the purpose of reforming it.

Seeing these things, then, am I prepared to discard the Company as an organ of government? I am not. Assuredly I will never shrink from innovation where I see reason to believe that innovation will be improvement. That the present Government does not shrink ftom innovations which it considers as improvements, the measure now before the House sufficiently shows. But surely the burthen of the proof lies on the innovators. They are bound to lay some ground; to show that there is a fair probability of obtaining some advantage before they call upon us to take up the foundations of the Indian government. I have no superstitious veneration for the Court of Directors or the Court of Proprietors. Find me a better Council: find me a better constituent body: and I am ready for a change. But of all the substitutes for the Company which have hitherto been suggested, not one has been proved to be better than the Company; and most of them I could, I think, easily prove to be worse. Circumstances might force us to hazard a change. If the Company were to refuse to accept of the government unless we would grant pecuniary terms which I thought extravagant, or unless we gave up the clauses in this Bill which permit Europeans to hold landed property, and natives to hold office, I would take them at their word. But I will not discard them in the mere rage of experiment.

Do I call the government of India a perfect government? Very far from it. No nation can be perfectly well governed till it is competent to govern itself. I compare the Indian government with other governments of the same class, with despotisms, with military despotisms, with foreign military despotisms; and I find none that approaches it in excellence. I compare it with the government of the Roman provinces—with the government of the Spanish colonies—and I am proud of my country and my age. Here are a hundred millions of people under the absolute rule of a few strangers, differing from them physically—differing from them morally—mere Mamelukes, not born in the country which they rule, not meaning to lay their bones in it. If you require me to make this government as good as that of England, France, or the United States of America, I own frankly that I can do no such thing. Reasoning *à priori*, I should have come to the conclusion that such a government must be a horrible tyranny. It is a source of constant amazement to me that it is so good as I find it to be. I will not, therefore, in a case in which I have neither principles nor precedents to guide me, pull down the existing system on account of its theoretical defects. For I know that any system which I could put in its place would be equally condemned by theory, while it would not be equally sanctioned by experience.

Some change in the constitution of the Company was, as I have shown, rendered inevitable by the opening of the China Trade; and it was the duty of the Government to take care that the change should not be prejudicial to India. There were many ways in which the compromise between commerce and territory might have been affected. We might have taken the assets, and paid a sum down, leaving the Company to invest that sum as they chose. We might have offered English security with a lower interest. We might have taken the course which the late Government designed to take. We might have left the Company in possession of the means of carrying on its trade in competition with private merchants. My firm belief is, that, if this course had been taken, the Company must, in a very few years, have abandoned the trade or the trade would have ruined the Company. It was not, however, solely or principally by regard for the interest of the Company, or of the English merchants generally, that the Government was guided on this occasion. The course which appeared to us the most likely to promote the interests of our Eastern Empire was to make the proprietors of India stock creditors of the Indian territory. Their interest will thus be in a great measure the same with the interest of the people whom they are to rule. Their income will depend on the revenues of their empire. The revenues of their empire will depend on the manner in which the affairs of that empire are administered. We furnish them with the strongest motives to watch over the interests of the cultivator and the trader, to maintain peace, to carry on with vigour the work of retrenchment, to detect and punish extortion and corruption. Though they live at a distance from India—though few of them have ever seen or may ever see the people whom they rule—they will have a great stake in the happiness of their subjects. If their misgovernment should produce disorder in the finances, they will themselves feel the effects of that disorder in their own household expenses. I believe this to be, next to a representative constitution, the constitution which is the best security for good government. A representative constitution India cannot at present have. And we have, therefore, I think, given her the best constitution of which she is capable.

One word as to the new arrangement which we propose with respect to the patronage. It is intended to introduce the principle of competition in the disposal of writerships; and from this change I cannot but anticipate the happiest results. The civil servants of the Company are undoubtedly a highly respectable body of men; and, in that body, as in every large body, there are some persons of very eminent ability. I rejoice most cordially to see this. I rejoice to see that the standard of morality is so high in England, that intelligence is so generally diffused through England, that young persons who are taken from the mass of society, by favour and not by merit, and who are therefore only fair samples of the mass, should, when placed in situations of high importance, be so seldom found wanting. But it is not the less true, that India is entitled to the service of the best talents which England can spare. That the average of intelligence and virtue is very high in this country, is matter for honest exultation. But it is no reason for employing average men where you can obtain superior men. Consider too, Sir, how rapidly the public mind of India is advancing, how much attention is already paid by the higher classes of the natives to those intellectual pursuits on the cultivation of which the superiority of the European race to the rest of mankind principally depends. Surely, under such circumstances, from motives of selfish policy, if from no higher motive, we ought to fill the Magistracies of our Eastern Empire with men who may do honour to their country—with men who may represent the best part of the English nation. This, Sir, is our object; and we believe, that by the plan which is now proposed this object will be attained. It is proposed that for every vacancy in the civil service four candidates shall be named, and the best candidate elected by examination. We conceive that, under this system, the persons sent out will be young men above par—young men superior either in talents or in diligence to the mass. It is said, I know, that examinations in Latin, in Greek, and in mathematics, are no tests of what men will prove to be in life. I am perfectly aware, that they are not infallible tests; but that they are tests I confidently maintain. Look at every walk of life—at this House—at the other House—at the Bar—at the Bench—at the Church—and see whether it be not true, that those who attain high distinction in the world are generally men who were distinguished in their academic career. Indeed, Sir, this objection would prove far too much even for those who use it. It would prove, that there is no use at all in education. Why should we put boys out of their way? Why should we force a lad, who would much rather fly a kite or trundle a hoop, to learn his Latin Grammar? Why should we keep a young man to his Thucydides or his Laplace, when he would much rather be shooting? Education would be mere useless torture, if, at two or three and twenty, a man who has neglected his studies were exactly on a par with a man who has applied himself to them—exactly as likely to perform all the offices of public life with credit to himself and with advantage to society. Whether the English system of education be good or bad is not now the question. Perhaps I may think that too much time is given to the ancient languages and to the abstract sciences. But what then? Whatever be the languages—whatever be the sciences, which it is, in any age or country, the fashion to teach, those who become the greatest proficients in those languages and those sciences, will generally be the flower of the youth—the most acute—the most industrious—the most ambitious of honourable distinctions. If the Ptolemaic system were taught at Cambridge, instead of the Newtonian, the senior wrangler would nevertheless be in general a superior man to the wooden spoon. If, instead of learning Greek, we learned the Cherokee, the man who understood the Cherokee best, who made the most correct and melodious Cherokee verses—who comprehended most accurately the effect of the Cherokee particles—would generally be a superior man to him who was destitute of these accomplishments. If astrology were taught at our Universities, the young man who cast nativities best would generally turn out a superior man. If alchymy were taught, the young man who showed most activity in the pursuit of the philosopher's stone, would generally turn out a superior man.

I will only add one other observation on this subject. Although I am inclined to think that too much attention is paid in the education of English gentlemen to the dead languages, I conceive, that when you are choosing young men to fill situations for which the very first and most indispensable qualification is familiarity with foreign languages, it would be difficult to find a better test of their fitness than their classical acquirements.

Some persons have expressed doubts as to the possibility of procuring fair examinations. I am quite sure, that no person who has been either at Cambridge or at Oxford can entertain such doubts. I feel, indeed, that I ought to apologize for even noticing an objection so frivolous.

Next to the opening of the China trade, the change most eagerly demanded by the English people was, that the restrictions on the admission of Europeans to India should be removed. In this measure, there are undoubtedly very great advantages. The chief advantage is, I think, the improvement which the minds of our native subjects may be expected to derive from free intercourse with a people far advanced beyond themselves in intellectual cultivation. I cannot deny, however, that the advantages of this great change are attended with some danger.

The danger is that the new comers, belonging to the ruling nation, resembling in colour, in language, in manners, those who hold supreme military and political power, and differing in all these respects from the great mass of the population, may consider themselves as a superior class, and may trample on the indigenous race. Hitherto there have been strong restraints on Europeans resident in India. Licences were not easily obtained. Those residents who were in the service of the Company had obvious motives for conducting themselves with propriety. If they incurred the serious displeasure of the Government, their hopes of promotion were blighted. Even those who were not in the public service, were subject to the formidable power which the Government possessed of banishing them at its pleasure.

The licence of the Government will now no longer be necessary to persons who desire to reside in the settled provinces of India. The power of arbitrary deportation is withdrawn. Unless, therefore, we mean to leave the natives exposed to the tyranny and insolence of every profligate adventurer who may visit the East, we must place the European under the same power which legislates for the Hindoo. No man loves political freedom more than I. But a privilege enjoyed by a few individuals in the midst of a vast population who do not enjoy it, ought not to be called freedom. It is tyranny. In the West Indies I have not the least doubt that the existence of the Trial by Jury and of Legislative Assemblies, has tended to make the condition of the slaves worse than it would otherwise have been. Or, to go to India itself for an instance, though I fully believe that a mild penal code is better than a severe penal code, the worst of all systems was surely that of having a mild code for the Brahmins, who sprang from the head of the Creator, while there was a severe code for the Sudras, who sprang from his feet. India has suffered enough already from the distinction of castes, and from the deeply rooted prejudices which those distinctions have engendered. God forbid that we should inflict on her the curse of a new caste, that we should send her a new breed of Brahmins, authorized to treat all the native population as Parihas.

With a view to the prevention of this evil, we propose to give to the supreme government the power of legislating for Europeans as well as for natives. We propose that the regulations of the Government shall bind the King's Court as they bind all other Courts, and that registration by the Judges of the King's Court shall no longer be necessary to give validity to those regulations within the towns of Calcutta, Madras, and Bombay.

I could scarcely, Sir, believe my ears when I heard this part of our plan condemned in another place. I should have thought, that it would have been received with peculiar favour in that quarter where it has met with the most severe condemnation. What, at present, is the case? If the Supreme Court and the Government differ on a question of jurisdiction, or of legislation within the towns which are the seats of Government, there is absolutely no umpire but the Imperial Parliament. The device of putting one wild elephant between two tame ones was ingenious; but it may not always be practicable. Suppose a tame elephant between two wild ones, or suppose, that the whole herd should run wild together. The thing is not without example. And is it not most unjust and ridiculous that on one side of a ditch the edict of the Governor General should have the force of law, and that on the other side it should be of no effect unless registered by the Judges of the Supreme Court? If the registration be a security for good legislation, we are bound to give that security to all classes of our subjects. If the registration be not a security for good legislation, why require it? Why give it to a million of them, and withhold it from the other ninety-nine millions? Is the system good? Extend it. Is it bad? Abolish it. But in the name of common sense do not leave it as it is. It is as absurd as our old law of sanctuary. The system of imprisonment for debt may be good or bad. But no man in his senses can approve of the ancient system under which a debtor who might be arrested in Fleet Street was safe as soon as he had scampered into Whitefriars. Just in the same way, doubts may fairly be entertained about the expediency of allowing four or five persons to make laws for India; but to allow them to make laws for all India without the Mahratta ditch, and to except Calcutta, is the height of absurdity.

I say, therefore, either enlarge the power of the Supreme Court and give it a general veto on laws, or enlarge the power of the Government, and make its regulations binding on all Courts without distinction. The former course no person has ventured to propose. To the latter course objections have been made,—but objections which to me, I must own, seem altogether frivolous. It is acknowledged, that of late years inconvenience has arisen from the relation in which the Supreme Court stands to the Government.

But, it is said, that Court was originally instituted for the protection of natives against Europeans. The wise course would, therefore, be to restore its original character.

Now, Sir, the fact is, that the Supreme Court has never been so mischievous as during the first ten years of its power, or so respectable as it has lately been. Every body who knows anything of its early history knows, that for a considerable time after its institution, it was the terror of Bengal, the scourge of native informants, the screen of European delinquents, a convenient tool of the government for all purposes of evil, an insurmountable obstacle to the Government in all undertakings for the public good;—that its proceedings were made up of pedantry, cruelty, and corruption;—that its disputes with the Government were at one time on the point of breaking up the whole fabric of society; and that a convulsion was averted only by the dexterous policy of Warren Hastings, who at last bought off the opposition of the Chief Justice for £8,000 a-year. It is notorious, that while the Supreme Court opposed Hastings in all his best measures, it was a thorough-going accomplice in his worst—that it took part in the most scandalous of those proceedings which fifty years ago roused the indignation of Parliament and of the country—that it assisted in the spoliation of the princesses of Oude—that it passed sentence of death on Nuncomar. And this is the Court which we are to restore from its present state of degeneracy to its original purity. This is the protection which we are to give to the natives against the Europeans. Sir, so far is it from being true that the character of the Supreme Court has deteriorated, that it has, perhaps, improved more than any other institution in India. But the evil lies deep in the nature of the institution itself. The Judges have in our time deserved the greatest respect. Their judgment and integrity have done much to mitigate the vices of the system. The worst charge that can be brought against any of them is that of pertinacity—disinterested, conscientious, pertinacity—in error. The real evil is in the state of the law. You have two supreme powers in India. There is no arbitrator except a Legislature ten thousand miles off. Such a system is in the face of it an absurdity in politics. My wonder is, not that this system has several times been on the point of producing fatal consequences to the peace and resources of India,—these, I think, are the words in which Warren Hastings describes the effect of the contest between his Government and the Judges—but that it has not actually produced such consequences. The most distinguished members of the Indian Government—the most distinguished Judges of the Supreme Court—call upon you to reform this system. Sir Charles Metcalfe, Sir Charles Grey, represent with equal urgency the expediency of having one single paramount council armed with legislative power. The admission of Europeans to India renders it absolutely necessary not to delay our decision. The effect of that admission would be to raise a hundred questions—to produce a hundred contests between the council and the judicature. The Government would be paralysed at the precise moment at which all its energy was required. While the two equal powers were acting in opposite directions, the whole machine of the state would stand still. The Europeans would be uncontrolled; the natives would be unprotected. The consequences I will not pretend to foresee. Every thing beyond is darkness and confusion.

Having given to the Government supreme legislative power, we next propose to give to it for a time the assistance of a Commission for the purpose of digesting and reforming the laws of India, so that those laws may, as soon as possible, be formed into a code. Gentlemen of whom I wish to speak with the highest respect, have expressed a doubt whether India be at present in a fit state to receive a benefit which is not yet enjoyed by this free and highly civilized country. Sir, I can allow to this argument very little weight beyond that which it derives from the personal authority of those who use it. For, in the first place, our freedom and our high civilization render this improvement, desirable as it must always be, less indispensably necessary to us than to our Indian subjects: and in the next place our freedom and civilization, I fear, render it far more difficult for us to obtain this benefit for ourselves than to bestow it on them.

I believe that no country ever stood so much in need of a code of laws as India, and I believe also that there never was a country in which the want might so easily be supplied. I said, that there were many points of analogy between the state of that country after the fall of the Mogul power, and the state of Europe after the fall of the Roman empire. In one respect the analogy is very striking. As in Europe then, so in India now, there are several systems of law widely differing from each other, but co-existing and co-equal. The indigenous population has its own laws. Each of the successive races of conquerors has brought with it its own peculiar jurisprudence: the Mussulman his Koran and its innumerable commentators—the Englishman his Statute-Book, and his Term Reports. As there were established in Italy, at one and the same time, the Roman law, the Lombard law, the Ripuarian law, the Bavarian law, and the Salic law, so we have now in our Eastern empire Hindoo law, Mahometan law, Parsee law, English law perpetually mingling with each other, and disturbing each other; varying with the person, varying with the place. In one and the same cause the process and pleadings are in the fashion of one nation, the judgment is according to the laws of another. An issue is evolved according to the rules of Westminster, and decided according to those of Benares. The only Mahometan book in the nature of a code is the Koran;—the only Hindoo book the Institutes. Every body who knows those books, knows that they provide for a very small part of the cases which must arise in every community. All beyond them is comment and tradition. Our regulations in civil matters do not define rights; they merely establish remedies. If a point of Hindoo law arises, the Judge calls on the Pundit for an opinion. If a point of Mahometan law arises, the Judge applies to the Cauzee. What the integrity of these functionaries is, we may learn from Sir William Jones. That eminent men declared, that he could not answer it to his conscience to decide any point of law on the faith of a Hindoo expositor. Sir Thomas Strange confirms this declaration. Even if there were no suspicion of corruption on the part of the interpreters of the law, the science which they profess is in such a state of confusion that no reliance can be placed on their answers. Sir Francis Macnaghten tells us, that it is a delusion to fancy that there is any known and fixed law under which the Hindoo people live; that texts may be produced on any side of any question; that expositors equal in authority perpetually contradict each other; that the obsolete law is perpetually confounded with the law actually in force, and that the first lesson to be impressed on a functionary who has to administer Hindoo law is, that it is vain to think of extracting certainty from the books of the jurists. The consequence is, that in practice the decisions of the tribunals are altogether arbitrary. What is administered is not law, but a kind of rude and capricious equity. I asked an able and excellent Judge lately returned from India how one of our Zillah Courts would decide several legal questions of great importance—questions not involving considerations of religion or of caste—mere questions of commercial law. He told me, that it was a mere lottery. He knew how he should himself decide them. But he knew nothing more. I asked a most distinguished civil servant of the Company, with reference to the clause in this

Act abolishing slavery, whether at present, if a dancing girl ran away from her master, the Judge would force her to go back. "Some Judges," he said, "send a girl back; others set her at liberty. The whole is a mere matter of chance. Every thing depends on the temper of the individual judge."

Even in this country, we have had complaints of judge-made law; even in this country, where the standard of morality is higher than in almost any other part of the world—where, during several generations, not one depositary of our legal traditions has incurred the suspicion of personal corruption—where there are popular institutions—where every decision is watched by a shrewd and learned audience—where there is an intelligent and observant public—where every remarkable case is fully reported in a hundred newspapers—where, in short, there is everything which can mitigate the evils of such a system. But judge-made law, where there is an absolute government and a lax morality—where there is no bar and no public—is a curse and a scandal not to be endured. It is time that the Magistrate should know what law he is to administer—that the subject should know under what law he is to live. We do not mean that all the people of India should live under the same law: far from it: there is not a word in the Bill—there was not a word in my right hon. friend's speech—susceptible of such an interpretation. We know how desirable that object is; but we also know that it is unattainable. We know that respect must be paid to feelings generated by differences of religion, of nation, and of caste. Much, I am persuaded, may be done to assimilate the different systems of law without wounding those feelings. But, whether we assimilate those systems or not, let us ascertain them, let us digest them. We propose no rash innovation; we wish to give no shock to the prejudices of any part of our subjects. Our principle is simply this—uniformity where you can have it—diversity where you must have it—but in all cases certainty.

As I believe that India stands more in need of a code than any other country in the world, I believe also that there is no country on which that great benefit can more easily be conferred. A code is almost the only blessing—perhaps it is the only blessing which absolute governments are better fitted to confer on a nation than popular governments. The work of digesting a vast and artificial system of unwritten jurisprudence, is far more easily performed, and far better performed, by few minds than by many—by a Napoleon than by a Chamber of Deputies and a Chamber of Peers—by a government like that of Prussia or Denmark, than by a government like that of England. A quiet knot of two or three veteran jurists is an infinitely better machinery for such a purpose than a large popular assembly divided, as such assemblies almost always are, into adverse factions. This seems to me, therefore, to be precisely that point of time at which the advantage of a complete written code of laws may most easily be conferred on India. It is a work which cannot be well performed in an age of barbarism—which cannot without great difficulty be performed in an age of freedom. It is the work which especially belongs to a government like that of India—to an enlightened and paternal despotism.

I have detained the House so long, Sir, that I will defer what I had to say on some parts of this measure—important parts, indeed, but far less important, as I think, than those to which I have adverted, till we are in Committee. There is, however, one part of the Bill on which, after what has recently passed elsewhere, I feel myself irresistibly impelled to say a few words. I allude to that wise, that benevolent, that noble clause, which enacts that no native of our Indian empire shall, by reason of his colour, his descent, or his religion, be incapable of holding office. At the risk of being called by that nickname which is regarded as the most opprobrious of all nicknames, by men of selfish hearts and contracted minds—at the risk of being called a philosopher—

I must say that, to the last day of my life, I shall be proud of having been one of those who assisted in the framing of the Bill which contains that clause. We are told that the time can never come when the natives of India can be admitted to high civil and military office. We are told that this is the condition on which we hold our power. We are told, that we are bound to confer on our subjects—every benefit which they are capable of enjoying?—no—which it is in our power to confer on them?—no—but which we can confer on them without hazard to our own domination. Against that proposition I solemnly protest as inconsistent alike with sound policy and sound morality.

I am far, very far, from wishing to proceed hastily in this most delicate matter. I feel that, for the good of India itself, the admission of natives to high office must be effected by slow degrees. But that, when the fulness of time is come, when the interest of India requires the change, we ought to refuse to make that change lest we should endanger our own power; this is a doctrine which I cannot think of without indignation. Governments, like men, may buy existence too dear. "Propter vitam vivendi perdere causas," is a despicable policy either in individuals or in states. In the present case, such a policy would be not only despicable, but absurd. The mere extent of empire is not necessarily an advantage. To many governments it has been cumbersome; to some it has been fatal. It will be allowed by every statesman of our time, that the prosperity of a community is made up of the prosperity of those who compose the community, and that it is the most childish ambition to covet dominion which adds to no man's comfort or security. To the great trading nation, to the great manufacturing nation, no progress which any portion of the human race can make in knowledge, in taste for the conveniences of life, or in the wealth by which those conveniences are produced, can be matter of indifference. It is scarcely possible to calculate the benefits which we might derive from the diffusion of European civilization among the vast population of the East. It would be, on the most selfish view of the case, far better for us that the people of India were well governed and independent of us, than ill governed and subject to us—that they were ruled by their own kings, but wearing our broadcloth, and working with our cutlery, than that they were performing their salams to English collectors and English Magistrates, but were too ignorant to value, or too poor to buy, English manufactures. To trade with civilized men is infinitely more profitable than to govern savages. That would, indeed, be a doting wisdom, which, in order that India might remain a dependency, would make it an useless and costly dependency—which would keep a hundred millions of men from being our customers in order that they might continue to be our slaves.

It was, as Bernier tells us, the practice of the miserable tyrants whom he found in India, when they dreaded the capacity and spirit of some distinguished subject, and yet could not venture to murder him, to administer to him a daily dose of the pousta, a preparation of opium, the effect of which was in a few months to destroy all the bodily and mental powers of the wretch who was drugged with it, and to turn him into an helpless idiot. The detestable artifice, more horrible than assassination itself, was worthy of those who employed it. It is no model for the English nation. We shall never consent to administer the pousta to a whole community—to stupify and paralyse a great people whom God has committed to our charge for the wretched purpose of rendering them more amenable to our control. What is that power worth which is founded on vice, on ignorance, and on misery—which we can hold only by violating the most sacred duties which as governors we owe to the governed—which as a people blessed with far more than an ordinary measure of political liberty and of intellectual light, we owe to a race debased by three thousand years of despotism and priestcraft? We are free, we are civilized, to little purpose, if we grudge to any portion of the human race an equal measure of freedom and civilization.

Are we to keep the people of India ignorant in order that we may keep them submissive? Or do we think that we can give them knowledge without awakening ambition? Or do we mean to awaken ambition and to provide it with no legitimate vent? Who will answer any of these questions in the affirmative? Yet one of them must be answered in the affirmative, by every person who maintains that we ought permanently to exclude the natives from high office. I have no fears. The path of duty is plain before us: and it is also the path of wisdom, of national prosperity, of national honour.

The destinies of our Indian empire are covered with thick darkness. It is difficult to form any conjecture as to the fate reserved for a state which resembles no other in history, and which forms by itself a separate class of political phenomena. The laws which regulate its growth and its decay are still unknown to us. It may be that the public mind of India may expand under our system till it has outgrown that system; that by good government we may educate our subjects into a capacity for better government, that, having become instructed in European knowledge, they may, in some future age, demand European institutions. Whether such a day will ever come I know not. But never will I attempt to avert or to retard it. Whenever it comes, it will be the proudest day in English history. To have found a great people sunk in the lowest depths of slavery and superstition, to have so ruled them as to have made them desirous and capable of all the privileges of citizens, would indeed be a title to glory all our own. The sceptre may pass away from us. Unforeseen accidents may derange our most profound schemes of policy. Victory may be inconstant to our arms. But there are triumphs which are followed by no reverses. There is an empire exempt from all natural causes of decay. These triumphs are the pacific triumphs of reason over barbarism; that empire is the imperishable empire of our arts and our morals, our literature and our laws.

MINISTERIAL PLAN FOR THE ABOLITION OF SLAVERY.*

JULY 24, 1833.

HE rose with feelings of regret upon the present occasion. Though he had taken no part in the discussion upon this Bill, yet there was no one who had with more patience watched, or with greater anxiety attended to, the provisions of a measure, which he could not but consider to contain a great mixture of good and evil. He should now express his opinions upon this Bill in general, and particularly on those parts in which Amendments had been introduced, and to which the hon. Member (Mr. Fowell Buxton) had referred. He should discharge his duty, he was afraid, very imperfectly, and he would therefore entreat the House to extend to him that indulgence on the present occasion which he had experienced on former occasions when he had addressed it with less harassed feelings, and more confidence than at present. He had every disposition not only to do the amplest justice to his Majesty's Ministers, but to give them the greatest credit—them, with whom he generally acted—for having framed every part of this measure with the purest and most benevolent intentions, even those parts of which he could not approve. To those parts of which he disapproved, he was anxious to state his objection, but, previous to doing that, he most solemnly disclaimed any unfriendly feeling towards any class of persons whose interests might be concerned in the proposed measure. He hoped that he should be able to prove, that he was not, on the one hand, disposed to

* Hansard, 3d Series, vol. xix. p. 1202–1209.

sacrifice principle to party, nor on the other, disposed to sacrifice the rights of the planters to popular clamour. Of the three objects which the Bill was intended to effect, the first had his fullest and most unqualified approbation—the abolition of slavery. He believed slavery to be the greatest of political evils; and when he thought of the horrid state of the slave, he sometimes felt ashamed of himself for the enthusiasm he had manifested in removing domestic grievances; such, for example, as the Catholic disabilities. They had seen guilt in many ages and in many countries; but where had they seen guilt in the hideous forms in which it had for so many years been exhibited in the West-India islands? Slavery there had been made to do the work of famine, of pestilence, and of war combined. It had accomplished more than they could accomplish, in putting an end to that disposition to increase and multiply which was manifested by the human race in every other part of the world. There had been fierce and prolonged wars in Europe, but population went on augmenting; and fresh life filled up the chasms caused by such fields as those of Leipzic, Borodino, and Waterloo. Ambition had done all it could to destroy; but it had been assisted by famine and pestilence; but the void which they created was speedily and completely filled up. The law of nature was not counteracted. As soon as the population became thinned by any powerful physical cause, early marriages increased, and the deficiency was soon supplied. In the West-India colonies alone was found a society in which the number of human beings was continually decreasing without the surviving labourers obtaining any advantages. In the West-India Colonies a state of society existed unparalleled in the history of the world. Fully believing in the necessity of demolishing slavery, he nevertheless thought, that his Majesty's Government had taken the right course in the Bill which his right hon. friend had introduced. The only fault which he found with that Bill was, that it had a leaning to mitigate an evil which ought to be demolished altogether. They had made attempts to mitigate slavery on former occasions. They had sent out to the negro a Church Establishment, while they left him to be bought and sold; but that mitigation was useless. The object of this Bill, he thanked God! was not a mitigation of that description; it attacked the foundation of the principle of slavery. Slavery was not a system which could be improved; it must be annihilated. Slavery was in itself the abuse. The principle of slavery, as Montesquieu had observed, was pure unmixed evil. Terror was the only motive that could operate upon the slave. Terror was the only mode by which the proprietor of the slave could hope to guard his own life or to save his wife and daughters from violation. If they abstracted terror from the system, the whole fabric of slavery was at once destroyed. The introduction of liberty was a new principle, not a mitigation of slavery. To mitigate slavery by introducing liberty, would be to take away the props without supplying pillars. When he heard persons say, that it would be madness immediately to put an end to slavery, and at the same time declare that it was frightful to continue its cruelties, it appeared to him as if they were the most inconsistent of men. He could not comprehend the mitigation of slavery. Its abolition would give the slave a motive for preserving the order by which he was to benefit. In this country where there were no slaves, where the lowest labourer was an intelligent being, we could afford to connive at the violence of a mob; we could laugh at Political Unions and speeches; even in cases of actual treason and rebellion we could punish the leaders and pardon their followers; but in such a country as the West Indies, to tell the masters to be merciful and moderate, was to tell them to submit to butchery. How was it possible that while they gave the negroes religious instruction, in order to educate them as men, they could continue to treat them as brutes? Of that part of the Bill, therefore, which abolished slavery, he cordially approved. There was another part of the Bill which he knew was most unpopular—he meant the Compensation Clause—to which, however, he gave his full consent. He regretted that, on this point, he felt it his duty to oppose those with whom he had generally had the happiness to act on this subject; but he was prepared to take his full share of whatever unpopularity might arise from this part of the Bill. He well knew, that there were in this country many excellent persons who detested the principle on which compensation to the planters was founded. It was not with those persons a question of money. They would be quite ready to give the twenty millions or thirty millions, or more, as charity, but they were strongly opposed to giving it as compensation. For his part, he held that the owners of the slaves had a distinct right to this compensation. He did not mean to say, that they had any right as against the slave; and if he had no alternative but to choose between the positions—that slavery should never be abolished, or that the planter should never be compensated, he should have no hesitation in deciding for the latter; for highly as he valued the rights of property, he could never put them in competition with the right of personal liberty. It had been most justly declared, that the property of man in his labour was the origin of all property, and ought to be held most sacred. Therefore, if there must be robbery at all, he would rather rob the planter of his property than the slave of his freedom. But to that alternative he was not reduced. With the question of compensation a slave had nothing to do. The State had solemnly sanctioned the property of the planter. The public faith had been pledged to its maintenance by proclamation, by treaty, by prescription. Could that House consent to violate it? He had heard that it was maintained that the planter ought to receive no compensation, because there ought to be no indemnity for the abandonment of crime. He protested against such a doctrine, as establishing principles that would be most extensively pernicious. He readily admitted, that no contract tending to crime was binding, and that to condemn men to slavery was criminal. If 100 Acts of Parliament had been passed to establish slavery, and if all the Members of that House had sworn at the Table to maintain slavery, slavery ought nevertheless to be abolished. But that was not the question to be considered. When crime entered into a contract between two parties equally criminal, it could not prevent the execution of the contract as it respected them. If the choice were solely between violating the public faith, or putting an end to slavery, which was a violation of the law of nature, it would be a very different matter; but here there was an alternative; and where there was that alternative, the violation of public faith would be subversive of all public and private morality. He was sorry to detain the House; but the principle was of so much consequence, not only at the present time, but with reference to the future, that he could not refrain from making a few further observations upon it. If they were to violate the public faith pledged to the West-India planter, they would establish a precedent of a most monstrous and injurious character. To illustrate this position, he would take an instance from the commonest life: suppose a Catholic gentleman had ordered an image for the decoration of his chapel to be sculptured by a first-rate artist, and that when, after immense skill and labour, the image was finished, he should say to the artist, "Take it back, since I ordered it my mind has been enlightened; I now believe that the Protestant is the true religion. I therefore consider the contract between you and me as sinful, and I cannot consent to perform my part of it." Would not the argument that would justly be used be: "If you are enlightened, so much the better; but you must pay for the contract into which you entered when you were in a state of darkness?" Or suppose a Mahometan, having three or four wives in his Harem, were to embrace Christianity, would he be entitled to break his contract with them, turn them all out into the world, and leave them to starve? Or, in the case of a lottery, which, as all gaming was vicious, ought never to be resorted to by a Government, would it not be the height of enormity, if, after all the tickets had been sold, Government were to declare that it had become sensible of its error, and were to leave the purchasers to digest their loss? Nay, if once such a doctrine as that which he was contravening were established, almost the whole of the public debt of this country ought to be wiped away; for he held that there was no national crime greater than to engage in wanton and unjustifiable wars; and the greater part of that debt was incurred in the prosecution of such wars. For instance,, during the American war we had borrowed 100 millions. The prosecution of that war was as wicked an act as the maintenance of slavery. What difference was there between keeping one set of men in a state of severe and unmerited bondage, and carrying fire and sword among another set of men who merely asserted their rights? If it was unjust to compel the slave to labour throughout life for his master, was it not unjust to spend money in sending the sabre of the Hessian, or the tomahawk of the Indian, into the fields of a people who were only struggling for liberty? If, therefore, the principle against which he was contending were established, those who admitted it would be at a loss to make out how the claims of almost any public creditor could be considered as valid. He repeated, therefore, that he was decidedly favourable to two of the principles of the Bill; the Abolition of Slavery, and the Compensation to the Planter. But as to the third principle of this Bill, which related to the transition state of the negro, before the total cessation of his slavery, he confessed that he entertained great, and in some respects, he feared, insurmountable doubts. There could be no question that it was the solemn duty of Parliament to do all they could to protect the planter; but he had great doubts if the provision in question would have that effect. If it could be proved, that what they were about to do was calculated to improve the morality of the slave, and thereby enable him, when he became wholly free, better to discharge the duties of a citizen, he should assent to it. He should not refuse to assent to it because it was severe, provided it could be shown that that severity was likely to be efficacious. What he objected to was this, that the restraints laid on the negro by the Bill were not so laid with the sole view of improving his moral character. His right hon. friend had, with perfect candour, admitted that. The ninth clause of the Bill contained a provision that it should be lawful for the slave at any time to purchase his freedom on the payment of a value legally fixed. Now that clause admitted a principle in which he could not acquiesce; namely, that the planters had a right to compensation from their slaves. The planters and the State had been accomplices in a crime, and it would be exceedingly hard and unjust to throw the burden of retribution on one party; but it would be still more hard and unjust to lay any portion of it on the third and injured party. By this clause a negro who was fit for all the duties of civil life, might still be kept in slavery. Why was he to give this money to his master? If the clause had provided, that when the slave had laid up a certain sum in the Savings' Bank he should become free, that would have been a fair proposition; but when they compelled him to pay it to the master, they compelled him to pay the price of a right—a principle—the justice of which he (Mr. Macaulay) could never admit. A man who had laid up 10*l.* was not rendered more or less fit for freedom by giving that money to his master, or by keeping it in his own chest. He denied the right of the State to demand any sacrifice whatever from the injured party. He would now say a few words with respect to the restraints which were imposed on slaves who were artizans, artificers, coopers, &c., or who, in the words of his right hon. friend, were non-predial. Even many of those who denied that the slaves engaged in agriculture were fit for freedom, admitted that the non-predial slaves were perfectly fit for freedom; and he was convinced that they might be instantly set free from all restraints, without any danger whatever to society. If so, it was impossible to justify the infliction upon them of a seven years' apprenticeship. With respect to the other class of slaves, who, it might be said, stood more in need of a transition state, he was apprehensive that the twelve years' apprenticeship would be found a bad and inefficient mode of training them for freedom. There had been no practical experience on this matter. Indeed, they might as well talk of practical experience of a nation of Amazons. There had been no example of such apprenticeships. He must say, however, that he thought the argument on the subject of his hon. friend, the member for Weymouth, very convincing; and that he did not think that his right hon. friend had met that argument in so direct a manner as was usual with him. Agricultural labour in the West-Indies was a most painful drudgery. The labourer, therefore, ought to have a strong motive for exertion. He was at a loss, however, to understand what that motive was to be. Even in this country, agricultural apprentices were not taken without a premium, and he understood that the great body of apprentices did not, for a considerable time, earn their own living. But what was to be the motive of the West-India apprentice to exert himself?—The Magistrate. It was he who was to superintend all the operations of society in the colonies. Every day in the week, and every hour in the day, whenever the master became harsh, or the slave became indolent, there was to be no recourse but to the Magistrate. It must be recollected, that in the colonies the negro and the master would always have opposite interests, and that those interests could not be reconciled by law. In this country it was quite different. Here a master had the choice of labourers, and a labourer the choice of masters; but in slavery it had always been found necessary to give despotic power to the master. By this Bill it was left to the Magistrate to keep the peace between the master and the slave. Every time that the slave took twenty minutes, to do that which the master thought he might have done in fifteen, recourse must be had to the Magistrate. Society day and night would be in a constant state of litigation, and all differences and difficulties were to be met by judicial interference. He did not entertain the apprehensions expressed by his hon. friend, the member for Weymouth, that such a state of things would lead to gross cruelty. It would, in his opinion, be merely a state of dead slavery, a state destitute of any vital principle. He did not see reason to apprehend any cruelty; for what motive could the stipendiary Magistrate have for hostility towards the slaves? The contrary would, he thought, be the case. The Magistrates would be accountable to the Colonial Office; the Colonial Office to the House of Commons, in which every whipping would, no doubt, be told. The object of the Magistrate, therefore, would be to be as lenient as possible. His apprehension was, that the result of continuing this state of society for twelve years would be, that the whole negro population would become inactive, would sink into weak and dawdling inefficiency, and would be much less fit for liberty at the end of the period than at its commencement. His hope was, that the system would die a natural death; that a few months' experience would establish its utter inefficiency, so as to induce the planters to abandon it, and to substitute a state of freedom. In his opinion, however, it would be much better, that that should be done by parliamentary enactment, rather than it should be left to the Colonial Authorities. He had voted for the second reading of the Bill, and he should vote for the third reading of it; but while it was in the Committee, he would join with other hon. Members in doing all that was possible to amend those points of the Bill to which he objected. He was aware how freely he had stated his opinions on this important question; but he was sure that the House would do justice to his motives, which, amidst conflicting feelings and opinions, prompted him honestly to endeavour to perform his duty.

ON THE BALLOT.*

JUNE 18, 1839.

HAVING been long absent from the House, he wished it had been in his power to be, at least for some weeks, a silent listener to their debates; but the deep interest which he took in this question, and his sense of what he owed to a large and respectable portion of his constituents, whose views on this subject concurred with his own, impelled him to trust to that indulgence which it was customary in that House to bestow. But before he made any remarks upon the question immediately before the House, he wished to advert, fc. a short time, to one topic which had excited the greatest interest throughout the country, and to which the hon. Gentleman who had just sat down had made some very sarcastic, and not, he thought, exceedingly well-judged allusions. It was generally understood that her Majesty's Ministers had determined that the question of the ballot should be an open question—that all the members of the Government should be free to speak and vote on that question according to their individual opinions. It was natural that this determination should excite censure on the one side of the House and applause on the other. For his own part, he must say, that, without any reference whatever to his opinion on this particular question, he was inclined, on higher and more general grounds, to approve of the determination of the Government. He rejoiced to see the number of open questions increasing; he rejoiced to see that they were returning to the wise, the honest, the moderate maxims which prevailed in that House in the time of their fathers and grand-

* Hansard, 3d Series, vol. xlviii. p. 462–476.

fathers. He said, that the practice of the House, in that respect, had undergone, in very recent times, a great change; he believed that another change was now taking place, and that they were reverting to a more prudent and rational system. To what precise extent it was desirable that the Ministers of the Crown should act in strict concert together in Parliament on the various legislative questions that came under consideration, was an exceedingly nice question, a question to which, so far as he was aware, no rigid and strictly drawn rule could be applied. Hon. Gentlemen on the other side, no doubt, possessed a great advantage over him; they were probably aware of much that might have passed during the last four or five years on this subject, with which he was unacquainted. But he was not aware that any speculative or practical statesman had ever been found, either in writing or speaking, to take any distinct line on this subject, and to trace out a definite line of action, for the guide of political prudence, in all cases, was, he believed, difficult, and perhaps impossible. It was perfectly plain, however, that there were but three courses possible with respect to the conduct of Ministers in dealing with legislative questions—either that they must agree on all questions whatever, or that they must pretend to agree where there was a real difference, or that they must leave each individual member of their body to take the course which his own opinion and inclination dictated. Now, that there should be a perfect agreement between Ministers on all questions, they knew to be impossible. That was not his expression, it was the expression of one who had long been the brightest ornament of that House—Lord Chatham. That great man said, "Talk of divided houses! Why, there never was an instance of an united Cabinet! When were the minds of twelve men ever cast in one and the same mould?" They knew that even if two men were brought up together from their childhood—if they followed the same course of study, mixed in the same society, communicated their sentiments to each other on all topics with perfect freedom, and exercised a mutual influence in forming each other's minds, a perfect agreement between them on political subjects could never be expected. How then was it possible that this agreement could subsist between a cabinet of several persons imperfectly acquainted with each other? Every Government—he spoke neither of the present Government, nor of the late Government, nor of the Government which seemed about to be formed the other day—was constructed in such a manner that forty or fifty gentlemen, some of whom had never seen each other's faces till they were united officially, or had been in hot opposition to each other all the rest of their lives, were brought into intimate connexion. He meant to cast no reflection whatever on either side of the House, but such was the general character of all Governments, and complete unanimity in any was out of the question. It would, in truth, be an absolute miracle. Only two courses, therefore, remained. Either there might be a semblance of unanimity, where unanimity really was not, or each person might be left to act on his own opinions. He did not profess any extraordinary degree of prudery on matters of political morality. He was perfectly aware that in Parliament it was impossible any thing great could be done without co-operation, and he was aware that there could be no co-operation without mutual compromise. He admitted, therefore, that men were justified, when united into a party, either in office or in opposition, in making mutual concessions, in opposing measures, which they might, as individuals, think desirable, in assenting to those which they might consider objectionable, and giving their votes, not with reference to the mere terms of the question put from the chair, but with reference to the general state of political parties. All this he admitted. If there were any person who thought it wrong, he respected the tenderness of his conscience, but that person's vocation was not for a public life. That person should select a quieter path for his passage through life, one in which he might play a useful and respectable part; but he was as completely unfitted for the turmoils of political strife as a Quaker, by his religious principles, was prevented from undertaking the command of a regiment of horse. Thus far he admitted the principle of party combinations, but he admitted that they might be carried too far—that they had been carried too far. That a Member of the House should say "No," to a proposition which he believed to be essentially just and necessary—that he should steadily vote through all its stages in favour of a bill that he believed would have pernicious consequences, was conduct which he (Mr. Macaulay) should think was not to be defended. Such a course of action was not reconcileable to a plain man, whose notions of morality were not drawn from the casuists. He only defended the principle of mutual action among political partisans as being a peculiar exception from the great general rules of political morality, and it was clear, that an exception from the great rules of political morality should be most strictly construed, that it should not be needlessly extended, and, above all, that it should not be converted into the rule. Therefore, he said, that in the members of a Government, any concession of opinion which was not necessary to the efficient conduct of affairs, to cordial co-operation, was to be looked upon as unjustifiable. In saying this, he was not pleading for any innovation, he was attacking a modern basis of action, and recommending a return to the sounder and better maxims of the last generation. Nothing was more common than to hear it said, that the first time when a great question was left open, was when Lord Liverpool's Administration left the Catholic question open. Now, there could not be a grosser error. Within the memory of many persons living, the general rule was this, that all questions whatever were open questions in a cabinet, except those which came under two classes—namely, first, measures brought forward by the Government as a Government, which all the members of it were, of course, expected to support; and, second, motions brought forward with the purpose of casting a censure, express or implied, on the Government, or any department of it, which all its members were, of course, expected to oppose. He believed that he laid down a rule to which it would be impossible to find an exception, he was sure he laid down a general rule, when he said that fifty years ago all questions not falling under these heads were considered open. Let gentlemen run their minds over the history of Mr. Pitt's administration. Mr. Pitt, of course, expected that every Gentleman connected with him by the ties of office should support him on the leading questions of his Government—the India Bill, the resolutions respecting the commerce of Ireland, the French commercial treaty. Of course, also, he expected, that no Gentleman should remain in the Government who had voted for Mr. Bastard's motion, of censure on the naval administration of Lord Howe, or for Mr. Whitbread's motion on the Spanish armament; but, excepting on such motions, brought forward as attacks on Government, perfect liberty was allowed to his colleagues, and that not merely on trifles, but on constitutional questions of vital importance. The question of Parliamentary reform was left open; Mr. Pitt and Mr. Dundas were in favour of it, Lord Mulgrave and Lord Grenville against it. On the impeachment of Warren Hastings, likewise, the different Members of Government were left to pursue their own course; that governor was attacked by Mr. Pitt, and defended by Lord Mulgrave. In 1790 the question, whether the impeachment should be considered as having dropped, in consequence of the termination of the Parliament, in which the proceedings were commenced, was left an open question; Mr. Pitt took one side, and was answered by his own Solicitor-general, Sir J. Scott, afterwards Lord Eldon. The important question respecting the powers of juries in cases of libel was left open; Mr. Pitt took a view favourable to granting them extensive powers, Lord Grenville and Lord Thurlow opposed him. The abolition of the slave trade was also an open question. Mr. Pitt and Lord Grenville were favourable to it; Mr. Dundas and Lord Thurlow were among the most conspicuous defenders of the slave trade. All these instances had occurred in the space of about five years. Were they not sufficient to prove how absurdly and ignorantly those persons spoke who told us, that the practice of open questions was a mere innovation of our own time? There were men now living—great men, held in honour and reverence—Lord Grey, Lord Wellesley, Lord Holland, and others, who well remembered, that at an early period of their public life, the law of libel, the slave trade, Parliamentary reform, were all open questions, supported by one section of the Cabinet, and opposed by another. Was this the effect of any extraordinary weakness or timidity on the part of the statesman then Prime Minister? No; Mr. Pitt was a man, whom even his enemies and detractors always acknowledge, possessed of manly, brave, and commanding spirit. And was the effect of this policy to enfeeble his Administration, to daunt his adherents, to render them unable to withstand the attacks of the Opposition? On the contrary, never did a ministry present a firmer or more serried front to Opposition, nor had he the slightest doubt but that their strength was increased in consequence of giving each Member more individual liberty. Where there were no open questions, opinions might be restrained for a time, but sooner or later they would show themselves, and when they did, what would be the consequence? Not, as in Mr. Pitt's time, when one Minister would speak against a measure and another for it—when one would divide with the ayes, and another with the noes, and as Mr. Pitt and Mr. Dundas did, all in perfect good humour, lest the Government should be dissolved. Now, as soon as one Cabinet Minister got up and declared that he could not support the view taken by another upon any question, what was the result? The result had been seen. They all remembered the manner in which the Government of the Duke of Wellington, in 1828, dispensed with the services of some members of the cabinet, in consequence of a difference of opinion upon a subject on which not one of Mr. Pitt's colleagues would have asked permission to vote against him. He did not pretend to draw the line precisely, but he was satisfied that of late the line had been drawn in an improper and inconsiderate manner. It was time they should return to better maxims, maxims which had been shown by experience to be sound and good. He was perfectly satisfied that the present Government would find, by taking this course on the present occasion, that they had increased their strength and raised their character. Now, to come to the particular question before the House, he should vote for the motion of the hon. Member for the city of London. He wished to explain that, in doing this, he was merely to be understood as giving a declaration in favour of the principle of secret voting. He desired to be understood as reserving to himself the right of withholding his support from any bill which, when he examined its details, did not appear to contain such provisions as would effect the object he had in view. He must reserve to himself, also, the right of considering how far he could, with propriety, give his support to any bill which should not be accompanied or preceded by some measure for improving the mode of revising the registration. He should think it most disingenuous to give a popular vote, saddling it with a condition which he thought either impossible or exceedingly difficult of fulfilment. Such was not his opinion. He had no doubt that it was possible to provide machinery which should give both to the voter and to the country all the security which the transactions of human life admitted, and he had as little doubt that it was possible to devise a tribunal, whose decision on a vote before the election would command as much public confidence as the decisions of committees of that House after elections. Subject to these two conditions he would give his support to the vote by ballot. He could not say that he did so upon the grounds on which many of the supporters of the ballot rested their case, because he by no means conceived, like many of them, that this was a case on which all the arguments lay on one side.

He admitted that, in his opinion, the advantages that would be derived from this measure would be very great; but, admitting and feeling this, still he was not surprised that very wise and very virtuous men hesitated on this subject, and that such men came, on this subject, to a conclusion different from his. They must in this, as in almost every other question of human affairs, balance the good with the good, and the evil with the evil. He fully admitted that the ballot would withdraw the voter from the influence of something that was good as well as from the influence of something that was bad. He admitted that it took away the salutary check of public opinion, as well as the pernicious effect of intimidation. He was compelled to strike a balance, and take refuge in the ballot, as the lesser of two evils. He did not, he must say, altogether agree with the Member for the city of London, if he perfectly understood him, in thinking that the ballot would secure that entire prevention of the bribery of voters which, on this subject, the hon. Member seemed inclined to hope. In small constituencies, he did think that bribery would continue, although, at the same time, it might not be so extensively entered into. He considered that the ballot was a remedy, a specific remedy, and the only remedy for the evils of intimidation; and upon this ground he gave it his support. There was a time when he, like the noble Lord who seconded the motion of the hon. Member for London, was inclined to hope that those evils, like many other evils which had yielded to the force of public opinion and the progress of intelligence, would die a natural death. That hope he had been compelled to relinquish. He believed the evil to be a growing evil, and he was satisfied that it had made progress within the last seven years. He believed it had made progress within the last three years. He could not disguise from himself that the growth of this evil was, in some measure, to be imputed to the Reform Act; and, in saying this, he only said it in common of the Reform Act, and of almost every great measure. The Reformation of the Church, they all knew, produced classes of society and moral evils that were unknown in the time of the Plantagenets. The Revolution produced a description of abuses that were unknown in the time of the Stuarts; and the Reform Act, although he believed no measure was more generally pleasing to the country, like the Reformation of the Church and the Revolution, produced some new, and aggravated some old, evils; it swept away many abuses, but it seemed to him to have given a deeper and more malignant energy to the abuses which it spared. It swept away many of the old channels of corrupt influence, but, in those channels which it had not swept away, the corrupt current not only still ran on, but it ran on deeper, and stronger, and fouler than ever. It destroyed, or, if it did not destroy, it restricted within narrow limits, the old practice of direct nomination; but, in doing so, he believed it gave a new impulse to the practice of intimidation, and this at the very moment when it conferred the franchise on thousands of electors, and thus placed them in a situation in which they were most open to influence and intimidation. It was impossible to close their eyes to the evidence that was offered to them on every side. If he believed the outcry raised, not by one party, or from one corner of the kingdom, but by Tories, Whigs, and Radicals, in England, Scotland, and Ireland, he must believe that there were, sitting in that House, Gentlemen who owed their seats to votes extorted by fear. And he said, that if there was any Gentleman in that House who owed his seat to such means, it were infinitely better that he sat there for Old Sarum; for, by sitting there for Old Sarum, he would be no Representative of the people, nor was he a Representative of the people now. At Old Sarum there were no threats of ejectments because a voter had more regard to his public duty than to his private interest. At Old Sarum the voter was never put to the alternative whether he would abandon his principles, or reduce his family to distress. All tyranny was bad; but the worst was that which worked with the machinery of freedom. Under an undisguised oligarchy, the people suffered only the evil of being governed by those whom they had not chosen; but, to whatever extent intimidation mixed itself up with the system of popular election, to that extent the people suffered both the evil of being governed by those whom they had not chosen, and the evil of being coerced into a professed choice. A great number of human beings were thus mere machines through whom the great proprietors expressed their pleasure, and the greater their number, the greater the extent of misery and degradation. The noble Lord who had seconded the motion said, and most justly said, that he did not wish, in supporting this motion, to deprive wealth of its legitimate influence. Wealth, under any system, must always retain its legitimate influence. Wealth was power, and power justly and kindly used necessarily inspired affection. Wealth, or that which was so, compared with what was possessed by the great mass of electors, was closely connected with intellectual superiority. It enabled its possessor to select and prosecute any study to which he might be inclined; to continue it when those who commenced life with him, under less favourable circumstances, were forced to drudge for their daily bread; to enlarge his mind by foreign travel: to acquire an intimacy with the history of nations, and with the arts and sciences. These were advantages to which it was impossible that constituencies could be blind; nay, going much below those who formed the present body of electors, and descending to the very lowest of the populace, it never was found that, even in their wildest aberrations, they chose a leader destitute of these recommendations. This was the natural, the indestructible, the legitimate, the salutary influence of wealth. Whatever was more than this was corruption; and if it were thought necessary, as it appeared from the speech of the hon. Member who had last spoken, that some persons in that House did think it necessary to maintain the influence of bribery in our elective system, then he said, that incomparably the best and least objectionable method was that of open bribery. But against bribery they enacted laws; against bribery they passed resolutions; for bribery, boroughs were disfranchised; for bribery, Members were unseated; for bribery indictments and informations were preferred; for bribery, the penalties extended both to the elector and the elected; one man was disqualified, another man fined. On what principle did they inflict penalties on the elector—on what principle but this, that, from having dealt in pecuniary corruption, the elector was no longer fit to exercise the right of voting? But what was the operation of intimidation? It was this—"Vote with me, or give up my custom. Vote with me, or give up your farm." Or it was thus—"Vote with me, and I will give you 20*l.* for a pair of boots." Why, surely it was notorious that this was one of the constant forms of corruption. "Vote with me, and I will give you 20*l.* for a pair of boots," was a common and constant form of corruption, though less so, perhaps, because less easy, than "Vote for me, or I will carry my custom to the boot-maker's in the next street." On what possible pretext could any man defend such an exercise of the power of wealth as this? And here he must say, that he almost dissented from the form of expression used by the hon. Member for London in his eloquent and excellent speech; he objected to the hon. Member making an antithesis between intimidation and corruption. He said, that intimidation was corruption in its worst and most loathsome form, stripped of every seduction, of every blandishment, of everything that had the appearance of liberality and good humour; a hard, strict, cruel corruption, seeking by means most foul, a most loathsome end. It was corruption working by barbarity; and this sort of corruption, this general sort of corruption, was, most unhappily, the easiest and cheapest of all. Corruption by gifts costs something, but corruption by threats cost nothing but the crime. It was only of a superfluity out of what was left after expending all that was necessary for the support of a family, that corruption by giving commenced: but how much worse was the corruption of taking away? The man who practised intimidation was under no necessity of mortgaging his estate to prepare for an election: nay, at the same time that he improved perhaps his lands, by the very mode of administering the economy of his family, he was able to effect by intimidation all the purposes of corruption to a greater extent, and with more complete demoralization, than had ever been seen in Grampound or East Retford. But not only was intimidation worked easily and cheaply, but it was also most trying to the virtue of the persons that were subjected to it, inasmuch as it was much more easy to refuse that which a man never had, than to submit to be pillaged of that which he was accustomed to have. Many men who would not hesitate to throw down a purse if it were offered to him to vote for a particular candidate, would nevertheless vote against his conscience for fear of an ejectment. And he found, that this corruption, which was the greatest, the easiest, the cheapest, and the most trying to the party, was also the safest of all. It was also that sort of corruption which they allowed and must allow with perfect impunity. They could punish to a certain extent that good-humoured corruption which corrupted by making men happy, but they could not punish that malignant corruption that corrupted by making men miserable. They could not set up an inquisitorial tribunal that would be entitled to ask these questions:—"Why did you not continue such a lease—what fault did you find—did not the tenant do justice to the land—did he not pay his rent—was he disrespectful—and if not for his vote, why did you turn him out?" Or, to take the instance of a tailor after the Westminster election, could you put such questions as these:—"Why have you left him—had he not suited you—did he not fit you well—were his charges too high—and if not for his vote, why did you leave him?" Such a remedy would be worse than the disease. Property ceased to be property, if they called upon the proprietor for any reasons other than mere will and caprice, to state why he discharged his tailor or other tradesman. In what position, then, did they stand? Here was, as it seemed to him, a great evil—a growing evil—an evil much more fearful than many which had undergone the direct censure of the law. But it was so intertwined with the institution of property, that if they attempted to strike at it by means of an enacting bill, they would inflict necessarily a wound upon the institution of property. It seemed to him, then, considering punishment out of the question, that they could only try means of prevention. What were the means of prevention suggested? Absolutely none, except the ballot. Here, then, or nowhere we can find means of reconciling the rights of property with the rights of suffrage. In this way, only, could they enable each party really to do what he liked with his own. The estate was the landlord's, the vote was the tenant's." "So use your own rights," was the language of all civil as well as moral law, "as not to interfere with the rights of others." But here, it should be remarked, they could not give the one right without infringing or rather destroying the other. Through a system of open voting, they could not give the landlord that dominion over his estate which he ought to have, without throwing in the dominion over his tenants' votes which he ought not to have, and under the same system of open voting they could not protect the tenant's vote without interfering with the landlord's property. Under a system of open voting, with rights opposed to each other, it was impossible to reconcile the differences between these two great principles on which depended the whole national prosperity, liberty and property. If, then, there was any mode of reconciling these principles, ought they not eagerly to embrace it, and most seriously to consider whether they would not find in the ballot the mode of reconciling them? Whether the ballot would not give equal and perfect protection to both? Whether it would not give to each just what they ought to have and nothing more than each ought to have? If this were, as he really believed it would be, the effect of the ballot, if here, and here only, they could find a solution of those difficulties, surely no slight objections ought to deter them from adopting it. The objection to the ballot, though by no means the only one raised in discussion, which appeared to throw any real difficulty in the way of carrying it, was, as had been said by an eloquent, ingenious, and lively speaker, that in the minds of the people there was a moral objection to it, otherwise nothing could prevent for a single session the carrying of the principle of vote by ballot. He must own that this objection, highly respectable as many of those who entertain it were, did not seem to him sound or well considered, because he hardly thought that it could be entertained by any respectable and sensible person, who considered for a moment what was the amount of the evil effected by the present system. Surely if it were immoral to tell an untruth, at least it was equally immoral, having received a great public trust for the public good, to employ that trust to an evil purpose. If it were un-English not to dare to own the vote that was given, surely it was more un-English not to dare to vote as he thought right. When the word un-English was used, they were compelled to contrast their idea of that bold and sturdy independence which had been their great pride as a national characteristic, with the situation of a man, who, holding his farm from year to year, is compelled by fear of pecuniary loss and ruin to poll against him whom he wished to see chaired, and to vote for the candidate whom, with all his heart, he would see well ducked. At present they knew that many dishonest votes were given, but let the system of secrecy in voting be introduced and they would have honest votes, although the parties might afterwards deny that they had given them. Which was the greater evil of the two? God forbid that he should say anything that should seem to extenuate the guilt of falsehood, but God forbid, also, that he should not make some allowance for the poor as well as for the rich. God forbid that he should see more distinctly the mote in the eye of the 10*l.* householder, than the beam in the eye of a baron or a bishop. If morality were anything more than capricious favour or mere pretext, they would have ample opportunities of exercising it, without waiting till the ballot became the law of the land, or without even descending below their own rank in life. If it were criminal in a man to utter an untruth for the purpose of guarding a secret against private curiosity, then he would say, that they would find many criminals of a far higher station, and of a far more cultivated intellect, than the bakers and butchers about whose veracity they were so anxious. He would take a single illustration from the case of anonymous writers. It was perfectly notorious that men of high consideration, men of the first distinction, had written books and published them without their names, and on being questioned, had denied that they were the authors of the works they had written; and yet this denial did not prevent them from being generally considered with respect and kindness in society. They had also seen casuists of great repute defend those parties. One illustrious name he would instance, which would no doubt suggest itself to all who heard him, the name of a first-rate man of genius, of excellent principles, and a noble spirit—he need hardly add the name of Sir Walter Scott. Sir Walter Scott published without his name that eminent and popular series of novels which had endeared him to all his countrymen, nay, almost all the world, and which he for one could not think upon without feelings of the deepest admiration and gratitude. Sir Walter Scott published this series of novels anonymously, and to all questions put to him on the subject, persisted in denying the authorship of them, till at length he consented to drop the veil of concealment, and acknowledged them to be the productions of his pen. Now he would ask—and he appealed to many who were personally acquainted with that great man—he would appeal to them and ask, did this concealment and subsequent avowal of his name reflect any shame on the character of Sir W. Scott?—did any one of the large circle of his friends and admirers consider that Sir W. Scott had dishonoured himself by this proceeding. All that he demanded was this, that we should, in the purity of our own moral feelings, think of the moral feelings of other classes, as well as of those belonging to that class to which we ourselves belonged; that we should have one weight and one measure; and that we should extend to those untruths by means of which the poor man seeks to protect himself from the encroachments of the gentleman, that pardon which we extend to the untruths by which one gentleman defends himself from the impertinent curiosity of another. He did not pretend to be a casuist, nor to be accustomed to weigh questions of this nature in a very nice balance, but he should hesitate, he almost thought, to advise an elector now-a-days to tell the truth and take the consequences. They had no right to expect sacrifices of that kind from every body, or count on the moral courage to make them. As for the honest electors, that class of men—village Hampdens, Grey would have called them—they would be honest still if this measure were adopted. The man who would utter untruths when he had the ballot, was the man who would now be ready to give a corrupt vote. In fact, there was the same breach of faith in the one course as in the other. He was for neither. Of the two alternatives—of the two chances of evil—he thought the latter was to be preferred. In short, if the voters could not at once keep faith with their country, and with their corruptors, he was one who wished that we should have a system by which their faith might be kept to their country, and broken to their corruptors. If there were one system under which, more than another, it were easy for the elector to break his faith to the country, while he kept it with his corruptor, that system was the present. Another objection, which was sometimes put forward, was contained in this question, "Will you disturb that settlement which was made by the Reform Bill, and which we were then told was to be final?" On this point he fully agreed with the hon. Member for the city of London. He thought that this question had been expressly reserved at the time of carrying the Reform Bill; nor was he aware that a single person considered himself, by supporting the Reform Bill, to be pledged to do without the ballot. Now, with regard to the finality of the Reform Bill; he had always regarded that great measure with reverence,—but a rational, not a superstitious reverence; and he conceived that the question, whether it should be amended or not, should be considered upon no other principles, but the ordinary principles of public good. He saw many and strong arguments against frequent and violent changes in our constitutional system. He could not conceal from himself that the great revolution of 1832—for revolution it was, and a most fearful and sanguinary revolution it would have been in any other nation than this—that revolution was effected here without civil disorder, and without the effusion of blood; but unquestionably the passing of the bill was attended with much excitement and danger. That excitement and that danger he was not desirous to renew. He would bear with many inconveniences rather than open a similar scene; nay, he would bear with many grievances rather than agree to re-open the whole representative system which was established by the Reform Act. But if any man argued that the Reform Act ought to be final, he must, at the same time, admit, that it ought to be effectual, otherwise they would have cut off one form of misrepresentation merely to have it replaced by another. They must not allow that which they meant as a franchise to be turned into a species of villein service, more degrading by far than any that belonged to the dark era of the 14th century. It was not that threats should be substituted in the place of bribery—it was not for that result that the aristocracy had been conquered in their own strongholds; but it was for the establishment of a genuine suffrage, and of real, not pernicious, rights, that the Church, the aristocracy, and the Court together had been made to give way before the determined voice of a united people. The object of that mighty movement was not that old abuses should be brought back under new denominations, that the place of Old Sarum, the rotten borough, should be supplied by other Old Sarums, under the respectable names of counties and divisions of counties. No, nor was the time far remote, when this nation, with a voice as imperative as that with which she demanded the Reform Bill, would demand that the Reform Bill be carried out in the truth of its noble principle, and when that just and reasonable demand was conceded, as conceded it would be, and the franchise of every voter should be made a franchise indeed, they would find, that instead of having led the way, by this step, to reckless spoliation and confusion, in truth they had strengthened the law, secured to property its just rights, drawn closer the ties which united the two great orders of society to each other, and attached both of them all the more to the law, the Parliament, and the Crown.

ON CONFIDENCE IN THE MINISTRY.*

JANUARY 29, 1840.

It is possible, Sir, that the House may imagine I rise under some little feeling of irritation, to reply to the personalities and accusations of the right hon. Baronet [Sir J. Graham]. I shall indulge in neither. It would be easy to reply to them—to recriminate would be still easier. Were I alone personally considered, I should think either course unworthy of me. I know that egotism in this House is always unpopular; on this occasion it would be singularly unseasonable. If ever I am under the necessity of addressing this House on matters which concern myself, I hope it shall be on some occasion when the dearest interests of the empire are not staked on the event of our debate. I do rise, Sir, to address you under feelings of deep anxiety, but in that anxiety there is not, if I know my own heart, any mixture of selfish feeling. I do feel, indeed, with the most intense conviction, that in pleading for the Government to which I belong, I am pleading for the deepest interests of the Commonwealth—for the reformation of abuses, and for the preservation of august and venerable institutions. I trust, Mr. Speaker, that the first Cabinet Minister who, when the question is, whether the Government be or be not worthy of confidence, offers himself in debate, will find some portion of that generosity and good feeling which once distinguished English gentlemen. But be this as it may, my voice shall be heard. I was saying that I am pleading, not only for the preservation of our institutions, but for liberty and order, for justice administered in mercy, for equal laws,

* Hansard, 3d Series, vol. li. p. 815–835

for the rights of conscience, and for the real union of Great Britain and Ireland. Sir, I wish first to address myself not to any matter relating to myself alone, but to those parts of the subject with which my name is bound up in some degree with the character of the Government to which I belong. My opinions are favourable to secret voting. The opinions of my noble Friend (Lord John Russell) are in favour of open voting. Notwithstanding, we meet as Members of one Government. This has been made a topic of charge against the Government by every Gentleman who has addressed the House, from the hon. Baronet who opened the debate, down to the right hon. Baronet who spoke last. Now, Sir, I say in the first place, that if on account of this difference of opinion we shall be considered by the House unworthy of its confidence, then no Government for many years has been worthy, is worthy, of the House of Commons: for the Government of Mr. Pitt, the Government of Mr. Fox, the Government of Lord Liverpool, the Government of Mr. Canning, the Government of the Duke of Wellington, have all had open questions on subjects of the greatest moment. I say that the question of Parliamentary Reform was an open question with the Government of Mr. Pitt. Mr. Pitt, holding opinions in favour of that question, brought into the Cabinet Lord Grenville, who did not. Mr. Pitt was opposed to the slave trade. Mr. Dundas, a defender of it, was a Member of his Government. I say Mr. Fox, in the same manner, in his Cabinets of 1782 and 1806, had open questions of similar importance; and I say that the Governments of Lord Liverpool, Mr. Canning, and the Duke of Wellington, left, as an open question, Catholic Emancipation; which, closely connected as it was with the executive Administration, was, perhaps, one of the last questions which should ever have been left an open one by any Government. But to take still more important ground, and to come to a question which more nearly interests us—suppose you dismiss the present Government, on what principle do you mean to constitute an Administration composed of hon. Gentlemen opposite? Is it proposed by you to leave the privileges of this House an open question? Is it intended that your proposed Government should consist of those amongst you who declare themselves favourable to our privileges? Will it be said, that the question of privilege is of less importance than the question of the ballot? It is from the question of privilege that the question of the ballot, and all similar questions, derive their importance. And of what consequence is the mode in which you are elected, if, when you meet, you do not possess the privileges necessary for your efficiency as a branch of the Legislature? Is anything more clear than that, if an address (which is likely) were presented to the Crown on the subject of our privileges, you could never agree as to the answer to be given to it? Why, can any question be more important than that which should determine in what relation we stand to our constituents in the Courts of Judicature, and to the other branches of the Legislature? And, on the other hand, what is more monstrous (if we take the view of those opposed to our privileges) than that we should assert our privileges by attacking the liberty of the subject, by infringing on the functions of the courts where her Majesty dispenses the law, and committing to prison persons guilty only of the crime of appealing to the laws of their country? Can you conceive anything more absurd than the Prime Minister, over night, sending men to prison, to whom his law officers and supporters pay complimentary visits in the morning? I seriously believe that the differences of opinion on the other side on the question of privilege would, if a Ministry were formed from that quarter, produce, practically, more inconvenience in a week, than leaving the ballot an open question is likely to produce in ten years. The right hon. Baronet asks in what does the present Government differ from the Chartists? One Member of the present Government has, it is true, declared himself favourable to the ballot. I objected to the use of the word pledged; for I never gave any constituent body a pledge.

It is alleged too, that because I maintained that a 10*l.* house being considered a sufficient proof of a man's stake in the country to fit him to be a voter, it was not desirable his locality should decide upon his right of voting—for this reason, I stand exactly in the same position as those who would abolish all pecuniary qualification. I cannot see, however, in what way I admit, in the least, the doctrine of those who would abolish all qualification whatever, by expressing a desire to see the present 10*l.* franchise extended. In my opinion, a pecuniary qualification is indispensably necessary to the safety of the empire. In my opinion the 10*l.* qualification has never proved too high; and supposing society to continue in its progress—supposing education to continue, and the distribution of property, and the value of money to remain as they are, if I can foresee anything in my public conduct, I shall abide by the opinion which I have just expressed as to the question of the franchise. This is my answer to the right hon. Baronet, and if it does not convey to him a proof that my opinions are different from those of the Chartists on this subject, his conception of their doctrines differs very widely from mine. I come to that which, through the whole debate, has formed the principal subject of observation; for it must be clear, that it is not on the conduct of Commissioner Lin, or of Captain Elliot, or on the hostilities on the river La Plata, or on any circumstance of this kind, that the result of this debate must turn. The main argument of the hon. Gentleman opposite, used by the hon. Baronet who opened the debate, repeated by his seconder, and constituting the substance of every speech which has been delivered, amounts to this:—"The country is in an unsatisfactory state—there is great turbulence—there is great disposition to extensive political change—and at the bottom of all lies the agitating policy of those Whigs. They raised themselves to power by means of agitation—they strengthened themselves in favour by means of agitation—they carried the Reform Bill by means of agitation—and we are now paying the fruits of their acts. All this

Chartism is but the effect of their conduct; and it is evident that from those who have caused the evil you cannot expect the remedy. We ought to dismiss them, and seek others who, never having excited the people to turbulence, will command the confidence of the country." I don't know whether I have stated it correctly, but this, as nearly as I could collect, is the substance of what has been urged by hon. Gentlemen opposite. Now, I might fellow the example set by my right hon. Friend (the Judge Advocate) in his most noble and eloquent speech, and content myself with stating that this agitation belonged principally to the Government of Lord Grey. Of that Government, the noble Lord, the Member for Lancashire, and the right hon. Member for Pembroke were Members. I might say—"they were then distinguished Members of this House. To them I leave the task of exculpation—to them I leave it to defend agitation—to them I leave it to decide on what principle, and to what extent, they shared in such means of carrying public questions." In spite of that challenge which my right hon. Friend gave the right hon. Baronet, he gives no explanation, but contents himself with the simple confession—"I liked the Reform Bill—I agitated for it. I was carried I admit far beyond prudence, and just on the verge of the law." Is it possible that any gentleman possessing only a very small part of the foresight of the right hon. Gentleman should not perceive, that as soon as this defence is admitted, this consequence must of necessity follow—that the only question is, whether the measures to be agitated for are good in themselves, and not whether agitation itself be good or bad. The right hon. Baronet admits, then, that agitation itself is a proper and legitimate mode of carrying any measure that is good. When the right hon. Baronet comes forward to charge the present Government with agitation, and directs his reproaches against no member of that Government more than myself, I confess I feel some inclination to remonstrate with the right hon. Gentleman for want of generosity: for my interest in this question is small indeed, compared with that of the right hon. Gentleman himself. I, Sir, was not a member of the Cabinet that brought in the Reform Bill —I was not one of those Ministers who told their Sovereign they would serve him no longer unless he would create a sufficient number of Peers to carry their measures. I, Sir, at that time was merely one of those hundreds within these walls, and of millions throughout the country, who were firmly and deeply impressed with the conviction that the Reform Bill was a great and salutary measure—who reposed the greatest confidence in the abilities, the integrity, and the patriotism of the Ministers; and I must add, that in no Member of that administration did I place greater confidence for the possession of those high qualities than in the noble Lord the Secretary for Ireland, and in the right hon. Gentleman the First Lord of the Admiralty. In none did I place greater confidence that they would take measures to guard against the evils inseparable from all great changes, and take heed that they did not produce consequences injurious to the community. Is it not extraordinary that we should be reproached with what was, in fact, confidence in the noble Lord and right hon. Gentleman, by the very men who are seeking to raise that noble Lord and right hon. Gentleman to power? If the provisions of the Reform Bill point to Chartism—if the doctrines of Chartism are to be traced to the spirit of that enactment, then, Sir, I am bound to say that none more than the noble Lord and the right hon. Gentleman are answerable for it. If men are to be deemed disqualified for places in the councils of their Sovereign, because they exerted themselves to carry that bill, because they appealed to the people to support that bill, because they employed means, certainly lying within the verge of the law, but certainly also, as has been observed, just within the confines of prudence, then, Sir, I do say that no men in this empire lie under a disqualification for office more complete, more entire, than the noble Lord and the right hon. Baronet. Sir, I leave to them the task of defending themselves; well are they qualified by their talents to do so; but if the noble Lord does not answer, then it will remain for the right hon. Baronet, who twice offered both of them places in his Cabinet, to do so. If the noble Lord and the right hon. Baronet (or, as I trust he will permit me, in spite of some few asperities this evening, to call him my right hon. Friend) will forgive me, I would offer some considerations in extenuation of their conduct. I would say, "You condemn agitation. Do you mean to say that abuses shall never be removed? If they are to be removed, then I ask, is it possible that any great abuse can, in a country like this, be removed till the public feeling is against it, or that the public feeling can be raised and kept up without arguments, without exertions, both by speech and writing, the holding of public meetings, and other means of a like nature?" Sir, I altogether deny that assertion or insinuation, which I heard over and over again, both yesterday and this night, in this House, that a Government which countenances, or does not discountenance, agitation will not punish rebellion. There may be a similarity in the simple act between the man who bleeds and the man who stabs; but is there no difference in the nature of the action—in its intent and in its effects? I do not believe there has been one instance of justifiable insurrection in this country for a century and a-half. On the other hand, I hold agitation to be essential, not only to the obtaining of good and just measures, but to the existence of a free Government itself. If you choose to adopt the principle of Bishop Horsley, that the people have nothing to do with the laws but to obey them, then, indeed, you may deprecate agitation; but, while we live in a free country, and under a free Government, your deprecation is vain and untenable. If a man lives in Russia and can obtain an audience of the Emperor Nicholas or of Count Nesselrode, and can produce proof that certain views he entertains are sound, certain plans he proposes would be attended with practical benefit, then, indeed, without agitation, without public discussion, with a single stroke of the pen, a great and important change is at once effected. Not so, Sir, in this country. Here the people must be appealed to—the public voice must be consulted. In saying this have I defended one party alone—have I not defended alike both the great parties in this House? Have we not heard of agitation against the Catholic claims? Has there been no agitation against the Poor-law? Has there been no agitation against Education? Has there been no agitation against the Catholic Privy Councillors? But to pass, Sir, from questions about which there may fairly exist a difference of opinion, to measures upon which we must all agree—to pass to a measure of the proudest, grandest nature that ever received the sanction of a legislature; I say that the Slave-trade would never have been abolished without agitation. I say that slavery would never have been abolished without agitation. Would your prison discipline, or the severities of your penal code, have been ameliorated without agitation? I am far, very far, Sir, from denying that agitation may be much abused—that it may be carried to a most unjustifiable length. But, Sir, so also may freedom of speech in this House, so also may the liberty of the press. What is agitation when it is examined, but the mode in which the people in the great outer assembly debate? Is it not as necessary that they should have their discussion without the walls of this House, as we who sit within them? There may, indeed, be occasional asperities in popular meetings, as experience has shown that there frequently are in debates in this House, but that is no reason why freedom of debate should be abridged in either. I know well that agitation is frequently used to excite the people to resist the law, but that that is a proper subject for animadversion upon the Magistrates, I deny—that the agitation of the present time is evidence of the agitation of the Government of Lord Grey, I deny. It is perfectly true that what is said in this House, or any other public assembly, though it may be moderate, reasonable, and may point only to the legal remedy for an abuse, may yet be taken up by the disingenuous man, and be so twisted, distorted, and perverted, that it may excite the populace to acts of crime. I have heard within the walls of this House, the right hon. Gentleman opposite—not, I am sure, with any improper motive—apply to secret meetings of men for lawless purposes, expressions which the noble Lord used only with respect to public and open meetings. The right hon. Gentleman ought to remember, that his own words have been applied by bad men for the delusion of the multitude. One of the speeches which has been used by the Chartists as a handle for their excesses, was a speech of the right hon. Baronet. Do I blame him for that? No. He said nothing which was not within the just line of his duty as a Member of this House. I allude to a speech which the right hon. Baronet made upon the subject of the emoluments divided among the Privy Councillors. I fully acquit the right hon. Gentleman of saying anything that was not in strict conformity with his duty, but it is impossible for any man so to guard his expressions that bad men shall not misconstrue, and ignorant men misunderstand them. I therefore throw no censure upon the right hon. Baronet, but I do say, that the very circumstance of his own speech having been perverted should make him pause, before bringing charges against men not less attached than himself to the peace and well-being of society—charges having no better foundation than bad reports of their speeches, and his own misapprehension of them. Now, Sir, to pass by many topics which, but for the lateness of the hour I would willingly advert to, I come to that which is really the point. This is not less a comparative than a positive question. The meaning of the vote is not, clearly, whether this House approves in all respects of the conduct of the Government—it is whether this House conceives that a better one can at present be formed. All government is imperfect, but some government there must be; and if the present Government were far worse than any hon. Gentleman on the other side would represent it to be, still it would be every man's duty to support it if he did not see that a better one would supply its place. Now, Sir, I take it to be perfectly clear that in the event of the resignation of the present Administration one must be formed, the first place of which must be filled by the right hon. Baronet opposite. Towards that right hon. Baronet, and towards many of those Noblemen and Gentlemen who, in such an event, would be associated with him, I entertain nothing but kindly and respectful feelings. I am far—very far I hope—from that narrowness of mind which can see merit in no party but his own. If I may venture to parody the old Venetian proverb, I would say, "Be first an Englishman, and then a Whig." Sir, I feel proud for my country when I think how much of integrity—how many virtues and talents which would adorn any station, are to be found among the ranks of my political opponents. Among them, conspicuous for his high character and ability, stands the right hon. Baronet. When I have said this, I have said enough to prove that nothing is further from me than to treat him with the smallest discourtesy in the remarks which, in the discharge of my public duty, I shall feel it necessary to make upon his policy and that of his party. But, Sir, it has been his misfortune, it has been his fate, to belong to a party with whom he has had less sympathy than any head ever had with any party. I speak of that which is a matter of history. I speak now of times long ago. He declared himself decidedly in favour of those principles of free trade which made Mr. Huskisson odious to a great portion of the community. The right hon. Baronet gave every facility for the removal of the disabilities of Protestant Dissenters. The right hon. Baronet brought in a Bill for the relief of Catholic disabilities; yet what we are charged with is bringing that enactment into practical operation. The right hon. Baronet declared himself in favour of the Poor-law; yet if a voice is raised against the "Whig bastiles," or "the tyrants of Somerset House," that cry is sure to proceed from some person who wishes to vote the right hon. Baronet into power. Even upon this great question of privilege, upon which the right hon. Baronet has taken a part which ought to render his name to the end of time honourable in the opinion of this House, and of all who value its privileges, I cannot but conceive that the right hon. Gentleman is at variance with the great body of his supporters. Sir, I have also observed that where the right hon. Baronet does agree with the great body of his supporters in conclusions, he seldom arrives at those conclusions by the same process of reasoning by which their minds are led. Many great questions which they consider as of stern and unbending morality, and of strict principle, have been viewed by him as mere points of expediency, of place, and of time. I have not heard one allegation against the Government of Lord Melbourne which would not enable a Government formed by the right hon. Baronet to bring in, with some little variation, the same measures. I listened to the right hon. Baronet—I always listen to him with pleasure—upon the subject of education, and I could not but be amused at the skill with which he endeavoured to give the reasons of a statesman for the course of a bigot; and my conclusion, as I listened, was that he thought as I did with respect to the Douay version and the Normal schools. Sir, I am irresistibly brought to this conclusion, that in a conjuncture like the present, the right hon. Baronet can conduct the administration of affairs with neither honour to himself, nor with satisfaction to that party who seek to force him into office. I will not affect to feel apprehensions from which I am entirely free. I will not say that I think the right hon. Baronet will act the part of a tyrant. I do not think he will give up this country to the tender mercies of the bigoted part—and which form so large a part—of his followers. I do not believe he would strike out the names of all Catholics from office and from the Privy Council. Nor, Sir, do I believe that the right hon. Baronet will come down to the House with a Bill for a repeal of his own great measure. But, Sir, what I think he will attempt to do is this—he will attempt to keep terms with that party which raises him to power by a course which would soon excite the gravest discontents in all parts of the empire. And at the same time I think, Sir, that he will not carry the course of his administration far enough to keep their steady support. The result I think, will be this—that the right hon. Baronet will lose the support of a great portion of his own party, and, at the same time, he will not gain the support of the other, till at last his Government will fail from causes purely internal. Sir, we have not to act in this merely upon conjecture. We have beheld the same piece performed on the same scene, and by the same actors, at no distant period. In 1827, the right hon. Baronet was, as now, at the head of a powerful opposition. He had a strong minority in this House, and a majority in the House of Lords; he was the idol of the Church and of the Universities; and all those who dreaded change—all those who were hostile to the principles of liberty and the rights of conscience, considered him their leader; he was opposed to those Members who were sometimes called Papists, and sometimes idolaters; he was opposed to a Government which was said to have obtained power by personal intrigue and Court favour. At last the right hon. Baronet rises to the principal place in this House. Free from those difficulties which had embarrassed him, he was in opposition when Tory bigotry had found for the greatest orator, and the most accomplished of Tory statesmen in the nineteenth century, a resting-place in Westminster Abbey, and the right hon. Baronet appeared at the head of Government upon this bench, and those who had raised him to power with the loudest acclamations, and deemed that their expectations must necessarily be accomplished. Is it necessary to say in what disappointment—in what sorrow—in what fury all those expectations ended? The right hon. Baronet had been raised to power by prejudices and by passions in which he had no share. His followers were bigots; he was a statesman. He was calmly balancing conveniences and inconveniences, whilst they were ready to prefer confiscation, proscription, civil war, to the smallest concession to public feeling. The right hon. Baronet attempted to stand well with his party, and at the same time to perform some part of his duty to his country. Vain effort! His elevation, as it had excited the hopes and expectations of his own party, awakened gloomy apprehensions in other quarters. Agitation in Ireland, which for a time had slumbered, awakened with renewed vigour, and became more formidable than ever. The Roman Catholic Association rose to a height of power such as the Irish Parliament in the days of its independence never possessed. Violence engendered violence; scenes such as the country for long years had not witnessed, announced that the time of evasion and delay was passed. A crisis was arrived, in which it was absolutely necessary for the Government of the day to take one part or the other. A plain and simple issue was proposed to the right hon. Baronet—either to disgust his party or ruin his country. He chose the good path; he performed a painful, in some sense a humiliating, but in point of fact a most truly honourable part. He came down himself to propose to this House the great measure of Roman Catholic Emancipation. Amongst the followers of the right hon. Baronet, there were some who, like himself, had considered opposition to the Catholic claims purely as a matter of expediency. These readily changed about, and consented to support his altered policy. But not so the great body of those who had previously followed the right hon. Baronet. With them, opposition to the Roman Catholics was a passion, which a mistaken sense of duty bound them to cherish. They had been deceived, and it would have been more agreeable to them to think, that they had been deceived by others than by one of their own sect—one whom they themselves had been the means of raising to a permanent place in the Administration of the country. How profound was their indignation! With what an explosion did their rage break forth! None who saw that time can ever forget the frantic fury with which the former associates of the right hon. Baronet assailed their quondam chief. Never was such a torrent of invective and calumny directed against one single head. All history and all fiction were ransacked by his own followers to furnish terms of abuse and obloquy. The right hon. Gentleman, whom I am sorry not now to see in his place on the bench opposite, unable to express his feelings in the language of English prose, pursued his late chief with reproaches borrowed from the ravings of the deserted Dido. Another, wresting to his use the page of holy writ, likened him to Judas Iscariot. The great university, which heretofore had been proud to confer upon him the highest marks of its favour, was now foremost to fix upon him the brand of disgrace and infamy. Men came up in crowds from Oxford to vote against him, whose presence a few days before would have set the bells of all their churches jingling. The whole hatred of the high Church party towards those to whom they had previously been opposed, was sunk and absorbed in this new aversion; and thence it happened that the Ministry, which in the beginning of 1828 was one of the strongest that the country ever saw, was at the end of 1829 one of the weakest that a political opponent could desire to combat. It lingered on another year, struggling between two parties, leaning now on the Whigs, now on the Tories—reeling sometimes beneath a blow from the right, sometimes from a blow on the left—certain to fall as soon as the two parties should unite in their efforts to defeat it. At last it fell, attacked by the whole body of the Church, and of the Tory gentry in England. Now, what I wish to know is this: What reason have we to believe, that from an Administration now formed by the right hon. Baronet we could anticipate any different result. The right hon. Baronet is still the same—he is still a statesman? Yes—still a statesman, high in intellect, moderate in opinions, calm in temper, free from the fanaticism which is found in so large a measure among his followers. I will not say, that the party which follows him is still the same, for in my opinion it has undergone a change, and that change is this—it has become fiercer and more intolerant even than in days gone by. I judge by the language and doctrines of its press; I judge by the proceedings of its public meetings; I judge by its pulpits—pulpits which are every week teeming with invective and slander that would disgrace the hustings. A change has of late come over the spirit of a part, I hope not the most considerable part, of the Tory party. It was once the boast of that party, that through all changes of fortune they cherished feelings of loyalty, which rendered their very errors respected, and gave to servitude something of the dignity and worthiness of freedom. A great Tory poet, who, in his lifetime, was largely requited for his loyalty, said—

> "Our loyalty is still the same,
> Whether it win or lose the game,
> True as the dial to the sun,
> Although it be not shone upon."

We see now a very different race of Tories. We have lived to see a new party rear its head—a monster of a party, made up of the worst points of the Cavalier and the worst points of the Roundhead. We have lived to see a race of disloyal tories. We have lived to see Toryism giving itself the airs of those insolent pipemen who puffed out smoke in the face of Charles the First. We have lived to see Toryism, which, because it is not suffered to grind the people after the fashion of Strafford, turns round and abuses the Sovereign after the fashion of—(the remainder of the sentence was lost in the cheers of the House.) It is my firm belief that the party by which the present motion is supported throughout the country desire the repeal of the Catholic Emancipation Act. For what I say, I will give my reasons, which I think are unanswerable. In what other way, am I to explain the outcry which has been raised throughout the whole of the country about the three Papist Privy Councillors? Is the Catholic Emancipation Act to be maintained? If it is to be maintained, execute it. Is it to be abandoned? If so, openly and candidly avow it. If it is not to be executed, can anything be more absurd than to retain it upon the statute book? The Tory party resent as a monstrous calumny the imputation that they wish to get rid of the Emancipation Act; but the moment that an attempt is made to execute it, even to a small extent, they set up a cry as if Church and State were going to ruin. For the repeal of the Emancipation Act, I can see a reason—in the desire to repeal it, I see a meaning—a baneful meaning—a pernicious meaning, but still a meaning; but I cannot see a particle of reason nor a glimpse of meaning, in the conduct of those who say, "We will retain the Emancipation Act; those who say we desire to repeal it are calumniators and slanderers; we are as sensible of the importance of that Act as any party in the country," but who, the moment that an attempt is made to execute one jot or tittle of it, exclaim, "No, if you attempt to put the Act in force, we will agitate against you, for we, too, have our agitation; we will denounce you in our associations, for we, too, have our associations; our oracles shall be sent forth to talk of civil war, of rebellion, of resistance to the laws, and to give hints about the fate of James 2nd—to give hints that a Sovereign who has merely executed the law may be treated like a Sovereign who has most grossly violated the law." I could understand a person who told me, that he had a strong objection to admit Roman Catholics to power or office in England; but how any man who professes not to think, that an invidious distinction should be made between Catholic and Protestant, can bring himself to the persuasion that the Roman Catholics in this country enjoy more than a fair share of official power and emolument, I own passes my comprehension. What is the proportion of Roman Catholics to the whole population of the kingdom? About one fourth. What is the proportion of Roman Catholic Privy Councillors? Perhaps three to two hundred. And what, after all, is the dignity of a Privy Councillor?—what power does the seat of a Privy Councillor, merely as such, confer? Are not the hon. Gentlemen opposite Privy Councillors? If a change of administration were effected to-morrow, and the right hon. Gentlemen opposite were to come into office, would not those whom they displaced, be still Privy Councillors? In point of fact, the seat of a Privy Councillor absolutely confers no power whatever. Yet, we are seriously called upon to believe, that men, who think it monstrous that this mere futile honorary distinction should be given to three Roman Catholics, do still in their hearts desire to maintain a law by which a Roman Catholic may become Commander-in-chief, with all the promotion of the army in his hands; First Lord of the Admiralty, with all the patronage of the navy—Secretary of State for the Foreign Department, entrusted with all the interests of the country, as connected with foreign states—Secretary for the Colonies, with the whole conduct of our remoter dependencies—or First Lord of the Treasury, possessing the chief influence in every department of the state. I say, therefore, that unless I suppose, that a great portion of the Opposition who have raised throughout England, the cry against the three Roman Catholic Privy Councillors—unless I suppose them more childish, more imbecile than I would willingly suppose any number of my fellow-countrymen to be, I must suspect that the abolition of the Catholic Emancipation Act, is the chief object of a great proportion of that party which now ranges itself in direct hostility to the Government. The right hon. Baronet (Sir R. Peel) is, in my opinion, the same that he was in 1829; but his party, instead of being the same, is worse than it was at that period. The difficulty of governing Ireland, in opposition to the feelings of the great body of the people, is, I apprehend, now as great as ever it was. The right hon. Baronet, last year, was deeply impressed with that difficulty. The impossibility of governing Ireland in conformity with the sense of the great body of the people, and, at the same time, in conformity with the views and opinions of his own followers, is now, I apprehend, as great as ever. What, then, is to be the end of an Administration of which the right hon. Baronet should be head? Supposing the right hon. Baronet to come into office by the vote to-night, should I be wrong if I were to prophesy that, three years hence, he would be more vilified by the Tory party, than the present Government has ever been? Should I be very wrong, if I were to prophesy, that all the literary organs of his party now forward to sound his praise, would be amongst the foremost, the boldest, and the loudest to denounce him? Should I be very wrong if I were to prophesy that he would be burnt in effigy by the very people who are now clamorous to toast his health? Should I be very wrong if I were to prophesy that the very party who now crowd the House to vote him into power, would then crowd the lobby to bring Lord Melbourne back? Yes, already have I seen the representatives of the Church, and of the Universities of England, crowding the lobby of the House, for the purpose of driving the right hon. Baronet from the place to which they had previously raised him. I went out with them myself, when the whole body of the Tory Gentlemen—all the Representatives of the Church and of the Universities—united to force the right hon. Baronet from the position which he occupied in the councils of his Sovereign. I went out into the lobby, as the right hon. Baronet, the Member for Pembroke (Sir James Graham), will bear me witness, when those Gentlemen went out for the purpose of bringing into power Lord Grey, Lord Althorp, Lord Brougham, and Lord Durham. You may say, that they reasoned ill—perhaps they were weak—perhaps they did not see all that would happen. But so it was; and what has been once may be again. As far as I can see my way, it is absurd to suppose, that the party of which the right hon. Baronet is the head, would be content with less from him than they would take from Lord Melbourne. I believe just the contrary. I believe, that of all men in the world, the right hon. Baronet is most the object of distrust to the party opposite. They suffer him to remain at their head, because his great abilities, his eloquence, his influence are necessary to them; but they distrust him, because they never can forget that in the greatest crisis of his public life, he chose rather to be the victim of their injustice than to be its instrument. It is absurd to say, that that party will never be propitiated by any partition amongst their chiefs of the power or fruits of office. They can truly adopt the maxim, "measures not men." They care not who has the sword of state borne before him at Dublin—they list not who wears the badge of Saint Patrick on his breast—what they dislike, what they are invincibly opposed to, are the two great principles which had governed the administrations of Lord Normanby and Lord Ebrington—justice and mercy. What they want is not Lord Haddington, or any other nobleman of their own party whom the right hon. Baronet (Sir Robert Peel) might appoint to the Viceroyalty of Ireland; but the tyranny of race over race, and creed over creed. Give them this power, and you convulse the empire; withhold it, and you break up the Tory party. Supposing the vote of to-night to be carried in the affirmative, the right hon. Baronet (Sir R. Peel) would not be a month in office before the dilemma of 1829 would be again before him. With every respect for his intentions, with the highest opinion of his ability, I believe that at this moment it would be utterly impossible for him to head the Administration of this country without producing the most dreadful calamities to Ireland. Of this I believe he was himself sensible when he was last year called upon to form an Administration. The state of the empire was not at that time very cheering. The Chartists were abroad in England—the aspect of Canadian affairs was not pleasing—an expedition was pending in the East which had not then ended in success—discontent prevailed in the West Indies. Yet, in the midst of all these troubles, the discerning eye of the right hon. Baronet left him in no doubt as to the quarter in which his real danger lay—he knew 'twas Ireland. The right hon. Baronet admitted that his great difficulty would be in the government of Ireland. I believe that the present ministry possessed the confidence of the great body of the people of Ireland; and I believe that what it does for the people of Ireland, it can do with less irritation from the opposite party in England, than the right hon. Baronet would find it possible to do. I believe that if, with the best and purest intentions, the right hon. Baronet were to undertake the Government of this country, he would find that it was very easy indeed to lose the confidence of the party which raised him to power; but very difficult indeed to gain that which the present Government happily possessed—the confidence of the people of Ireland. It is upon these grounds, and principally upon the question of Ireland, that I should be inclined to rest the case of the present Ministry. I know well, how little chance there is of finding here or anywhere an unprejudiced audience upon this subject. Would to God that I were speaking to an audience that would judge this great controversy fairly and with an unbiassed mind, and as it will be judged by future ages. The passions which inflame us—the sophistries which delude us, will not last for ever. The paroxysms of faction have their appointed season, even the madness of fanaticism is but for a day. The time is coming when our conflicts will be to others as the conflicts of our forefathers are to us; when our priests who convulse the State—our politicians who make a stalking-horse of the Church, will be no more than the Harleys and Sacheverells of a by-gone day; and when will be told, in a language very different from that which now draws forth applause at Exeter Hall, the story of these troubled years. Then it will be said that there was a portion of the empire which presented a striking contrast to a portion of the rest. Not that it was doomed to sterility, for the soil was fruitful and well watered—not that it wanted facilities for commerce and trade, for its coasts abounded in havens marked by nature to be the marts of the whole world—not that the people were too proud to improve these advantages or too pusillanimous to defend them, for in endurance of toil and gallantry of spirit they were conspicuous amongst the nations—but the bounty of nature was rendered unavailable from the tyranny of man. In the twelfth century this fair country was a conquered province, the nineteenth found it a conquered province still. During the interval many great changes took place in other parts of the empire, conducing in the highest degree to the happiness and welfare of mankind; but to Ireland they brought only aggravation and misery. The Reformation came, bringing with it the blessings of Divine truth and intellectual liberty. To Ireland it brought only religious animosity, to add flame and fuel to the heats of national animosity, and to give, in the name of "Papist," another war-cry to animate the struggle between England and Ireland. The Revolution came, bringing to England and Scotland civil and religious liberty—to Ireland it brought only persecution and degradation. In 1829 came Catholic Emancipation, but it came too late, and came too ungraciously—it came as a concession made to fear; it was not followed nor accompanied by a suitable line of policy. It had excited many hopes—it was followed by disappointment. Then came irritation and a host of perils on both sides. If agitation produced coercion, coercion gave rise to fresh agitation: the difficulties and danger of the country thickened on every hand, until at length arose a Government which, all other means having failed, determined to try the only means that have never yet been fairly and fully applied to Ireland—humanity and justice. The State, so long the step-mother of the many, and the mother only of the few, became now the common parent of all the great family. The great body of the people began to look upon the Government as a kind and beneficent parent. Battalion after battalion—squadron after squadron—was withdrawn from the shores of Ireland; yet every day property became more secure, and order more manifest. Such symptoms as cannot be counterfeited—such as cannot be disguised —began to appear; and those who once despaired of that great portion of the commonwealth, began to entertain a confident hope that it would at length take its place among the nations of Europe, and assume that position to which it is entitled by its own natural resources, and by the wit and talent of its children. This, I feel, the history of the present Government of Ireland will one day prove. Let it thus go on; and then as far as I am concerned, I care not what the end of this debate may be, or whether we stand or fall. That question it remains with the House to decide. Whether the result will be victory or defeat I know not; but I know that there are defeats not less glorious than even victory itself; and yet I have seen and I have shared in some glorious victories. Those were proud and happy days—even my right hon. Friend who last addressed you will remember them,—those were proud and happy days when, amidst the praises and blessings of millions, my noble Friend led us on in the great struggle for the Reform Bill—when hundreds waited around our doors till sun-rise to hear the tidings of our success—and when the great cities of the empire poured forth their populations on the highways to meet the mails that were bringing from the capital the tidings whether the battle of the people was lost or won. Those days were such days as my noble Friend cannot hope to see again. Two such triumphs would be too much for one life. But, perhaps, there still awaits him a less pleasing, a less exhilarating, but not a less honourable task, the task of contending against superior numbers, through years of discomfiture, to maintain those civil liberties—those rights of conscience which are inseparably associated with the name of his illustrious house. At his side will not be wanting men who, against all odds, and through all the turns of fortune, amidst evil days and evil tongues, will defend to the last, with unabated spirit, the noble principles of Milton and Locke. He may be driven from office—he may be doomed to a life of opposition—he may be made the mark for all the rancour of sects which may hate each other with a deadly hate, yet hate his toleration more—he may be exposed to the fury of a Laud on one side, and to the fanaticism of a Praise-God-Barebones—but a portion of the praise which we bestow on the old martyrs and champions of freedom will not be refused by posterity to those who have, in these our days, endeavoured to bind together in real union, sects and races, too long hostile to each other, and to efface, by the mild influence of a parental Government, the fearful traces which have been left by the misrule of ages.

THANKS TO THE INDIAN ARMY.*

FEBRUARY 6, 1840.

He could not refrain from expressing his high gratification at the unanimity of the House on this very interesting occasion, and at the manner especially in which the right hon. Baronet [Sir R. Peel] had expressed himself in reference to the conduct of the British in India. It was not his intention to enter into any of the political questions which might be considered in connection with this expedition, but he wished to make a remark upon what had fallen from the right hon. Baronet in reference to Lord Auckland. The right hon. Gentleman had omitted all mention of a case of the highest importance—the case of Lord Minto—to whom, after the reduction of Java, the thanks of the House were awarded for the part which he had taken in superintending the military arrangements; nor was the right hon. Baronet correct in supposing that Lord Wellesley had only received the thanks of Parliament as Captain-general, since he also received the thanks of the House in connection with the taking of Seringapatam, when he did not act as Captain-general. He quite conceded to the right hon. Baronet the right, and he fully admitted the propriety, of reserving his opinion as to the general policy under which the expedition took place, till the results were known; but his own conviction was, that this great event would be found, in its results, highly conducive to the prosperous state of our finances in India, and that, as a measure of economy, it would be found not less deserving of praise than it confessedly was in a military point of view. He could bear witness

* Hansard, 3d Series, vol. li. p. 1334–1336.

to some of the circumstances to which his right hon. Friend had alluded. Among many peculiarities of our Indian empire there was no one more remarkable than this—that the people whom we governed there were a people whose estimate of our power sometimes far exceeded the truth, and sometimes fell far short of it. They knew nothing of our resources; they were ignorant of our geographical position; they knew nothing of the political condition of the relative power of any of the European states. They saw us come and go, but it was upon an element with which they were not acquainted, and which they held in horror. It was no exaggeration to state that not merely the common people, but the upper classes—nay, even the ministers of the native provinces—were, almost without exception, so profoundly ignorant of European affairs that they could not tell whether the King of the French or the Duke of Modena was the greatest potentate. Further, he could tell the House this—when he was in India there was a restless, unquiet feeling existing in the minds of our subjects, neighbours, and subsidiary allies—a disposition to look forward to some great change, to some approaching revolution; to think that the power of England was no longer what it had been proved to be in former times. There was a disposition to war on the part of Ava and other states; on every side, in short, there had prevailed a feeling in the public mind in India, which, unchecked, might have led the way to great calamities; but this great event, this great triumph at Ghuznee, acted so signally by the British troops, had put down, with a rapidity hardly ever known in history, this restless and uneasy feeling; and there never was a period at which the opinion of our valour and skill, and what was of equal importance, the confidence in our "star," was higher than it now was in India. He believed that the right hon. Baronet opposite would find reason to think that all the expense incurred by these thousands of camels and thousands of troops was sound and profitable economy. He had seen something of the brave men who defended our Indian empire, and it had been matter of great delight to him to see the warm attachment to their country and their countrymen which animated them in that distant land, and which added a ten-fold force to the zeal and vigour with which they performed their arduous duties. While he was on this point, let him remark that there was a disposition in that gallant service to imagine that they were not sufficiently appreciated at home; to think that the Indian service was not so highly considered in England as other services not less able, nor performed with less jeopardy, in other countries. It was extraordinary to see the interest, with what gratification, the smallest scrap, the merest line, in an English newspaper, conveying any praise on this service, was received by them, and their delight would be extreme when they came to read the vote of thanks which had been conferred on them unanimously by the House of Lords, and which he trusted would be passed as unanimously by the House of Commons, the more especially accompanied as it was by the testimony to their merits borne by the greatest general that England ever produced. At the same time that this well-merited tribute conferred the highest pleasure on the brave men who shared in the expedition, it would serve as a powerful inducement to every other man in that gallant service to expose himself to every peril and every privation when the interests of the empire required it.

PRIVILEGE—STOCKDALE *v.* HANSARD—BILL TO SECURE PUBLICATION.*

MARCH 6, 1840.

He promised not to detain the House for more than a few minutes, but he confessed he had listened with so much pain to the expressions of his noble Friend, and of one or two other Gentlemen with whom, during the former proceedings upon this subject, he had most cordially concurred, that he was exceedingly unwilling to allow the question to go to a division without explaining, very briefly, the ground upon which he should give his vote. He had not as yet taken any part in the discussions upon this question. He would not again go over the ground which others had already trod with an ability and eloquence which he was sensible he could only feebly imitate. He would only say, in general, that he believed the House of Commons to be, by the law of the land, the sole judge of its own privileges—that he believed the privilege of publication to be by the law of the realm one of the privileges of the House—that he believed it to be a privilege essential to the due discharge of the duties of the House—that he believed the decision of the Queen's Bench, which attacked that privilege, to have been a decision founded not on law nor on reason, and that he never could give his support to any proposition that he conceived would tend to render that privilege doubtful. If the proposition now before the House were for a law to provide that henceforth this privilege should belong to the House of Commons, to such a proposition he should give the strongest opposition.

* Hansard, 3d Series, vol. 52, p. 1010–1016.

But such was not the proposition of his noble Friend. He could perfectly understand, that by proposing to enact that such or such should be the right and privilege of the House, a question might be raised as to whether such a right or privilege had previously existed. The declaration that it should exist hereafter might appear to carry with it the implication that it had not existed previously. But the proposition in the present case was altogether different. All that was now proposed was by a new law to provide a new remedy for enforcing an old and well-established and undoubted privilege. He would take instances from cases perfectly familiar to every one. Suppose any Gentleman should propose to bring in a law to provide that a person holding a bill of exchange for a good consideration, should be entitled to have an action against the acceptor of that bill, to recover payment. The consequence of such a proceeding would be to throw into a state of doubt the whole of the negotiable paper current throughout the kingdom. But if, on the other hand, a bill were proposed to this effect—that the means of holders of bills of exchange not being sufficient to enable them to recover payment, therefore other means should, by a new enactment, be extended to them—would any person tell him that a measure of such a nature, acknowledging the right to recover in the fullest extent, but giving to the holders of negotiable papers an additional remedy—would any one tell him that such a measure would, in the smallest degree, bring into question the previously existing right of the holders of bills of exchange to proceed against the acceptors to recover payment? In point of fact, the proposition now before the House was not to provide, by a new law, that the House should have the privilege of publication—not to affect any of the existing remedies which the House already possessed for the vindication of its privileges—but simply to superadd a new remedy. It was not even proposed to substitute the new remedy for the old ones. The bill proposed by his noble Friend left the old remedies absolutely untouched. If, after the passing of this bill, any other person should think fit to imitate the example of Mr. Stockdale, and to set the privileges of the House at defiance, it would be as much as ever in the power of the House to send that person to prison. As he understood the bill, it did not acknowledge, did not in any way imply, that the House would not retain that power. It was founded merely upon this—that the remedies which the House now possessed, were in some respects imperfect, in some respects inconvenient. Did not every Member of the House acknowledge that fact? The noble Lord had referred to conversations which took place out of that House. Was there a single Member of the House who, when he went into the lobby, would hesitate to admit that there were some imperfections—some inconveniences in the remedies which it at present possessed for the vindication of its privileges? Was that a perfect remedy which applied only to one half of the year—which protected the privilege of the House during the sitting of Parliament, but left it wholly unguarded during the recess? Was that a perfect remedy which could only be applied by means of so large and so divided an assembly as the House of Commons? The noble Lord had stated what he thought to be the cause why so many Gentlemen on the opposite side of the House had ranged themselves against, what he conceived to be, the undoubted privilege of the House. But, whatever the cause, could there be any doubt as to its effect? Was there any doubt that there was within the walls of that House, a large body of Gentlemen who had done everything in their power to prevent the House from enforcing its privileges? What had been the loss of time upon this question? Was it not a matter of regret, that more time than had been occupied in the discussion of the most important measures—measures in which the interests of every part of the empire were deeply concerned—had this year been devoted to the discussion of a subject vexatious and troublesome in itself, important no doubt in many particulars, but singularly likely to be misconstrued and misunderstood by the people? His noble Friend said, he thought it necessary for the vindication of the privileges of the House to imprison the sheriffs; but at the same time he said he acquitted them of all moral blame. Was it not a matter of regret that the House to vindicate itself should be obliged to imprison persons guilty of no moral blame? Was that a convenient course? Let the House consider the case of the sheriff. He was not a person who sought his office—not a person who was fined for his office. He was taken and compelled to serve whether he would or not. He often made great interest to be exempted. "No matter," said the right hon. Gentleman, "you take him and compel him to serve you—you place him between two opposite forces—he receives commands and counter commands from both—he cannot obey both, and the moment he obeys one he is sent to prison for not obeying the other." Was that a state of the law desirable to be continued? Was it a state of the law in which the great body of the people were likely to acquiesce? He admitted that the House had no choice in the matter; it was compelled to imprison the sheriffs. He admitted, also, that the noble Lord the member for Lancashire had stated last night, that if the House had not imprisoned the sheriffs, the Court of Queen's Bench would have imprisoned them. But that fact, so far from being an argument against the course now proposed by his noble Friend, appeared to him to furnish a strong ground in support of it. If a nation were forced to go to war, it was oftentimes compelled to make the innocent suffer with the guilty. If, for instance, there were a small neutral Power situated between two hostile and belligerent nations, however anxious that small power might be to preserve its neutrality, and to keep itself distinct from the quarrels of its neighbours, it would almost inevitably happen, that one or other of the two great Powers would find it necessary for the protection of its own immediate interests, or for the better prosecution of its hostilities, to encroach on the independence of the smaller State, and to make it an instrument in the advancement of its own views. This was conspicuous during the last war in the case of Holland. We know how little Holland liked Bonaparte—how it detested his continental system, how it hated his dominion—yet we were at last forced to blockade her ports, and to treat her with severity, because it was essential to the preservation of our own interests and our own independence. In the same way did he (Mr. Macaulay) defend the necessity which compelled the House of Commons to send the sheriffs to prison. But he maintained that this was a state of things which rendered it absolutely necessary for the House to resort to some legislative enactment to prevent a recurrence of similar difficulties for the future. He did not understand what a Legislature existed for, if not to meet such cases as these. If there were two powers in the State, neither of which was in the nature of a Court of Appeal from the other—if these two powers gave counter orders to the same officer, and had the power of imprisoning him if he disobeyed—if the officer, distracted between the two, obeyed one and was immediately imprisoned by the other, surely, if ever there was a case in the world for legislative interference, that was one. Nay, he would go further: the Solicitor-General stated last night that the House had the power of commitment; and then went on to contend that all experience had shown that that power was sufficient to enable it to vindicate its privileges. No doubt it would be sufficient, if it were vested in the hands of a party who were ready to exercise it unsparingly and unmercifully. If the House were in all cases to do that, he certainly believed that it would have no difficulty in carrying its point. They all knew how the ancestor of his noble Friend the Member for Cornwall (Lord Eliot) was treated—how he was kept in prison till his spirits, health, and strength gave way—how his imprisonment was continued even to the hour of his death. But in the present day it was impossible for the House of Commons to pursue so harsh a course. Their own good nature would not allow them to do so. The feelings of the people would not permit them to do so. The very moment that the health or spirits of a prisoner began to suffer, that moment the House began to relent, and either upon the instant, or shortly afterwards, the prisoner was set at liberty. So that when the House possessed itself of a prisoner of a robust and hardy constitution, it might have the power of completely vindicating its privileges, by detaining him in prison till the question at issue was arranged; but if it happened to have a prisoner of a bilious and apoplectic habit, in that case its privileges must be abandoned, or only feebly asserted, because the health of the prisoner suffered from confinement. Even if the health of Mr. Stockdale himself should appear to be seriously affected by his imprisonment, it was certain that he would not long be detained in custody. Under these circumstances, it appeared to him, that the House was absolutely compelled to seek some other mode of protecting and vindicating its privileges. The noble Lord had asked, what would be the effect if this bill should be carried through the House of Commons, and lost in the House of Lords. He hoped that the bill would be carried through both branches of the Legislature. He hoped—most earnestly hoped—that the other House of Parliament would interfere to save the country from the scandals and the horrors that would necessarily follow, if it drove the House of Commons, in absolute self-defence, to use the whole of the extreme power which it possessed for the protection of its privileges. But if the Bill should unhappily miscarry in the House of Lords, then he said this, that the House of Commons would be absolved. They would have gone to the other House, not in a degrading or humiliating manner—they would have said, "We do possess the power of vindicating our privileges—we have the power, if we please, of throwing the whole of the country into confusion—we can stop the supplies—we can stop the Mutiny Act—there is no power which any political body can possess which we do not possess—we have the power of imprisoning every man who invades our privileges—we can commit every judge in the country, not being a peer, if he do not respect our privileges. We have the power of confining every ministerial officer who shall execute the sentence of any court, if that sentence be at variance with our privilege; but it is not our wish, by means like these, to enforce even the most necessary of our privileges. We apply for a new remedy, not because we have not in our power remedies that are sufficiently stringent and effective, but because those remedies are such, that some of them cannot be applied without the dissolution of society, and a cruel pressure upon individuals; we have remedies sufficiently severe—we look to you, my Lords, to assist us in adopting one of a milder nature; we have remedies sufficiently powerful to enable us to attain our ends, but which, from their severity, would be disagreeable to the great body of the people—we ask you, my Lords, to give us a remedy which the whole of the people, without exception, will unite in approving." He believed that by going before the House of Lords in that manner, they would have the post of no mean suitors. He believed that there would be nothing degrading on the part of the House of Commons, in bringing forward a measure the object of which was to secure the liberties of the people, and at the same time to enable the House to act with greater lenity in all its dealings with those who, from the misfortune of their situations, or from some other cause over which they had little or no control, had been guilty of violating its privileges. He believed that, if the House of Lords refused to give its assent to such a measure, the House of Commons would then be fairly supported by public opinion in the adoption of measures much stronger than any to which it had yet resorted. He believed that measures stronger even than those suggested by the hon. and learned member for Dublin, would find a support out of the House greater than was imagined by any who sat within the House, if, having proposed a mild remedy for the protection of its privileges, the House should be told by the Lords, that to that mild remedy they would not give their assent.

THE ARMY ESTIMATES.*

MARCH 9, 1840.

His noble Friend (Lord John Russell) had relieved him from the necessity of making some remarks which otherwise he should have thought necessary in reply to the speech of the hon. Member for Kilkenny. He should, therefore, at present only say that any person who had heard that speech, and who was unacquainted with the previous transactions of the country, would have been very slow to believe that the military establishment proposed this year was actually lower in men and charge than that for which the hon. Gentleman himself both voted and spoke. It was only on the 2d of August last, when his noble Friend proposed a supplemental estimate of 75,000*l.* and an addition of men amounting to 5,000, that the hon. Gentleman declared he would not take on himself the responsibility of refusing that sum of money and those men, which his noble Friend declared necessary for the peace and honour of the state. He should be glad to know why the arguments which the hon. Gentleman had used that evening might not, on the 2d of August last year, have been urged with equal effect. All the hon. Gentleman had said respecting the refusal of justice to Canada, all he had said as to the refusal of justice to England, all he had said of those monopolies, some of which he, like the hon. Gentleman, disapproved, as pressing severely on the people of this country, and all he had said as to the condition of the country, might be said exactly with equal propriety and effect on the 2nd of August last year, as it was now. In bringing

* Hansard, 3d Series, vol. lii. p. 1087–1096.

forward the estimates, which he should have the honour of proposing to be laid on the table, he should have the satisfaction, at all events, of thinking that he could not be found liable to the charge of profusion, if the Hon. Gentleman was acquitted of it. The estimate brought forward by his noble Friend, the Member for Northumberland, in February, was 6,119,068*l.* To that sum, in August, was added 75,000*l.*, making the whole charge 6,194,068*l.* The whole charge this year would be 40,000*l.* more; but in this sum there was included a considerable charge for Indian troops, which would be defrayed out of the Indian revenues. The whole force estimated in February, 1839, including the force for India, was 109,818 men, and this year it was 121,112, making an addition of 11,294, but of these 7,746 were employed in defence of India, and chargeable on the revenues of that country. There remained an increase of 3,548 to be added to the 5,000 men voted last August. The additional force that he should have to propose was 4,088. It might be proper to explain the mode in which this addition was made, and the more so, because it would refute, he thought, conclusively, an invidious insinuation of the hon. Member for Kilkenny. About 500 were to be added by an increase of three companies to the 1st West-Indian regiment, and he trusted that such a sum as was requisite would not be refused for raising a force which would spare our own countrymen from the hardships inseparable from foreign service. About 102 men were provided for Malta, which the local authorities declared to be absolutely necessary, not only for the garrison but for port-guard. A small militia (so to speak) was required for Bermuda. It was thought desirable that a portion of the youth of Bermuda should be formed, not as a separate company, but as a sort of body appended to the best troops from England, and thus initiated in the best system of military discipline; and after having been for some time so attached, to return to the mass of the population, being relieved by a new set of young men. So that, in the course of a few years, every man would be trained to the use of arms, and be capable of bearing them should the public service require it. In this manner was made the addition of 500 men which he had spoken of. The remaining addition was made by 65 men being added to every one of the 81 battalions of infantry in the United Kingdom; thus raising each from 835 to 900 men. These 65 men consisted of 4 serjeants, 4 corporals, and 57 privates. To every one of the 20 battalions engaged last year in India 250 men were added, raising each from 853 to 1,103 men; and, lastly, of the two battalions transferred to India, the increase was made from 835 to 1,103, being an addition of 268. And now he wished particularly to call the attention of the House to this circumstance, because the hon. Gentleman the Member for Kilkenny had said, he had observed that every Government had an interest in proposing an increased force, because it placed at their disposal many comfortable things. Now the whole additional regimental charge for the increase to the 81 battalions he had referred to, did not afford the Government or the Horse Guards, the means of obliging a single acquaintance, or conferring a favour on one ten-pound householder. He wished the House to understand, that if the number of 4,408 which were to be added to the army, were struck off, no means of disarming opposition, or gaining support, would be taken away from the Crown. If any Gentleman took the trouble of looking through the different ranks of the service, he would find that the charge for officers this year was diminished by 2,000*l.* The only addition to the foreign force which would come out of the revenues of this country was the three additional companies added to the 1st West-Indian Regiment. Of the 121,112 men, who it was proposed should compose the military establishment, 28,213 would be charged on foreign revenue, leaving 92,899, for whose maintenance this country was to provide. This estimate was somewhat confused, by having included in it 572 men, who were not actually charged on this country, but who, as recruiting companies of Indian regiments, were included in the Mutiny Act. Any man disposed to approve of this measure, would have no difficulty in approving of the many parts of the estimate which contributed to it. The increase in the force sufficiently explained the increase in the regimental charge in the medical department, and the small increase for religious books and tracts granted to the soldiers. Considering that 20,000 men had been raised within the last year, that the applications for works of this nature had been numerous and pressing, and the assistance of benevolent societies not sufficient to supply this want, he thought he was justified in allotting 200*l.* to this purpose. Here was one item about which he believed it was usual to make some statement, and he should say a few words respecting it. As to the good-conduct pay, there was not an increase but a diminution. The full effect of it would not be felt until 1843. The principle of a good conduct-warrant was this, that a soldier who had behaved well during seven years, received an additional 1*d.* a-day to his pay. Every soldier, since 1836, had the option of calling the old additional pay the good-conduct pay. The former was superior in this respect, that it could not be taken away unless by court-martial, and it was no less honourable than secure, for the soldier entitled to it had the power of wearing the good-conduct badge. The consequence was, that in 1840, at which time the soldiers enlisted in 1833 would have completed their seven years, we might expect a considerable addition to the soldiers receiving good-conduct pay. But it was not until 1843 that the effects of the new system, which he confidently expected would be found highly beneficial, could be ascertained. The number of the men wearing the good-conduct badge was about 13,000. He had felt it necessary to make a slight addition to the article of provisions, forage, &c. This he had estimated at 245,000*l.*, and he saw little reason to expect a falling off in that charge. The reason was this: It was known to the committee that the Australian colonies had suffered severely from calamities, which seemed to be a set off against the physical blessings with which they were endowed. The men had suffered from the effects of a most cruel drought; they had been excluded from the benefits of tea, and of vegetables in their soup, and in consequence of the high price of provisions they had been reduced from three to two meals a day, one of which was scanty and unpalatable, consisting only of oatmeal. These privations had fallen with the utmost cruelty upon those to whom our gallant men were most attached, and the medical men reported that the effects of the scarcity were visible upon the women and children attached to the regiments. Under these circumstances, it would be impossible to maintain proper and efficient discipline, and therefore, if even all considerations of humanity were discarded, policy alone would dictate attention to that point. In fact, to a certain and partial extent, discipline had already given way, and in one regiment the crime of theft had spread to some extent. It was, in consequence, therefore, of the distress which the gallant and deserving men serving in the colonies had suffered that he had made this addition of 5,000*l.* to the estimates. In the estimate there were three charges upon which, as they were perfectly new, it would be necessary to enter somewhat into detail. The first was a charge of 3,500*l.* for schoolmistresses. He saw some of his hon. Friends near him smiled, but they were perhaps not aware, as indeed he himself was not until a few weeks ago, of the strong reason there existed for this charge. The number of female children actually accompanying our regiments, was not less than 10,000. Those children were in the most emphatic manner called "the children of the State." For the public service they were hurried from place to place—from Malta to Gibraltar, from Gibraltar to the West-Indies—from the West Indies to Halifax, as the common weal might require. It would, therefore, be inexcusable if we did not provide these, at a small expense, with some means of instruction. Ever since 1811 a schoolmaster had been attached to every regiment, and he thought that there should be a dépôt for the instruction of female children also, under the superintendence of a schoolmistress, who might be probably the wife of a serjeant, and whose duty would be to instruct them in reading, writing, needlework, and the rudiments of common knowledge; with such simple precepts of morality and religion as a good plain woman of that rank might be supposed capable of imparting to them. The next vote to which he had to call the attention of the committee was 10,000*l.* for the formation of a veteran battalion in Canada, where desertions had occurred to an extent unknown elsewhere. About six years ago an inquiry had been made, and it was found—there being there at that time 2,500 rank and file—that desertions had taken place to the number of 663, while, during the same period, the desertions from the whole British army had been only 2,240. These desertions in Canada had not been confined to bad and disreputable characters—non-commissioned officers and men of respectability and good conduct had deserted. Nor was this symptom of desertion to be ascribed to distress, for many had gone away leaving behind them their necessaries and arrears of pay. Why desertion should take place more frequently in North America than in any other part of the empire it was not difficult to explain. In this country, the situation of the soldier was as comfortable, he might say more so, than that of the labourer, to which class generally the soldier belonged. In many of the colonies physical difficulties opposed themselves to flight. When in Malta, the soldiers were surrounded by sea; when at the Cape, they could only escape from their quarters to fly to the dwellings of savages; and as to India, he could imagine no situation more miserable than that of a deserter in that country, wandering amidst its vast regions, amongst a people of a strange race and colour, and his footsteps pursued by the power of British law. But with respect to the American colonies, the case was widely different. There the facilities of escape to the United States were many, and the temptation strong. The soil was flourishing, and the wages of labour high. The consequence was that the high wages, but still more the exaggerated representations that were put forth of the ease and luxury enjoyed by the labourer in America, had constantly drawn away our soldiers from Canada. Several plans had been proposed for meeting this evil. It had been proposed, and he thought wisely, that Canada should be the last point in rotation, to which the troops on colonial service should be sent. There would then be a great number of men with additional pay and good conduct pay, and those higher advantages would tend to keep the men faithful to their colours. It had also been thought that advantages would arise, and the temptation to which he had adverted be counteracted, if the Government were to hold out to the oldest and most tried of the troops in Canada a sort of military retirement, which should serve as a reward to those who remained faithful to their colours. Such had been the opinion of his noble Friend, the late Secretary at War, and of Lord Seaton, and he had reason to believe that that opinion was generally entertained amongst those who possessed the best information upon the subject. The precise details of the plan had not yet been made out, and much correspondence must take place before it could be produced; but as it was not improbable that, before the House again assembled, some regiments would be removed from Canada, it would be desirable that some men of good character should be induced to remain there. On these grounds he was induced to ask the House for the additional grant of 10,000*l.* on account. There was also a sum of 5,000*l.* on account, for the purpose of forming a corps for service in St. Helena—a place which required to be defended not according to the ordinary system. The whole charge for the land force then was 3,511,870*l.* for the present year. That applied for last year, including the supplemental estimate, was 3,496,382*l.* 11*s.* The increase, therefore, on this part of the charge was 15,487*l.* He now came to the staff, in which, in the Home Department, there was an increase, but a corresponding decrease on the foreign staff. On the whole there was an increase of about 550*l.* the reasons for which were to be found in the state of the provinces of New Brunswick and Nova Scotia, where it had been thought desirable that that which had hitherto been a major-general's command should be changed into a lieutenant-general's command, and it was thought that, in consequence of the high responsibility attached to that station, it should be filled by an officer of great talents, and receiving additional pay. Why the charge for Canada was increased, it was unnecessary for him to state. He did not know whether hon. Gentlemen were aware how this part of the estimates was formed—they were framed from the actual expenditure of the last year of which they had the accounts—thus the estimate for 1839 was framed upon that of 1837, and that of 1840 upon that of 1838. With respect to Jamaica, the addition was occasioned by the refusal of the Assembly to vote those allowances which used to be considered as matters of course. The whole charge for the staff in 1839 was, in round numbers, 155,000*l.*, while that for the present year was 164,000*l.* being an increase of 9,000*l.* He was sorry to say, that in consequence of the haste with which these estimates had been prepared, there was an error in the third line of the page, containing the head Public Departments. The item stood there at 5,016*l.* 17*s.* 6*d.*, but it ought to be 6,016*l.* 17*s.* 6*d.* With respect to the Royal Military College, it was unnecessary for him to say anything; and with respect to the Royal Military Asylum, the estimate for this year was 16,701*l.* 9*s.* 8*d.*, while that for last year was 17,486*l.* 3*s.* In the next item there was an increase; it was in the charge for volunteer corps. The vote for last year was 79,136*l.* 18*s.*, while that he asked in the present estimate was 92,993*l.* This had arisen from the expenses of calling out the yeomanry in aid of the civil power. He believed all would admit that, in the trying scenes of last year, the yeomanry exhibited all the valour and firmness for which those corps were distinguished; but in no instance, he believed, had they behaved with rigour and harshness, or otherwise than with propriety and discretion. While, then, the whole charge for effective estimates for last year was 3,807,073*l.*, the charge for the present year was 3,845,450*l.*; being an increase of 39,377*l.* He now came to the non-effective estimates. Under the head of Rewards for Service, there was a small reduction. The amount in 1839 was 16,041*l.* 18*s.*; while for the present year it was 15,815*l.* 10*s.* 1*d.*, being a decrease of 226*l.* The pay for unattached general officers last year was 102,000*l.*; this year it was 92,000*l.*, being a reduction of 10,000*l.* The number of general officers deceased who had received that pay last year was fifteen, and the number promoted to regiments nine. The number of Chelsea pensioners had decreased upwards of 1,000, and he understood there was a balance in the hands of the hospital, and he thought they might venture to make a reduction of 16,667*l.* Before he sat down, he could not help making some few observations on what had fallen from the hon. Member for Kilkenny. He knew well how zealous that hon. Gentleman was in the cause of economy; but he must be permitted to say that that hon. Gentleman had never given a vote so truly in favour of the cause of economy and of civil liberty, as when last August he voted for the increase of the army by 5,000 men, by which he now proposes to reduce it. He believed that that was a just and an economical vote. He had never for a moment doubted, that, on any great crisis that might befal this country, the force marshalled on the side of law and order would be found to be irresistible, and that this great country never could be given over to the hands of freebooters; but at the same time, when he considered the wealth of our great cities, it was not utterly impossible that a mob, exacerbated and infuriated by dishonest leaders, might have inflicted calamities that might have led to a crisis which the ingenuity and good fortune of years could scarcely have effaced. Once and once only, had this great metropolis been in the power of a mob, who for a short time had shown themselves to be stronger than the law, and that was on the occasion of the No Popery Riots in the time of Lord George Gordon. It was a matter of history that, at that time, a sum was awarded for compensation for injuries done to a single house, in a single street, greater in amount than that which was voted last year for the additional 5,000 men. Therefore he would repeat that the hon. Member for Kilkenny had never given a more economical vote than he did in the August of last year. It had been well remarked by Adam Smith, that though standing armies were found hostile to the liberty of the subject, yet that principle must be laid down with qualification. He believed that the remarks of that great man upon this subject were both ingenious and just. He believed that the question before the House a few months ago was simply, whether the force should be increased, or whether the Government should revert to the policy that had been tried by the administration of Mr. Pitt. He would say, then, that whoever voted on that occasion for that increase of force, voted for the House of Commons itself—for the freedom of the people—for the liberty of the press—for the security of property—in fact, for all the characteristics of a free state. Firmly was he convinced that the most happy and beneficial effects flowed from that vote. Nothing had since occurred that could justify her Majesty's Ministers in diminishing their means or their power of upholding and maintaining intact and uninjured the peace, the honour, the dignity and security of this realm. He therefore would place the vote in the hands of the Chairman, with the strongest confidence that it would receive the approbation of the Committee. The right hon. Gentleman concluded by moving, "That a number of land forces, not exceeding 93,471 men (exclusive of the men employed in the Territorial Possessions of the East India Company), commissioned and non-commissioned officers included, be maintained for the service of the United Kingdom of Great Britain and Ireland, from the 1st day of April, 1840, to the 31st day of March, 1841."

THE WAR WITH CHINA.*

APRIL 7, 1840.

If the right hon. Baronet (Sir J. Graham), in rising as the proposer of an attack, owned that he felt overpowered with the importance of the question, one who rose in defence, might certainly, without any shame, make a similar declaration. And he must say, that the natural and becoming anxiety which her Majesty's Ministers could not but feel as to the judgment which the House might pass upon the papers which had been presented to them, had been considerably allayed by the terms of the motion of the right hon. Baronet. It was utterly impossible to doubt the power of the right hon. Baronet, or his will to attack the proceedings of the present Administration; and he must think it a matter on which her Majesty's Ministers might congratulate themselves, that, on the closest examination of a series of transactions so extensive, so complicated, and on some points so disastrous, such an assailant could produce only such a resolution. In the first place, the terms of the resolution were entirely retrospective, and not only so, but they related to no point of time more recent than a year ago; for he conceived that the rupture between this country and China must date from the month of March, 1839, and there had been no omission and no despatch of a later date that could have been the cause of the rupture of our friendly relations. He conceived, therefore, that the present resolution was one which related entirely to past transactions, and while he did not dispute the right of the right hon. Baronet to found a motion, or the right of the

* Hansard, 3d Series, vol. liii. p. 704–720.

House to pass any vote censuring any bygone misconduct on the part of her Majesty's Ministers, he must at the same time feel gratified that the right hon. Baronet did not censure any portion of the present policy of the Government, and that he did not think fit in the present motion to raise any question as to the propriety of the measures, which, since the year 1839, her Majesty's Ministers had adopted. He saw, also, with pleasure that the right hon. Gentleman charged the Administration with no offence of commission; that he imputed to them no impropriety of conduct, no indiscretion, no step which had either lowered the national honour or given to China any just cause of offence. All the complaint was, that they had not foreseen what circumstances might by possibility arise, and that they had not given power to the representative of her Majesty to meet any such unforeseen circumstances; and he must say that such a charge was one which required, and which ought to receive, the most distinct, the fullest, and the most positive proof, because it was of all charges the easiest to make, and the easiest to support by specious reasoning, and, at the same time, it was one of the most difficult to refute. A man charged with a culpable act might defend himself from that act, but it was not possible in any series of transactions that an objection might not be made, that something might not have been done which, if done, would have made things better. The peculiarity of the case then before them was, that a grave charge had been brought against her Majesty's Ministers, because they had not sent sufficient instructions, and because they had not given sufficient power to a representative at a distance of fifteen thousand miles from them; that they had not given instructions sufficiently full, and sufficiently precise, to a person who was separated from them by a voyage of five months. He was ready to admit, that if the papers then on the table of the House related to important negotiations with a neighbouring state, that if they related, for instance, to negotiations carried on in Paris, during which a courier from Downing-street could be dispatched and return in thirty-six hours, and could be again dispatched and again return in as short a period; if such were the nature of the facilities for the parties negotiating, he would say without hesitation that a foreign secretary giving instructions so scanty and so meagre to the representative of the British Government was to blame. But he said, also, that the control which might be a legitimate interference with functionaries that were near, became an useless and a needless meddling with the functionaries at a distance. He might with confidence appeal to Members on both sides of the House who were conversant with the management of our Indian empire, for a confirmation of what he had stated. India was nearer to us than was China; with India, we were better acquainted than we were with China, and yet he believed that the universal opinion was, that India could be governed only in India. Indeed, the chief point which occupied the attention of the authorities at home was to point out the general line of conduct to be pursued; to lay down the general principles, and not to interfere with the details of every measure. If hon. Members only thought in what a state the political affairs of that country would be if they were placed under the sole guidance of a person at a distance of even less than 15,000 miles, they would at once see how absurd such a proposition was. They would see a dispatch written during the first joy at the news of the peace of Amiens received while the French invading army was encamped at Boulogne. They would find a despatch written while Napoleon was in Elba, arriving when he was the occupant of the Tuilleries; and they would have positive instructions sent whilst he was in the Tuilleries to come into operation when he was removed to St. Helena. In India, also, occurrences were continually and rapidly taking place, so that the state of things in Bengal or in the Carnatic would have changed long before the specified instructions could have arrived, and they all knew that the great men who had retained for us that country, Lord Clive and Lord Hastings, had done so by treating particular instructions from a distance as so much waste paper; if they had not had the spirit so to treat them, we should now have no empire in India. But the state of China made a stronger case still. Nor was this all. With regard to India, a politician sitting in Leadenhall-street, or in Cannon-row, might not know the state of things at the distance of India, but he might be acquainted with the general state of the country, its wants, its resources; but with regard to China it should be recollected that that country was not only removed from us by a much greater distance than India, but that those who were permitted to go nearest knew but little of it; for over the internal policy of China a veil was thrown, through which a slight glimpse only could be caught, sufficient only to raise the imagination, and as likely to mislead as to give information. The right hon. Baronet had honourably told the House that the knowledge of Englishmen residing at Canton resembled the notions which might be acquired of our government, our army, our resources, our manufactures, and our agriculture, by a foreigner, who, having landed at Wapping, was not allowed to go further. The advantages of literature even, which in other cases presented an opportunity of holding personal intercourse as well as looking into the character and habits of remote ages, afforded but little help in the case of China. Difficulties unknown in other countries there met the student at the very threshold; so that they might count upon their fingers those men of industry and genius, one of whom had been referred to that night, who had surmounted those difficulties, which were unequalled in the study of any other language which had an alphabet. And under these circumstances, with a country so far removed, and yet as little known to the residents at Canton itself as the central parts of Africa—under these circumstances, he said, in spite of the jeers of hon. Gentlemen opposite, the Secretary of State for Foreign Affairs could not be expected to give the same precise instructions to the representative of his Sovereign as he could to our Ministers at Brussels or the Hague. This was evidently the feeling of the Government of Earl Grey, of that Government to which the right hon. Baronet belonged, and for the acts of which he claimed, and rightly claimed, a full share of responsibility. The instructions, to which the right hon. Baronet was a party, did not go into detail—they laid down the broadest general principles—they simply told the representative of her Majesty to respect the usages of China, and to avoid by all means giving offence to the prejudices or the feelings of the Chinese. As for precise instructions, they never gave any. When the Duke of Wellington came into office, that great man, well versed as he was in great affairs, and knowing as he did, that even a man of inferior ability on the spot could judge better than the ablest man at a distance of 15,000 miles, in the only despatch which he addressed to a resident at Canton, contented himself with referring the Superintendent to the instruction of Lord Palmerston. Now, what he wished to impress on hon. Gentlemen was, that when charges were brought against the Government of omitting to give instructions, or omitting to empower our representative, or that by this omission had been produced a great and formidable crisis in the relations between this country and China, this charge ought to be sustained by the clearest, by the fullest, and by the most precise proof that such was one of the causes, if not the principal cause of such a crisis, and that proof the right hon. Baronet in the course of his long and elaborate speech had altogether failed to give. He had selected from the evidence on the table a great mass of information that was interesting, and much that was by no means applicable to the only point on which the present motion could rest. What were the omissions in the instructions and in the power given to our representative? The right hon. Baronet had read some despatches of the East India Company in 1832; and he had also discussed the conduct of Captain Elliott subsequent to the rupture; but he conceived that neither the one nor the other was before the House; that he had entirely forgotten to notice what act the Government might have done which it had not, and which might have prevented the present unfortunate position of affairs. What, however, were the omissions of which the right hon. Baronet complained? They were four in number. First, that the Government had omitted to correct a point in the Order in Council, which directed the Superintendent to reside in Canton; secondly, that they had omitted to correct the Order in Council on the point which showed the Superintendent a new channel of communication with the Chinese government; thirdly, that they had omitted to act upon the suggestion of the memorandum made by the Duke of Wellington to keep a naval force in the neighbourhood of Canton; and, fourthly, what was most important of all, that they did not give sufficient power to the superintendent to put down the illicit trade. He believed that there was not one other omission specifically mentioned in the able speech of the right hon. Gentleman. With regard to the first omission, the answer was simple. It was true that the order in council, directing the superintendent to reside at Canton, had not been revoked by her Majesty's Government. But it was also true, that no dispute as to the residence of the superintendent had anything to do with the unfortunate rupture; it was true that that dispute was perfectly accommodated. Captain Elliott said, in a letter dated Macao, March 18, 1837:—

"My Lord—A ship upon the point of sailing for Bengal, affords me a prospect of communicating rapidly with your Lordship, by the means of an overland mail of May. I seize this opportunity to transmit the translation of an edict, just procured through a private channel, containing the imperial pleasure, that I shall be furnished with a passport to proceed to Canton for the performance of my duties. The official notification may be expected from Canton in the course of a few days. For the first time in the history of our intercourse with China, the principle is most formally admitted, that an officer of a foreign sovereign, whose functions are purely public, should reside in a city of the empire. His Majesty's Government may depend upon my constant, cautious, and earnest efforts to improve the state of circumstances. I have, &c.

(Signed) "CHARLES ELLIOTT."

Therefore, this point of omission which the right hon. Baronet made an article of charge against the Government was no charge at all; for two years before the rupture the point had been fully conceded in the most formal and honourable manner by the Chinese authorities. And he would venture to say, that in no subsequent letter was there any document which indicated that the place of residence of the superintendent was any point in question. Therefore, he said with confidence, that the first of the right hon. Baronet's omissions had not any groundwork on which it could rest. The second charge was, that the Government did not alter the order in council to direct the superintendent as to his future communications with the Government, and did not tell him not to communicate as the supercargos used to do with the Chinese Government. To that alleged case of omission the answer was, that the Chinese Government had fully conceded the point. Negotiations had taken place between Captain Elliott and the Chinese authorities, and the dispute was, in fact, at an end. As to the question which arose, it was about the use of the word "Pin;" the point was easily answered, because Captain Elliott did not adhere to the construction which was put upon it. He must say, that Captain Elliott, acting under the discretion which it was absolutely necessary that every Government should give to their officers at a distance, had given up the point of superscription, and, therefore, the second omission imputed to the British Government by the right hon. Baronet had nothing to do with the present state of affairs. The third charge brought forward was, that the Government had not provided a vessel of war to be stationed upon the Chinese coast to be ready to act upon any emergency which might arise. What was the recommendation of the Duke of Wellington, in reference to this very subject? It was, that a vessel of war should be off Canton ready to act until the trade of the British merchants should return to its proper channel. He wrote in reference to the state of things which existed at that time, but there was not one syllable in the despatch of the noble Duke which showed that that advice should extend beyond the continuance of the existing circumstances. His Grace said, that he should recommend that, until trade should resume its ordinary course, there should always be within reach of Canton a stout frigate or vessel of war ready to act in case of necessity; but this charge was not made until four years after that advice was given, in the course of which Sir George Robinson had declared that affairs had been restored to their usual condition. The Duke of Wellington recommended that the frigate should be there only until trade should take its regular course. The right hon Baronet had told the House that, subsequently to that, Sir George Robinson had brought about a peaceable state of affairs; and then, after that, when circumstances had occurred which he would venture to say no human mind could have foreseen, it was wondered at, and fault was found, that no vessel was at the spot pointed out. He was confident that nothing was contained in any of the Duke of Wellington's prior despatches which could be taken to exhibit any desire on his part that there should be a naval force constantly upon the Canton station, to await any calamitous event which might take place. Then he came to the fourth charge, which he thought was the most important; for those to which he had already referred he conceived that there existed no ground whatsoever. The fourth point was, that the English Government, having legal authority to do so, had omitted to send to the superintendent at Canton proper powers for the purpose of suppressing the illicit trade which they knew was carried on there. In the first place, during a considerable portion of time since the present administration had been in office, there were stronger reasons in existence than there had been in the time of Lord Grey, or when the Duke of Wellington was Minister for Foreign Affairs, against sending over such powers. There was this plain and obvious reason, that down to the month of May, 1838, the Foreign Secretary had very strong reasons to believe that it was in the contemplation of the government of China immediately to legalize the opium trade, which had undoubtedly been carried on in disobedience to the existing law. It was quite clear from these papers, though it was not easy to follow all the windings of Chinese policy, that in 1836, the attention of the government of that country was called in a very peculiar manner to the opium trade. The system under which that trade had been carried on was this—it had been prohibited by law, but connived at in practice. The Chinese Government appeared to think that a worse state of things could not exist; that it produced all the evils of a contraband trade; that it gave rise to as much intemperance as if there were no prohibition; and, what they looked upon with equal regret, that the exportation of silver was likewise as great as if there was no prohibition upon it. That the then existing system could not last, seemed to have been the opinion of the Chinese authorities. Tang-Tzee, the able and ingenious President of the Sacrificial Offices, who he was sorry to perceive had been dismissed, because dismissal in China, he believed, was a much more severe punishment than in England, had argued that it was unwise to prohibit the introduction of the drug; that if it were desired by the people, whatever might be the abuse of it by intemperance, no prohibition could keep it out; and that as both the revenue and the morals of the people would suffer by the continuance of a contraband trade, it was desirable to make the trade legitimate, and tax the importation of the article. But Tchu-Sung appeared to be one of that class of statesmen, who, when they found that the laws were rendered nugatory, and that it was impossible to carry them into execution by altering their machinery, and by opposing public feeling, made them more stringent.

Tchu-Sung informed the Emperor that he had discovered in the course of his ministerial studies that the mode in which Europe had established her empire in several parts of Asia was, by the introduction of opium, which so weakened the intellect and enervated the bodies of the inhabitants, that they were easily pounced upon and made prisoners of by the Europeans. The opinion that the trade would be legalized was entertained by Captain Elliott, and he could himself vouch for the fact, that the mercantile community of Calcutta, during a part of the year 1837, decidedly believed that notification of the authorisation of the traffic by the Chinese government might be expected from day to day. It was not until the month of May, 1838, that a despatch arrived at the Foreign office, interfering with, or putting an end to that expectation. That being the case, it was not strange that his noble Friend, the Secretary for Foreign Affairs, should have hesitated to send out an order to put down a trade which he had every reason to believe would have been made legitimate before such order could have reached the Chinese seas. But he (Mr. Macaulay) did not think it would have been at all desirable or right that such an order should have been sent out even in 1838. He thought that that House would have required of the Government a very clear account indeed, a very strong proof of the necessity or policy of such order, and that if they could not have furnished that proof the House would have been justified in calling them to a sharp reckoning for sending out powers to the Superintendent authorising him to seize and send home any British subject who should have been found carrying on a trade which that superintendent might have prohibited. Without meaning to deny that there were extreme cases which authorised extreme powers, he must say, that he conceived such powers as these were not to be lightly granted by any British Minister. He certainly should be convinced, before he agreed to a vote of censure upon any Government for not granting them, that, in the first place, there were grounds for supposing them to have been absolutely necessary; and in the next, that their having been withheld was the cause of the unfortunate circumstances in which we were now placed with regard to China. He, however, felt satisfied, that whether their powers had been granted or withheld, those unfortunate circumstances would have taken place: nay more, he ventured to say, that if those powers had been granted we should now find ourselves involved in hostilities with China under circumstances of peculiar calamity and national dishonour. With regard to the practicability of carrying the order, if it had been given, into effect, he must say, that it would have been impossible to put down the trade, except by the exertions of the Chinese themselves. The right hon. Baronet was far too experienced a member of the Government to suppose that, to suppress a lucrative trade, it was only necessary to issue a written edict. In England we had a preventive service, which cost half a million of money, which employed 6,000 effective men, and upwards of fifty cruisers, and yet every one knew well that every article which was reasonably portable, which was much desired, and on which severe duties were imposed, was smuggled to a very great extent. It was known that the amount of brandy smuggled had been ordinarily 600,000 gallons every year, and of tobacco an amount not much less than the whole quantity regularly imported through the Custom-house, was conveyed into the country by clandestine means. It has been proved, also, before a Committee of the House that no less than 4,000,000lbs. of tobacco had been smuggled into Ireland in opposition to the most effective preventive laws which existed in the world. Knowing this—knowing that the whole power of King, Lords, and Commons could not put an end to a lucrative traffic; could the House believe that a mere order could put a stop to the trade in opium? Did they suppose that a traffic supported on the one hand by men actuated by the love of a drug, from the intoxicating qualities of which they found it impossible to restrain themselves; and on the other, by persons actuated by the desire of gain, could be terminated by the publication of a piece of paper signed "Charles Elliott." There never was a stronger proof of the impotence of Chinese power to keep out an article of traffic than that afforded by the year 1839. If the trade could have been stopped by them, it was impossible to suppose that Mr. Commissioner Lin would have caused the seizure of certain individuals, against some of whom there existed mere suspicion, whilst against others there was no hesitation in supposing that there was not the slightest ground for believing them implicated in the traffic which had been carried on. Could it be supposed even that if the orders of Elliott had failed, the preventive service of China, had it been as effectual and as trustworthy as our own, would have been able to overcome the affection of the opium-eater for the drug upon which he feasted, or the longing of the merchant for the profit which he obtained? If it could not be supposed to produce so good a result, he would ask whether it were to be considered that it would produce no effect at all? He believed that it would, and that the effect would have been this—that it would have driven the opium trade from Canton; but would have spread it throughout the coast of the whole country. The traffic would not have been carried on, indeed, any longer under the very eye of the commissioner, or in such a manner as that the traders might afterwards be called upon to answer for their offences in some English court, but they would remove from Canton, where an English society being collected, their proceedings would be watched with unremitting jealousy, but they would have found that the lawless trade would have been carried on all along the coast, by means infinitely more lawless than those which had been already adopted. The traders would have gone to a distance from the great port, the whole east coast would have been covered with smugglers, and in their efforts to secure the object which they had in view, they would have undoubtedly come in contact with the local authorities, who would be unaccustomed to deal with European traders;

the *mala prohibita* of a contraband traffic would be converted into the *mala per se*, and smuggling would be turned into piracy, a crime of a much more heinous description. If under the eye of an English society—consisting certainly of persons, some of whom were suspected of being concerned in the trade, but many of whom were of the highest respectability—the traffic could not long be carried on without producing acts having some appearance of piracy, what could they expect when no man would have any judge of his own conduct but himself? It would be found that men being congregated in vessels for the purpose of carrying on the trade, would land for the purpose of procuring fresh supplies of provisions; that their demands would be refused; that they would attempt to seize them; wells would be poisoned, or four or five sailors, perhaps, going to fill their water casks, would be captured, and that the demand for their liberation not being complied with, their comrades would proceed to burn and sack the neighbouring village. Similar circumstances had occurred in former instances, and he saw no reason why, at the present time, scenes of equal atrocity should not occur. He believed, therefore, that if the smuggling trade had been removed from Macao, and scattered along the coast in the manner which he had described, hostilities with China would have been the speedy and the inevitable consequence. What did they see in the proceedings of the Chinese government, or of Mr. Commissioner Lin, to induce them to suppose that those hostilities would not have taken place? Commissioner Lin had not hesitated to inflict severe punishment upon men whose characters were totally unsuspected, and was it likely, that if the events which he had endeavoured to describe, had occurred along the coast of China, Lin would have been more scrupulous? Would he not have published some proclamation, setting forth, that Captain Elliott had undertaken to put a stop to the contraband trade, but that he had deceived him; that he had pretended to command the discontinuance of the traffic, but that he had issued false edicts—for that it had been carried on along the whole coast, to an extent even greater than that to which it had before gone, and that therefore he would hold all Englishmen, who ought to have had the power to prevent all this, whether blameable or not blameable, as hostages, until the wrong which had been committed should have been remedied. That would have been the spirit of Mr. Commissioner Lin; and therefore he said that, so far as he had been able to form a judgment, he believed that the positive prohibition of the opium trade by Captain Elliott, unsupported by physical force, would have been inadequate to put the trade down. Did the right hon. Baronet mean, that this country should pay the expense of a preventive service for the whole coast of China? He knew that it was impossible that he, or any one else, could for one moment advocate a doctrine so absurd; and he could not but repeat his firm belief, that by any course but that which had been adopted, the existing evils would only have been aggravated, and the rupture which had taken place would have been brought about in a manner still more calamitous, and still more dreadful. He had now gone, he thought, through the four charges on which the right hon. Baronet rested his case; and he declared most solemnly, that it did not appear to him that, according to the terms of the motion which was before the House, to any one of the four omissions which were alleged to have been made, was to be attributed that interruption of our friendly relations which was so deeply and so universally deplored. If he could believe that hon. Gentlemen would vote, keeping in mind really what the proposition was, he should not have the smallest hesitation as to the result; but he could not refrain from saying, that some persons, for whose feelings of humanity he entertained the highest respect, might possibly imagine, that in giving their assent to the motion, they were marking their disapprobation of the trade, which he regretted as deeply as they did. They had seen it asserted over and over again, that the Government was advocating the cause of the contraband trade, in order to force an opium war on the public; but he thought that it was impossible to be conceived that a thought so absurd and so atrocious should have ever entered the minds of the British Ministry. Their course was clear. They might doubt whether it were wise for the government of China to exclude from that country a drug which, if judiciously administered, was powerful in assuaging pain, and in promoting health, because it was occasionally used to excess by intemperate men—they might doubt whether it was wise policy on the part of that Government to attempt to stop the efflux of precious metals from the country in the due course of trade. They learned from history—and almost every country afforded proof, which was strengthened by existing circumstances in England, to which he had already alluded—that no machinery, however powerful, had been sufficient to keep out of any country those luxuries which the people enjoyed, or were able to purchase, or to prevent the efflux of precious metals, when it was demanded by the course of trade. What Great Britain could not effect with the finest marine, and the most trustworthy preventive service in the world, was not likely to be effected by the feeble efforts of the mandarins of China. But, whatever their opinions on these points might be, the Governor of China alone, it must be remembered, was competent to decide; that government had a right to keep out opium, to keep in silver, and to enforce their prohibitory laws, by whatever means which they might possess, consistently with the principles of public morality, and of international law; and if, after having given fair notice of their intention to seize all contraband goods introduced into their dominions, they seized our opium, we had no right to complain; but when the government, finding, that by just and lawful means, they could not carry out their prohibition, resorted to measures unjust and unlawful, confined our innocent countrymen, and insulted the Sovereign in the person of her representative, then he thought, the time had arrived when it was fit that we should interfere. Whether the proceedings of the Chinese were or were not founded on humanity, was not now to be decided. Let them take the case of the most execrable crime that had ever been dignified by the name of a trade—the African slave trade. The prosecution of that trade was made a misdemeanour, a felony, and finally piracy. We made treaties with foreign powers and paid large sums of money to secure the object which we had in view; and yet it was perfectly notorious, that notwithstanding all the efforts which we had made, slaves had been introduced from Africa into our colony of the Mauritius. Undoubtedly it was our duty to put down the traffic which had so long been carried on with rigour, and to bring all persons engaged in it to punishment; but suppose a ship under French colours was seen skulking under the coast of the island, and that the Governor had his eye upon it, and was satisfied that it was a slaver, and that it was waiting for an opportunity by night to run its cargo; suppose the Governor, not having a sufficient naval force to seize the vessel, should send and take thirty or forty French gentlemen resident in the island, some of them, perhaps, suspected of having been engaged in the trade, and some who had never fallen under any suspicion, and lock them up. Suppose amongst others, he had laid violent hands on the Consul of France, saying that they should have no food till they produced the proprietor of the vessel, would not the French government be in a condition to claim reparation, and, if so, would not the French government have a right to exact reparation if refused by arms? Would it be enough for us to say, "Oh, but it is such a wicked trade, such a monstrous trade, that you have no right to quarrel with us for resorting to any means to put it down?" The answer would be, "Are you not trampling upon a great principle by doing so?" If such would be the answer of France, was it not fit and right that her Majesty should demand reparation from China? They had seen the success of the first great act of injustice perpetrated by that government produce its natural effect on a people ignorant of the relative places they and we held in the scale of nations. The Imperial Commissioner began by confiscating property; his next demand was for innocent blood. A Chinese was slain; the most careful inquiry had been made, but was insufficient to discover the slayer, or even the nation to which he belonged; but it was caused to be notified that, guilty or not, some subject of the Queen's must be given up. Great Britain gave an unequivocal refusal to be a party to so barbarous a proceeding. The people at Canton were seized; they were driven from Macao, suspected or not. Women with child, children at the breast, were treated with equal severity, were refused bread, or the means of subsistence; the innocent Lascars were thrown into the sea; an English gentleman was barbarously mutilated, and England found itself at once assailed with a fury unknown to civilized countries. The place of this country among nations was not so mean or ill ascertained that we should trouble ourselves to resist every petty slight which we might receive. Conscious of her power, England could bear that her Sovereign should be called a barbarian, and her people described as savages, destitute of every useful art. When our Ambassadors were obliged to undergo a degrading prostration, in compliance with their regulations, conscious of our strength, we were more amused than irritated. But there was a limit to that forbearance. It would not have been worthy of us to take arms upon a small provocation, referring to rites and ceremonies merely; but every one in the scale of civilized nations should know that Englishmen were ever living under the protecting eye of their own country. He was much touched, and he thought that probably many others were so also, by one passage contained in the dispatch of Captain Elliott, in which he communicated his arrival at the factory at Canton. The moment at which he landed he was surrounded by his countrymen in an agony of despair at their situation, but the first step which he took was to order the flag of Great Britain to be taken from the boat and to be planted in the balcony. This was an act which revived the drooping hopes of those who looked to him for protection. It was natural that they should look with confidence on the victorious flag which was hoisted over them, which reminded them that they belonged to a country unaccustomed to defeat, to submission, or to shame—it reminded them that they belonged to a country which had made the farthest ends of the earth ring with the fame of her exploits in redressing the wrongs of her children; that made the Dey of Algiers humble himself to the insulted consul; that revenged the horrors of the black hole on the fields of Plessey; that had not degenerated since her great Protector vowed that he would make the name of Englishman as respected as ever had been the name of Roman citizen. They felt that although far from their native country, and then in danger in a part of the world remote from that to which they must look for protection, yet that they belonged to a state which would not suffer a hair of one of its members to be harmed with impunity. All were agreed upon this point of the question. He had listened with painful attention to the speech of the right hon. Baronet, but he had not detected in it one word which implied that he was not disposed to insist on a just reparation for the offence which had been committed against us. With respect to the present motion, whatever its result might be, he could not believe that the House would agree to a vote of censure so gross, so palpable, or so unjust as that which was conveyed in its terms; and he trusted that even if there was to be a change of men consequential upon the conclusion of the debate, there would at all events be no change of measures. He had endeavoured to express his views and his opinions upon this subject, and he begged in conclusion to declare his earnest desire that this most rightful quarrel might be prosecuted to a triumphal close—that the brave men to whom was entrusted the task of demanding that reparation which the circumstances of the case required, might fulfil their duties with moderation, but with success—that the name, not only of English valour, but of English mercy, might be established; and that the overseeing care of that gracious Providence which had so often brought good out of evil, might make the crime which had forced us to take those measures which had been adopted the means of promoting an everlasting peace, alike beneficial to England and to China.

COLONIAL PASSENGERS' BILL.*

JUNE 4, 1840.

HE entertained so high a respect for his right hon. and learned friend [Sir S. Lushington], and knew so well the services he had rendered to the cause of freedom, that he felt much pain in differing from him. But after the speech they had just heard, he was unwilling to give his vote without stating the grounds of it. He believed, that with respect to the general principle there was little difference between his right hon. friend and himself. None knew better than his right hon. friend how important it was to remove labourers from districts where the population was thick and wages were low, to districts where the land was widely spread, and labour in demand. He would admit, there might be exceptions—he thought, that wheresoever slavery existed there ought to be restrictions placed upon immigration; he was also of opinion, that while slavery existed in the West Indies, it was in the highest degree pernicious to the labouring population to permit the emigration from parts where the demand for labour was small to those where it was great. And he considered, that the system of slavery, separating, as it did altogether, the interest of the capitalist from that of the labourer, depriving the latter of the fair advantage, which in a free condition he had a right to expect from the fertile soil, and a great demand for his labour, rendered it necessary to impose a restriction upon the passage of the labourer from one country to another. But now, if there was any one part of the empire from which it was desirable to encourage emigration, it was

* Hansard, 3d Series, vol. liv. p. 941–944.

India, and if there was any part to which the tide should flow, it was the Mauritius. The wages in the latter place would be fifty times what the labourer received in his native place. When he considered the state of the native peasantry of India, he would say, with every respect for the sincere feelings of humanity which actuated those who were opposed to the present measure, that they might be betrayed by those very feelings into committing a great wrong upon that unfortunate population. He could state it as a fact, that at the time when the debates on the subject of these peasants were going on—while persons were speaking with the greatest horror of the new system of slave-trade, the Governor-general was obliged to turn out of his road to avoid the sight of these wretched peasants dying in the ditches from starvation, in consequence of low wages. He understood his right hon. friend to say, that as a general principle, they ought not to interfere with the free labourers removing from one part of the country to another, therefore it would appear as if he contended, that in the present case, there were circumstances which counterbalanced the difference between famine and plenty, and between two-pence a day as wages and one shilling. His right hon. friend had spoken of the disparity between the sexes. Had he heard the statement of his noble friend, he would have heard that measures were in view which would remedy that great evil. His right hon. friend had also spoken of the artifices, blameable in the highest degree, practised by the agents in the Mauritius; but had he heard the speech of his noble friend, he would have discovered that no agency would now be permitted, except such as was authorized by the government in India or the government in the Mauritius. Had his right hon. friend heard the speech, he would also have discovered that it was intended to limit the contracts entered into to such a degree that the labourers would be at liberty to choose their masters, and that no contract was to last for a longer term than twelve months. That was a state of things under which evils would arise, such as those anticipated by his right hon. friend. With regard to the point that the language of these people was not understood in the Mauritius, his right hon. friend seemed to have overlooked the fact, that in that island were constantly to be found a considerable number of the civil servants of the East India Company, men of high respectability, character, and attainments. Those persons understood the language of the emigrants, and would naturally be disposed to feel a strong interest in their welfare. That circumstance alone would constitute a strong distinction between the case of the Mauritius and of the West Indies, which his right hon. friend had paralleled. With respect to some unfortunate circumstances in the past history of the Mauritius he would say, without attempting to impute to his right hon. friend any other motives than those by which he was guided, and which were the purest and most humane, that both his right hon. friend, and the hon. Member for Bridport, had insisted too much upon that point. It was worth while to consider whether the last slave trade, so long carried on in the Mauritius, were to be attributed entirely to a lawless disposition and contempt for the mother country, or whether it were not to be attributed to the fact that the Mauritius was close to the slave market, while other colonies were more distant. There were many general local circumstances to induce the belief that the emigrants would be better off in the Mauritius, and return to their own country afterwards under better circumstances from the Mauritius than from the West Indies. He would say, then, looking at the papers, if he were asked whether the evils he saw there were those of the slave trade such as existed between Africa and the West Indies, or those of the slave trade as it existed between this country and the colonies on the other side of the Atlantic, he should say that the evils, though great and requiring correction, certainly belonged to the latter class. He would only add that he believed no persons—or few at least—had felt more strongly than he had felt during the contest that took place on the subject of negro slavery. He would not say that he did not feel for those persons who were connected with colonial property; and he declared that since that time, so far from regarding those proprietors with unfriendly feelings, there was no interest in the empire which he was more desirous to see in a flourishing and prosperous condition; because he believed that on the fate of the great experiment that had been tried depended the fate of slaves throughout the civilized world. If, twenty years hence, those colonies in which slavery continued, should be able to point to those in which it had been abolished, ruined, and the plantations in them abandoned, then he would say that although we should indeed have wiped a stain from our own land, he questioned whether we should have conferred a great and signal boon upon humanity in general. Believing, then, that the measure of his noble friend would have a tendency to promote the prosperity of the colonies by means at once just towards the labourer, and compatible with his freedom and comfort, he should give it his most cordial support.

REGISTRATION OF VOTERS—IRELAND.*

JUNE 19, 1840.

He entertained so great a respect for the eminent talents and legal acuteness of the right hon. Gentleman who had just sat down [Sir E. Sugden], that it was with great diffidence he ventured to oppose his opinion to that of the right hon. and learned Gentleman on the construction of a single clause. But when the right hon. and learned Gentleman had emphatically, distinctly, and repeatedly assured the Committee that the question on which they were to divide was, whether a person now on the register was to remain on it all his life, he (Mr. Macaulay) could not but say that it appeared to him that the words of his noble Friend's amendment by no means bore out such a statement. His reading of the words was, that the voter should be continued on the register so long as his right of voting and the registry were to remain in force, which under the present law were not for the term of his life, but for the period of eight years. If he was correct in conceiving that the right hon. and learned Gentleman had thus, from reading it but cursorily, mistaken his noble Friend's amendment, he might well suppose that the right hon. and learned Gentleman had not been altogether correct in his other remarks. He utterly denied, that the smallest imputation of unfairness, of violation of Parliamentary rule, or of want of perfect candour, could be brought against his noble Friend. The question which his noble Friend had brought forward was one of the gravest importance; it was the question of re-investigation or no re-investigation, and

* Hansard, 3d Series, vol. liv. p. 1349–1357.

was one which the Committee would repeatedly have to decide on during the progress of the bill. It was a question which it was possible for any Member of that House, without the slightest infringement of Parliamentary rule, to bring forward on the discussion of any clause in which it could with propriety be inserted. Considering the history of the noble Lord's bill—considering that on the question of going into Committee the noble Lord had a majority of but three, and that of that majority two hon. Members declared themselves unfavourable to the principle of re-investigation, two used language such as gave the House to understand that should the bill come to a third reading, still containing that principle, they would vote against it—he thought his noble Friend was justified on the first occasion which presented itself in taking the opinion of the Committee on the great question of whether re-investigation was to remain the prominent defect of the bill? Although it was the intention of Government to go fully and fairly into the Committee on the bill, he entertained no expectation of any good result. He did not hope that any good measure could be made out of one so laboriously, so elaborately, bad as that of the noble Lord; but if any effectual alteration could be made, it must be made by a series of amendments like the present. By such alterations the bill might, perhaps, leave the Committee what it purported to be, a bill to amend the Registration. At present he could designate it by no other name than a bill to take away the right of voting under the pretence of ascertaining it. He need hardly say, that it was to no purpose that the bill did not directly affect the right of voting, because there was no right which could not be annulled by indirect as well as by direct means, or by providing a tedious, troublesome, and costly mode of obtaining it. That was seen in all questions relating to the rights of property. It was to no purpose, by the substantive law of the land, particular estates or sums of money belonged to a certain person, if that law were so expensive as only to obtain his right at a greater expense than the object was worth. There was not an hon. Member in that House who had not at some time or other submitted to an unjust demand rather than run the risk of vexatious proceedings. If a law were brought into that House for the purpose of making justice expensive, he should be justified in calling it a law of spoliation, and so he thought he was justified in designating a bill the object of which was disfranchisement under the name of registration. At the same time he had not the smallest doubt but that the bill of the noble Lord would remove some persons from the register who had not the smallest right to be there, in the same way as if they made a law making the Court of Requests as expensive as the House of Lords. Many a groundless action would be driven out of it, but the question was, whether they would not be throwing difficulties in the way of the just as well as of the unjust claimant. Let the noble Lord satisfy him that the impediments provided by this bill would lie only in the way of fraudulent claimants, and he would give him his support. But he saw no provision to that effect in the bill. He saw that it went to make registration costly and difficult both for the fraudulent and the just claimant, and it was on the distinction between the two that the sense of the Committee would be taken. It provided repeated hearings of the same question—first before a subordinate, and then before an appellate tribunal. He would beg of the committee to consider to what extent that abuse might be carried under the bill. Even the legal knowledge of the right hon. and learned Gentleman would not enable him to find a parallel in any law, British or foreign, ancient or modern. It would not be necessary to select as matter of objection some point which had not been investigated before, for one and the same objection might be raised every time a new assistant barrister came to the country, or as often as a new judge went the circuit. If he rightly understood the noble Lord's bill, an objection might be made in 1840 before the assistant barrister, from that there might be made an appeal to the Court of Queen's Bench; in 1841 it might be again brought before the assistant-barrister, and from him to the Court of Common Pleas; in 1842 it might again come before the assistant-barrister, and then there was an appeal to the Court of Exchequer. Nay, further, should there be a new Chief Justice, it might be tried another year in the Court of Common Pleas. Now, he would venture to ask if the whole jurisprudence of the world contained anything which afforded a parallel to such a system of legislation? He would venture to assert that there was no parallel, because, although there was something like it in the English system—and it was the vice of the system—yet there was only one trial, but in any other respect he defied the noble Lord to find a parallel in any country that ever called itself civilized. The noble Lord said, if that power of objection was not given, persons would get upon the registry who had no legal right to be there. Did the noble Lord imagine that there were no persons in possession of property in this country the judgments in whose favour were by no means justified? Did the noble Lord imagine that all the damages awarded to plaintiffs by juries, and that all the large sums which had been paid by the Courts of Law, were sanctioned by truth and justice? Did he not believe that there were many estates which were in the possession of wrong owners? But the Courts of Law could not and ought not to set these matters right by eternal re-investigation. Suppose an injured man had come and said that the judgment obtained against him was erroneous—that he had procured the evidence—that he had found in the bottom of a chest an old paper which would establish his claim—that he had been taken by surprise; the court might naturally say, that they regretted the hardship of the case, but it would be impossible for them to go on hearing and re-hearing the case twenty or thirty or fifty times; that the noble Lord's bill admitted, and it required no great stretch of imagination to suppose a case in which the voter might be objected to 120 or 130 times in the course of his life. He had not the smallest doubt that if they went on hearing criminal cases over and over again, they would at length hang some great ruffians. He had no doubt that if a man brought an action over again for the same cause, some cases of importance might be set right; but it had been ruled over and over again that it was better occasionally that some wrong should be endured than that the rights of society should be constantly interfered with; and why should they depart from that principle in the single case of the franchise? No doubt the bill would exclude many dishonest voters, but the question was, what would be its effect on the honest voter? All the objections in the bill were common to the rightful and the wrongful claimant. The vexation and expense of travelling, of appearing before the judge, of severe cross-examinations, of brow-beatings, and reflections upon his integrity, were all common to the rightful as well as the wrongful claimant. But did the noble Lord believe that a case never broke down unless when a man went with a fraudulent intention? Did he not know that the accidental absence of a witness, or direct perjury—(for if the noble Lord imputed so much on the side of the claimant, surely he might allow a little on the side of the objectors)—would break down the claim? Was he not aware that men, who thought they had a good right, were frequently withheld from pressing it in a court of law, because they were in doubt whether they could establish it satisfactorily; or had the noble Lord never heard of the uncertainty of the law? If out of one hundred honest claimants only four or five were defeated, or saddled with costs, could any one doubt that that would act to the injury of the honest claimant? Almost every clause of the noble Lord's bill for keeping out the wrongful, acted just as effectually against the rightful claimant. The noble Lord had drawn a pretty picture of an unfortunate claimant being opposed by a pauper; but the noble Lord should recollect that property was the best of qualifications—that the claim of the rich man must be a valid one, and that it was much more likely that the case might be reversed. He would suppose another case, the case of a man of great wealth, and of imperious, obstinate, and arbitrary temper—one of those men, who, as had been said by his lamented and valued friend, in words which should be engraven on his tomb, thought much of the rights of property, and little of its duties. He would suppose that man willing to spend £6,000 or £7,000 a year in securing the command of a county; that, every man knew, would not be impossible even in England. He would not mention any recent transaction; he did not wish to mix up personalities with that serious debate; but they all knew that a certain man now dead, provoked by the opposition he received in a certain town, vowed that he would make the grass grow in its streets, and he kept his vow. Another ejected 400 voters in one county, and entered 15 criminal and 225 civil actions. Such a man could easily command an Irish county. It would only be a picture less in his gallery, or an antique gem the less in his collection. The cost would be but as dust under his feet, compared with the pleasure of domination. He had no hesitation in saying that every clause in the noble Lord's bill tended to harass and obstruct the voter in obtaining his just rights. The effect, in short, would be, that a great many would abandon the claim altogether. The franchise was a sacred public trust, which should be used for the benefit of the public, and yet when honestly seeking that, their pecuniary interests were to be seriously affected. They should also take into consideration that men did not go to the registry with the same spirit with which they went to the poll. There had been few registrations since 1826, at which a general election was expected; and men who, when the candidates were declared, and when perhaps the fate of a ministry was to be sealed, would pay £50 or run any trouble to record their votes in a hard-fought election, would hardly go across the street to register. Therefore, you ought rather to encourage than discourage registration. Yet, supposing a Parliament to last seven years, the noble Lord's bill would expose the voter to fourteen law-suits, against which what human fortitude or human patriotism could stand out?—and this was the principle which the House was now called upon to assert or reject. Sir, (continued the right hon. Gentleman), there is another consideration which applies specially to Ireland; that is, the state of the franchise. It is impossible to separate that from the subject of registration—it is impossible to have a perfect law of registration, that is, one which shall throw the greatest difficulties in the way of the wrongful, and every facility in the way of the rightful claimant: but it is still open for you to distinguish as clearly as possible which are the rightful and which are the wrongful claimants, and how can I decide upon a question like this without looking at the state of the franchise? It is impossible not to feel how much more the Irish franchise is restricted, as compared with the English, even by the Reform Bill—how much it is restricted even below what Pitt, and Castlereagh, and Grenville, and Windham, considered to be just. Looking at statistics, I find that Westmoreland, with little more than 50,000 inhabitants, and covered by naked hills and barren moors, has more voters than any Irish county—than Tipperary with 400,000 inhabitants, or Cork with 800,000. Sir, I cannot think that even the superiority of England in point of property can explain so enormous a disparity; and, whatever way I look at the question, I think that the Irish franchise ought to be rather extended than restricted—if it is to be altered at all—and I do not pledge myself to support any proposition for its extension; but if I hesitate to interpose to make it better, I will not lay violent hands upon it to make it worse—and strong as is my regard for the great settlement of 1832, I will never consent to make it final as against the people alone; and if not restoring what it took away, I will not consent to withdraw the smallest portion of what it gave. But, Sir, this is not an Irish merely, it is an imperial question. I hope and trust that if the bill is to pass at all, it will pass modified by the amendment proposed to-night, and by others conceived in the same spirit. But if not, I shall regard it as the first step in a great retrograde movement—as the beginning of a scheme of which the object is to undo what was done by the Reform Bill. I do not believe the Reform Bill would be directly attacked. Much as hon. Gentlemen have talked of re-action, they well know that there has been no re-action here—they well know that it would not be safe to attempt to despoil our great cities and towns of political power, and confer it again on old walls and mouldering towers. But what cannot be done directly may be done indirectly—it matters not what franchise is conferred if the means of acquiring it are restricted. It matters not how well the law of rights is framed, if not accompanied by as efficient a law of remedies—power that can be obtained only by wealth or time, though nominally given to the many, is really given only to the few. Let us have the most democratic Reform Bill, and let the noble Lord frame our registration, and political power may yet be in the hands of the aristocracy and its tools. The Opposition begin with Ireland, and they are wise. Distance, difference of religious belief—perhaps that unfriendly feeling, the natural effect of much wrong inflicted, and much wrong endured—may have deterred the people of this country from resenting the insult offered to the Irish nation as they would have resented the same insult to themselves. But, Sir, I grieve for the short-sightedness of my countrymen; Ireland is the first field—it will not be the last. I believe this struggle is just as much for Yorkshire and Kent as for Cork and Kerry. And the day when the constituencies, worked upon this bill, shall send up to this House representatives regarded by the Irish people as enemies, will be dark and dreary for the liberties of England. But it is not necessary that I should resort to topics like these. The derisive expressions of Gentlemen opposite, I suppose intimate, that they would be unjust to Ireland alone. Well, whether they mean this injustice to be confined to Ireland or to extend to England, I hardly know how to express my reprobation of so odious and disgusting a measure. The people of Ireland have been already hardly enough used. When we granted them religious emancipation, we took away their franchise. By the Reform Bill, a very small portion of what was before taken away was restored; and now the noble Lord by this bill would take away the little which the Reform Bill bestowed. There is only one bill on the table relative to the registration in England, a bill laid on the table by the same hand that laid the Reform Bill there, and one worthy of that hand. But as regards Ireland, we are now discussing a bill made up of the very worst features of all the bills that have been of late years introduced on the subject of registration—of the English system, of the system at present existing in Ireland, and of the ill-considered plan of Sir Michael O'Loghlen. Yes! the ill-considered plan of Sir Michael O'Loghlen. Each and all of these systems have been made to contribute their evil, but not one of their redeeming qualities; and the noble Lord, out of those evil qualities, has framed his bill. What must be the feelings of the people of Ireland when they compare that bill with the bill laid on the table by my noble Friend for the settlement of the registration system in England? To perpetuate differences and to excite discord seems to be the object of the noble Lord. Not such was the spirit in which the great minister who carried the act of Union treated the people of Ireland. The words which he quoted seem to have been forgotten by the noble Lord.

"Paribus se legibus ambæ
Invictæ gentes æterna in fœdera mittant."

These were the sentiments of the promoter of the act of Union. I venerate that great measure. I am ready to defend it against the open enmity of the hon. and learned member for Dublin, as against the still more dangerous friendship of the noble

Lord. I am satisfied that for every repealer made by the eloquence of the hon. and learned Member for Dublin, ten would be produced by the bill of the noble Lord if it passed in its present shape, and unmitigated. Should an universal cry for repeal of the Union arise in Ireland on the passing of the bill, I should not regard it in any other light than as the natural succession of effect and cause. It would be puerile, nay it would be hypocritical, to go on misgoverning, and to pretend to hope that the results of good government would follow—to assume that those whom we treat as aliens, ought to feel towards us as brothers—to oppose agitation and multiply the grievances by which agitation is alone supported, and by which it was originated—to raise the cry of civil war whereon the people of Ireland called for a repeal of the legislative Union, and at the very time when you are taking steps to annul all those rights and privileges, without which the legislative Union would be but an empty name.

THE COPYRIGHT BILL.*

FEBRUARY 5, 1841.

THOUGH, Sir, it is in some sense agreeable to approach a subject with which political animosities have nothing to do, I offer myself to your notice with some reluctance. It is painful to me to take a course which may possibly be misunderstood or misrepresented as unfriendly to the interests of literature and literary men. It is painful to me, I will add, to oppose my hon. and learned Friend on a question which he has taken up from the purest motives, and which he regards with a parental interest. These feelings have hitherto kept me silent when the law of copyright has been under discussion. But as I am, on full consideration, satisfied that the measure before us will, if adopted, inflict grievous injury on the public, without conferring any compensating advantage on men of letters, I think it my duty to avow that opinion and to defend it.

The first thing to be done, Sir, is to settle on what principles the question is to be argued. Are we free to legislate for the public good, or are we not? Is this a question of expediency, or is it a question of right? Many of those who have written and petitioned against the existing state of things, treat the question as one of right. The law of nature, according to them, gives to every man a sacred and indefeasible property in his own ideas, in the fruits of his own reason and imagination. The legislature has indeed the power to take away this property, just as it has the power to pass an act of attainder for cutting off an innocent man's head without a trial. But as such an act of attainder would be legal

* Hansard, 3d Series, vol. lvi. p. 344–357.

murder, so would an act invading the right of an author to his copy be, according to these gentlemen, legal robbery. Now, Sir, if this be so, let justice be done, cost what it may. I am not prepared, like my hon. and learned Friend, to agree to a compromise between right and expediency, to commit an injustice for the public convenience. But I must say, that his theory soars far beyond the reach of my faculties. It is not necessary to go, on the present occasion, into a metaphysical inquiry about the origin of the right of property; and certainly nothing but the strongest necessity would lead me to discuss a subject so likely to be distasteful to the House. I agree, I own, with Paley in thinking that property is the creature of the law, and that the law which creates property can be defended only on this ground, that it is a law beneficial to mankind. But it is unnecessary to debate that point. For even if I believed in a natural right of property, independent of utility and anterior to legislation, I should still deny that this right could survive the original proprietor. Few, I apprehend, even of those who have studied in the most mystical and sentimental schools of moral philosophy, will be disposed to maintain that there is a natural law of succession older and of higher authority than any human code. If there be, it is quite certain that we have abuses to reform much more serious than any connected with the question of copyright. For this natural law can be only one, and the modes of succession in the Queen's dominions are twenty. To go no further than England, land generally descends to the eldest son. In Kent the sons share and share alike; in many districts the youngest takes the whole. Formerly a portion of a man's personal property was secured to his family. It was only of the residue that he could dispose by will. Now he can dispose of the whole by will. But a few years ago you enacted, that the will should not be valid unless there were two witnesses. If a man dies intestate, his personal property generally goes according to the statute of distributions. But there are local customs which modify that statute. Now which of all these systems is conformed to the eternal standard of right? Is it primogeniture, or gavelkind, or borough English? Are wills *jure divino?* Are the two witnesses *jure divino?* Might not the *pars rationabilis* of our old law have as fair a claim to be regarded as of celestial institution? Was the statute of distributions enacted in Heaven long before it was adopted by Parliament? Or is it to Custom of York, or to Custom of London, that this pre-eminence belongs? Surely, Sir, even those who hold that there is a natural right of property must admit that rules prescribing the manner in which the effects of deceased persons shall be distributed, are purely arbitrary, and originate altogether in the will of the legislature. If so, Sir, there is no controversy between my hon. and learned Friend and myself as to the principles on which this question is to be argued. For the existing law gives an author copyright during his natural life; nor do I propose to invade that privilege, which I should, on the contrary, be prepared to defend strenuously against any assailant. The point in issue is, how long after an author's death the State shall recognise a copyright in his representatives and assigns, and it can, I think, hardly be disputed by any rational man that this is a point which the legislature is free to determine in the way which may appear to be most conducive to the general good. We may now, therefore, I think descend from these high regions, where we are in danger of being lost in the clouds, to firm ground and clear light. Let us look at this question like legislators, and after fairly balancing conveniences and inconveniences, pronounce between the existing law of copyright and the law now proposed to us. The question of copyright, Sir, like most questions of civil prudence, is neither black nor white, but grey. The system of copyright has great advantages, and great disadvantages, and it is our business to ascertain what these are, and then to make an arrangement under which the advantages may be as far as possible secured, and the disadvantages as far as possible excluded. The charge which I bring against my hon. and learned Friend's bill is this,—that it leaves the advantages nearly what they are at present, and increases the disadvantages at least four fold. The advantages arising from a system of copyright are obvious. It is desirable that we should have a supply of good books; we cannot have such a supply unless men of letters are liberally remunerated: and the least objectionable way of remunerating them is by means of copyright. You cannot depend for literary instruction and amusement on the leisure of men occupied in the pursuits of active life. Such men may occasionally produce pieces of great merit. But you must not look to them for works which require deep meditation and long research. Such works you can expect only from persons who make literature the business of their lives. Of these persons few will be found among the rich and the noble. The rich and the noble are not impelled to intellectual exertion by necessity. They may be impelled to intellectual exertion by the desire of distinguishing themselves, or by the desire of benefiting the community. But it is generally within these walls that they seek to signalize themselves and to serve their fellow creatures. Both their ambition and their public spirit, in a country like this, naturally take a political turn. It is then on men whose profession is literature, and whose private means are not ample, that you must rely for a supply of valuable books. Such men must be remunerated for their literary labour. And there are only two ways in which they can be remunerated. One of those ways is patronage; the other is copyright. There have been times in which men of letters looked, not to the public, but to the Government, or to a few great men, for the reward of their exertions. It was thus in the time of Mæcenas and Pollio at Rome, of the Medici at Florence, of Louis the Fourteenth in France, of Lord Halifax and Lord Oxford in this country. Now, Sir, I well know that there are cases in which it is fit and graceful, nay, in which it is a sacred duty, to reward the merits or to relieve the distresses of men of genius by the exercise of this species of liberality. But these cases are exceptions. I can conceive no system more fatal to the integrity and independence of literary men, than one under which they should be taught to look for their daily bread to the favour of ministers and nobles. I can conceive no system more certain to turn those minds which are formed by nature to be the blessings and ornaments of our species into its scandal and its pest. We have then only one resource left. We must betake ourselves to copyright, be the inconveniences of copyright what they may. Those inconveniences, in truth, are neither few nor small. Copyright is monopoly, and produces all the effects which the general voice of mankind attributes to monopoly. My hon. and learned Friend talks very contemptuously of those who are led away by the theory that monopoly makes things dear. That monopoly makes things dear is certainly a theory, as all the great truths which have been established by the experience of all ages and nations, and which are taken for granted in all reasonings, may be said to be theories. It is a theory in the same sense in which it is a theory that day and night follow each other, that lead is heavier than water, that bread nourishes, that arsenic poisons, that alcohol intoxicates. If, as my hon. and learned Friend seems to hold, the whole world is in the wrong on this point, if the real effect of monopoly is to make articles good and cheap, why does he stop short in his career of change? Why does he limit the operation of so salutary a principle to sixty years? Why does he consent to anything short of a perpetuity? He told us that in consenting to anything short of a perpetuity he was making a compromise between extreme right and expediency. But if his opinion about monopoly be correct, extreme right and expediency would coincide. Or rather why should we not restore the monopoly of the East-India trade to the East-India Company? Why should we not revive all those old monopolies which, in Elizabeth's reign, galled our fathers so severely that, maddened by intolerable wrong, they opposed to their sovereign a resistance before which her haughty spirit quailed for the first and for the last time? Was it the cheapness and excellence of commodities that then so violently stirred the indignation of the English people? I believe, Sir, that I may safely take it for granted that the effect of monopoly generally is to make articles scarce, to make them dear, and to make them bad. And I may with equal safety challenge my hon. Friend to find out any distinction between copyright and other privileges of the same kind,—any reason why a monopoly of books should produce an effect directly the reverse of that which was produced by the East-India Company's monopoly of tea, or by Lord Essex's monopoly of sweet wines. Thus, then, stands the case. It is good, that authors should be remunerated; and the least exceptionable way of remunerating them is by a monopoly. Yet monopoly is an evil. For the sake of the good we must submit to the evil; but the evil ought not to last a day longer than is necessary for the purpose of securing the good. Now, I will not affirm, that the existing law is perfect, that it exactly hits the point at which the monopoly ought to cease, but this I confidently say, that it is very much nearer that point than the law proposed by my hon. and learned Friend. For consider this; the evil effects of the monopoly are proportioned to the length of its duration. But the good effects for the sake of which we bear with the evil effects are by no means proportioned to the length of its duration. A monopoly of sixty years produces twice as much evil as a monopoly of thirty years, and thrice as much evil as a monopoly of twenty years. But it is by no means the fact that a posthumous monopoly of sixty years, gives to an author thrice as much pleasure and thrice as strong a motive as a posthumous monopoly of twenty years. On the contrary, the difference is so small as to be hardly perceptible. We all know how faintly we are affected by the prospect of very distant advantages, even when they are advantages which we may reasonably hope that we shall ourselves enjoy. But an advantage that is to be enjoyed more than half a century after we are dead, by somebody, we know not whom, perhaps by somebody unborn, by somebody utterly unconnected with us, is really no motive to action. It is very probable, that in the course of some generations, land in the unexplored and unmapped heart of the Australian continent, will be very valuable. But there is none of us who would lay down five pounds for a whole province in the heart of the Australian continent. We know, that neither we, nor anybody for whom we care, will ever receive a farthing of rent from such a province. And a man is very little moved by the thought that in the year 2000 or 2100, somebody who claims through him, will employ more shepherds than Prince Esterhazy, and will have the finest house and gallery of pictures at Victoria or Sydney. Now, this is the sort of boon which my hon. and learned Friend holds out to authors. Considered as a boon to them, it is a mere nullity; but, considered as an impost on the public, it is no nullity, but a very serious and fatal reality; I will take an example. Dr. Johnson died fifty-six years ago. If the law were what my hon. and learned Friend wishes to make it, somebody would now have the monopoly of Dr. Johnson's works. Who that somebody would be, it is impossible to say, but we may venture to guess. I guess, then, that it would have been some bookseller, who was the assign of another bookseller, who was the grandson of a third bookseller, who had bought the copyright from Black Frank, the Doctor's servant, in 1785 or 1786. Now, would the knowledge, that this copyright would exist in 1841, have been a source of gratification to Johnson? Would it have stimulated his exertions? Would it have once drawn him out of his bed before noon? Would it have once cheered him under a fit of the spleen? Would it have induced him to give us one more allegory, one more life of a poet, one more imitation of Juvenal? I firmly believe not. I firmly believe that a hundred years ago, when he was writing our debates for the Gentleman's Magazine, he would very much rather have had twopence to buy a plate of shin of beef at a cook's shop underground. Considered as a reward to him, the difference between a twenty years' term, and a sixty years' term of posthumous copyright, would have been nothing or next to nothing. But is the difference nothing to us? I can buy Rasselas for sixpence; I might have had to give five shillings for it. I can buy the Dictionary—the entire genuine Dictionary—for two guineas, perhaps for less; I might have had to give five or six guineas for it. Do I grudge this to a man like Dr. Johnson? Not at all. Show me that the prospect of this boon roused him to any vigorous effort, or sustained his spirits under depressing circumstances, and I am quite willing to pay the price of such an object, heavy as that price is. But what I do complain of is that my circumstances are to be worse, and Johnson's none the better; that I am to give five pounds for what to him was not worth a farthing. The principle of copyright is this. It is a tax on readers for the purpose of giving a bounty to writers. The tax is an exceedingly bad one; it is a tax on one of the most innocent and most salutary of human pleasures; and never let us forget, that a tax on innocent pleasures is a premium on vicious pleasures. I admit, however, the necessity of giving a bounty to genius and learning. In order to give such a bounty, I willingly submit even to this severe and burdensome tax. Nay, I am ready to increase the tax, if it can be shown that by so doing I should proportionably increase the bounty. My complaint is, that my hon. and learned Friend doubles, triples, quadruples, the tax, and makes scarcely any perceptible addition to the bounty. To recur to the case of Dr. Johnson,—what is the additional amount of taxation which would have been levied on the public for Dr. Johnson's works alone, if my hon. and learned Friend's bill had been the law of the land? I have not data sufficient to form an opinion. But I am confident that the taxation on his Dictionary alone would have amounted to many thousands of pounds. In reckoning the whole additional sum which the holders of his copyrights would have taken out of the pockets of the public during the last half century at twenty thousand pounds, I feel satisfied that I very greatly under-rate it. Now, I again say, that I think it but fair that we should pay twenty thousand pounds in consideration of twenty thousand pounds' worth of pleasure and encouragement received by Dr. Johnson. But I think it very hard that we should pay twenty thousand pounds for what he would not have valued at five shillings. My hon. and learned Friend dwells on the claims of the posterity of great writers. Undoubtedly, Sir, it would be very pleasing to see a descendant of Shakespeare living in opulence, on the fruits of his great ancestor's genius. A house maintained in splendour by such a patrimony would be a more interesting and striking object than Blenheim is to us, or than Strathfieldsaye will be to our children. But, unhappily, it is scarcely possible that, under any system, such a thing can come to pass. My hon. and learned Friend does not propose that copyright shall descend to the eldest son, or shall be bound up by irrevocable entail. It is to be merely personal property. It is therefore highly improbable that it will descend during sixty years or half that term from parent to child. The chance is that more people than one will have an interest in it. They will in all probability sell it and divide the proceeds. The price which a bookseller will give for it will bear no proportion to the sum which he will afterwards draw from the public, if his speculation proves successful. He will give little, if any thing, more for a term of sixty years than for a term of thirty or five-and-twenty. The present value of a distant advantage is always small; but when there is great room to doubt whether a distant advantage will be any advantage at all, the present value sinks to almost nothing. Such is the inconstancy of the public taste, that no sensible man will venture to pronounce, with confidence, what the sale of any book published in our days will be in the years between 1890 and 1900. The whole fashion of thinking and writing has often undergone a change in a much shorter period than that to which my hon. and learned Friend would extend posthumous copyright. What would have been considered the best literary property in the earlier part of Charles the Second's reign? I imagine Cowley's poems. Overleap sixty years, and you are in the generation of which Pope asked, "who now reads Cowley?" What works were ever expected with more impatience by the public than those of Lord Bolingbroke, which appeared, I think, in 1754. In 1814, no bookseller would have thanked you for the copyright of them all, if you had offered it to him for nothing. What would Paternoster-row give now for the copyright of Hayley's Triumphs of Temper, so much admired within the memory of many people still living? I say, therefore, that, from the very nature of literary property, it will almost always pass away from an author's family; and I say, that the price given for it to the family will bear a very small proportion to the tax which the purchaser, if his speculation turns out well, will in the course of a long series of years levy on the public. If, Sir, I wished to find a strong and perfect illustration of the effects which I anticipate from long copyright, I should select,—my hon. and learned Friend will be surprised,—I should select the case of Milton's grand-daughter. As often as this bill has been under discussion, the fate of Milton's grand-daughter has been brought forward by the advocates of monopoly. My hon. and learned Friend has repeatedly told the story with great eloquence and effect. He has dilated on the sufferings, on the abject poverty, of this ill-fated woman, the last of an illustrious race. He tells us that, in the extremity of her distress, Garrick gave her a benefit, that Johnson wrote a prologue, and that the public contributed some hundreds of pounds. Was it fit, he asks, that she should receive, in this eleemosynary form, a small portion of what was in truth a debt? Why, he asks, instead of obtaining a pittance from charity, did she not live in comfort and luxury on the proceeds of the sale of her ancestor's works? But, Sir, will my hon. and learned Friend tell me that this event, which he has so often and so pathetically described, was caused by the shortness of copyright? Why, at that time, the duration of copyright was longer, than even he, at present, proposes to make it. The monopoly lasted not sixty years, but for ever. At the time at which Milton's grand-daughter asked charity, Milton's works were the exclusive property of a bookseller. Within a few months of the day on which the benefit was given at Garrick's theatre, the holder of the copyright of Paradise Lost, I think it was Tonson, applied to the Court of Equity for an injunction against a bookseller, who had published a cheap edition of the great epic poem, and obtained his injunction. The representation of Comus was, if I remember rightly, in 1750—the injunction in 1752. Here, then, is a perfect illustration of what I conceived to be the effect of long copyright. Milton's works are the property of a single publisher. Everybody who wants them, must buy them at Tonson's shop, and at Tonson's price. Whoever attempts to undersell Tonson is harassed with legal proceedings. Thousands who would gladly possess a copy of Paradise Lost, must forego that great enjoyment. And what, in the meantime, is the situation of the only person for whom we can suppose that the author, protected at such a cost to the public, was at all interested? She is reduced to utter destitution. Milton's works are under a monopoly. Milton's grand-daughter is starving. The reader is pillaged; but the writer's family is not enriched. Society is taxed doubly. It has to give an exorbitant price for the poems; and it has at the same time to give alms to the only surviving descendant of the poet. But this is not all. I think it right, Sir, to call the attention of the House to an evil, which is perhaps more to be apprehended when an author's copyright remains in the hands of his family, than when it is transferred to booksellers. I seriously fear, that if such a measure as this should be adopted, many valuable works will be either totally suppressed or grievously mutilated. I can prove that this danger is not chimerical; and I am quite certain that, if the danger be real, the safeguards which my hon. and learned Friend has devised are altogether nugatory. That the danger is not chimerical may easily be shown. Most of us, I am sure, have known persons who, very erroneously, as I think, but from the best motives, would not choose to reprint Fielding's novels, or Gibbon's *History of the Decline and Fall of the Roman Empire.* Some Gentlemen may perhaps be of opinion, that it would be as well if *Tom Jones* and Gibbon's History were never reprinted. I will not, then, dwell on these or similar cases. I will take cases respecting which it is not likely that there will be any difference of opinion here, cases too in which the danger of which I now speak is not matter of supposition, but matter of fact. Take Richardson's novels. Whatever I may, on the present occasion, think of my hon. and learned Friend's judgment as a legislator, I must always respect his judgment as a critic. He will, I am sure, say that Richardson's novels are among the most valuable, among the most original works in our language. No writings have done more to raise the fame of English genius in foreign countries. No writings are more deeply pathetic. No writings, those of Shakespeare excepted, show such profound knowledge of the human heart. As to their moral tendency, I can cite the most respectable testimony. Dr. Johnson describes Richardson as one who had taught the passions to move at the command of virtue. My dear and honoured Friend, Mr. Wilberforce, in his celebrated religious treatise, when speaking of the unchristian tendency of the fashionable novels of the eighteenth century, most distinctly excepts Richardson from the censure. Another excellent person whom I can never mention without respect and kindness, Mrs. Hannah More, often declared in conversation, and has declared in one of her published poems, that she first learned from the writings of Richardson those principles of piety, by which her life was guided. I may safely say that books celebrated as works of art through the whole civilised world, and praised for their moral tendency by Dr. Johnson, by Mr. Wilberforce, by Mrs. Hannah More, ought not to be suppressed. Sir, it is my firm belief, that if the law had been what my hon. and learned Friend proposes to make it, they would have been suppressed. I remember Richardson's grandson well; he was a clergyman in the city of London; he was a most upright and excellent man; but he had conceived a strong prejudice against works of fiction. He thought all novel-reading not only frivolous but sinful. He said,—this I state on the authority of one of his clerical brethren, who is now a bishop;—he said that he had never thought it right to read one of his grandfather's books. Suppose, Sir, that the law had been what my hon. and learned Friend would make it. Suppose that the copyright of Richardson's novels had descended, as might well have been the case, to this gentleman. I firmly believe, that he would have thought it sinful to give them wide circulation. I firmly believe, that he would not for a hundred thousand pounds have deliberately done what he thought sinful. He would not have reprinted them. And what protection does my hon. and learned Friend give to the public in such a case? Why, Sir, what he proposes is this: if a book is not reprinted during five years, any person who wishes to reprint it may give notice in the *London Gazette:* the advertisement must be repeated three times: a year must elapse; and then, if the proprietor of the copyright does not put forth a new edition, he loses his exclusive privilege. Now, what protection is this to the public? What is a new edition? Does the law define the number of copies that make an edition? Does it limit the price of a copy? Are twelve copies on large paper, charged at thirty guineas each, an edition? It has been usual, when monopolies have been granted, to prescribe numbers and to limit prices. But I do not find that my hon. and learned Friend proposes to do so in the present case.

And, without some such provision, the security which he offers is manifestly illusory. It is my conviction, that under such a system as that which he recommends to us, a copy of *Clarissa* would have been as rare as an Aldus or a Caxton. I will give another instance. One of the most instructive, interesting, and delightful books in our language is Boswell's *Life of Johnson.* Now it is well known that Boswell's eldest son considered this book, considered the whole relation of Boswell to Johnson, as a blot in the escutcheon of the family. He thought, not perhaps altogether without reason, that his father had exhibited himself in a ludicrous and degrading light. And thus he became so sore and irritable, that at last he could not bear to hear the *Life of Johnson* mentioned. Suppose that the law had been what my hon. and learned Friend wishes to make it. Suppose that the copyright of Boswell's *Life of Johnson* had belonged, as it well might, during sixty years to Boswell's eldest son. What would have been the consequence? An unadulterated copy of the finest biographical work in the world would have been as scarce as the first edition of Camden. These are strong cases. I have shewn you that, if the law had been what you are now going to make it, the finest prose work of fiction in the language, the finest biographical work in the language, would very probably have been suppressed. But I have stated my case weakly. The books which I have mentioned are singularly inoffensive books,—books not touching on any of those questions which drive even wise men beyond the bounds of wisdom. There are books of a very different kind,—books which are the rallying points of great political and religious parties. What is likely to happen if the copyright of one of these books should by descent or transfer come into the possession of some hostile zealot? I will take a single instance. It is fifty years since John Wesley died; his works, if the law had been what my hon. and learned Friend seeks to make it, would now have been the property of some person or other. The sect founded by Wesley is the most numerous, the wealthiest, the most powerful, the most zealous, of sects. In every election it is a matter of the greatest importance to obtain the support of the Wesleyan Methodists. Their numerical strength is reckoned by hundreds of thousands. They hold the memory of their founder in the greatest reverence; and not without reason, for he was unquestionably a great and a good man. To his authority they constantly appeal. His works are in their eyes of the highest value. His doctrinal writings they regard as containing the best system of theology ever deduced from Scripture. His journals, interesting even to the common reader, are peculiarly interesting to the Methodist: for they contain the whole history of that singular polity which, weak and despised in its beginning, is now, after the lapse of a century, so strong, so flourishing, and so formidable. The hymns to which he gave his imprimatur are a most important part of the public worship of his followers. Now suppose that the copyright of these works belonged to some person who holds the memory of Wesley and the doctrines and discipline of the Methodists in abhorrence. There are many such persons. The Ecclesiastical Courts are at this very time sitting on the case of a clergyman of the Established Church who refused Christian burial to a child baptized by a Methodist preacher. I took up the other day a work which is considered as among the most respectable organs of a large and growing party in the Church of England, and there I saw John Wesley designated as a forsworn priest. Suppose that the works of Wesley were suppressed. Why, Sir, such a grievance would be enough to shake the foundations of Government. Let Gentlemen who are attached to the Church reflect for a moment what their feelings would be if the Book of Common Prayer were not to be reprinted for thirty or forty years,—if the price of a Book of Common Prayer were run up to five or ten guineas. And then let them determine whether they will pass a law under which it is possible, under which it is probable, that so intolerable a wrong may be done to some sect consisting perhaps of half a million of persons. I am so sensible, Sir, of the kindness with which the House has listened to me, that I will not detain you longer. I will only say this,—that if the measure before us should pass, and should produce one-tenth part of the evil which it is calculated to produce, and which I fully expect it to produce, there will soon be a remedy, though of a very objectionable kind. Just as the absurd acts which prohibited the sale of game were virtually repealed by the poacher, just as many absurd revenue acts have been virtually repealed by the smuggler, will this law be virtually repealed by piratical booksellers. At present the holder of copyright has the public feeling on his side. Those who invade copyright are regarded as knaves who take the bread out of the mouth of deserving men. Every body is well pleased to see them restrained by the law and compelled to refund their ill-gotten gains. No tradesmen of good repute will have anything to do with such disgraceful transactions. Pass this law: and that feeling is at an end. Men of a character very different from that of the present race of piratical booksellers will soon infringe this intolerable monopoly. Great masses of capital will be constantly employed in the violation of the law. Every art will be employed to evade legal pursuit; and the whole nation will be in the plot. On which side indeed should the public sympathy be when the question is whether some book as popular as Robinson Crusoe, or the Pilgrim's Progress, shall be in every cottage, or whether it shall be confined to the libraries of the rich for the advantage of the great grandson of a bookseller who, a hundred years before, drove a hard bargain for the copyright with the author when in great distress? Remember too that when once it ceases to be considered as wrong and discreditable to invade literary property, no person can say where the invasion will stop. The public seldom makes nice distinctions. The wholesome copyright which now exists will share in the disgrace and danger of the new copyright which you are about to create. And you will find that, in attempting to impose unreasonable restraints on the reprinting of the works of the dead, you have, to a great extent, annulled those restraints which now prevent men from pillaging and defrauding the living. If I saw, Sir, any probability that this bill could be so amended in the committee that my objections might be removed, I would not divide the House in this stage. But I am so fully convinced that no alteration which would not seem insupportable to my hon. and learned Friend, could render his measure supportable to me, that I must move, though with regret, that this bill be read a second time this day six months.

END OF VOL. I.

www.ingramcontent.com/pod-product-compliance
Lightning Source LLC
LaVergne TN
LVHW020109110826
845151LV00001B/114

* 9 7 8 1 4 2 5 5 4 3 6 7 9 *